T0330267

THE EMERGENCE OF ECONOMIC IDEAS

ECONOMISTS OF THE TWENTIETH CENTURY

General Editors: Mark Perlman, *University Professor of Economics, Emeritus, University of Pittsburgh* and Mark Blaug, *Professor Emeritus, University of London; Professor Emeritus, University of Buckingham and Visiting Professor, University of Exeter*

This innovative series comprises specially invited collections of articles and papers by economists whose work has made an important contribution to economics in the late twentieth century.

The proliferation of new journals and the ever-increasing number of new articles make it difficult for even the most assiduous economist to keep track of all the important recent advances. By focusing on those economists whose work is generally recognized to be at the forefront of the discipline, the series will be an essential reference point for the different specialisms included.

A list of published and future titles in this series is printed at the end of this volume.

The Emergence of Economic Ideas

Essays in the History of Economics

Nathan Rosenberg

Fairleigh S. Dickinson Jr Professor of Public Policy
Department of Economics
Stanford University, US

ECONOMISTS OF THE TWENTIETH CENTURY

Edward Elgar

© Nathan Rosenberg 1994.

All rights reserved. No part of this publication may be reproduced, stored in a retrieval system, or transmitted in any form or by any means, electronic, mechanical, photocopying, recording, or otherwise without the prior permission of the publisher.

Published by
Edward Elgar Publishing Limited
Gower House
Croft Road
Aldershot
Hants GU11 3HR
England

Edward Elgar Publishing Company
Old Post Road
Brookfield
Vermont 05036
USA

British Library Cataloguing in Publication Data
Emergence of Economic Ideas: Essays in the
History of Economics. − (Economists of
  the Twentieth Century Series)
  I. Rosenberg, Nathan   II. Series
  330.109

Library of Congress Cataloguing in Publication Data
The emergence of economic ideas : essays in the history of economics /
  edited by Nathan Rosenberg.
      p.   cm. — (Economists of the twentieth century)
    Includes bibliographical references and index.
    1. Economics—History. I. Rosenberg, Nathan, 1927− .
  II. Series.
  HB75.E54   1994
  330′.09—dc20   94−21289
                                                                           CIP

ISBN 1 85898 047 X

Printed in Great Britain at the University Press, Cambridge

Contents

Acknowledgements

The publishers wish to thank the following who have kindly given permission for the use of copyright material.

Basil Blackwell Publishers for article: 'Adam Smith on the Division of Labour: Two Views or One?', *Economica*, May 1965, pp. 127–39.

Cambridge University Press for articles: 'Charles Babbage: Pioneer Economist', *Exploring the Black Box: Technology, Economics, and History*, 1994, pp. 24–46; 'Joseph Schumpeter: Radical Economist', *Exploring the Black Box: Technology, Economics, and History*, 1994, pp. 47–61.

Duke University Press for article: 'Adam Smith and the Stock of Moral Capital', *History of Political Economy*, **22**(1), Spring 1990, pp. 1–17.

Johns Hopkins University Press for article: 'Mandeville and Laissez-Faire', *Journal of the History of Ideas*, April 1963, pp. 183–96.

Monthly Review Foundation for article: 'Marx as a Student of Technology', *Monthly Review*, July–August 1976, pp. 56–77. Copyright © 1976 by Monthly Review Inc.

University of Chicago Press for articles: 'Some Institutional Aspects of the *Wealth of Nations*', *The Journal of Political Economy*, **LXVIII**(6), December 1960, pp. 557–70; 'Adam Smith, Consumer Tastes, and Economic Growth', *The Journal of Political Economy*, June 1968, pp. 361–74; 'Adam Smith on Profits – Paradox Lost and Regained', *The Journal of Political Economy*, November–December 1974, pp. 377–89; 'Another Advantage of the Division of Labor', *The Journal of Political Economy*, **84**(4), 1976, pp. 861–8; 'Karl Marx on the Economic Role of Science', *The Journal of Political Economy*, July–August 1974, pp. 713–28; 'George Stigler: Adam Smith's Best Friend', *The Journal of Political Economy*, **101**(5), October 1993, pp. 833–48.

Every effort has been made to trace all the copyright holders but if any have been advertently overlooked the publishers will be pleased to make the necessary arrangements at the first opportunity.

Introduction

The reprinting of these papers in the history of economics raises the obvious question: What do they share beyond a common authorship? It is a fair question.

The most persistent theme of these papers, uniting my interest in certain economists from Mandeville to Stigler, is a concern with the emergence and diffusion of new ideas. Indeed, the first seven chapters are really concerned with an 'idea' no less than the discipline of economics itself. Mandeville should perhaps be regarded as a precocious, or even 'premature', economist. He had a number of penetrating insights into the spontaneous forces underlying the organization of economic activity, but he had no analytical apparatus. He was not yet, to use the felicitous phrase of his contemporary, Isaac Newton, 'standing on the shoulders of giants'. George Stigler, by contrast, writing more than 200 years after Mandeville, was not only a major contributor of ideas to a mature economic profession; he was also intensely interested in the historical evolution of the discipline itself. A great deal of his professional energies were absorbed in the study of the giants on whose shoulders he knew he stood.

Stigler's interests in his predecessors went far beyond some of the usual historiographic interests such as intellectual priority – who influenced whom and who first formulated some idea with a high degree of internal consistency and logical coherence. Stigler well understood that it is not enough merely to enunciate a new idea; a discipline can progress only when new ideas are accepted by a community of scholars and when that community in turn undertakes to utilize these ideas. And utilization included, for Stigler, drawing implications and testing them empirically. More than this, Stigler believed that there were, in fact, laws of evolution in the development of disciplines, and that these laws were, themselves, discoverable and testable. This represents a powerful challenge to which the economics profession has yet to respond.

As I attempt to show in my chapter on Stigler, he addressed the highly influential work of T.S. Kuhn (*The Structure of Scientific Revolutions*), who argued that scientific progress takes the form of occasional but highly significant paradigm shifts, rather than being a simple cumulative process (Kuhn does not deny that 'normal' science, science within a given paradigm, is cumulative in nature). Stigler asserts, however, that Kuhn has so far failed to specify the nature and content of a paradigm in sufficient detail such that the notion of paradigm *shifts* could be subjected to empirical testing. Until this is done, he concludes, Kuhn's 'fascinating hypotheses' can be neither accepted nor rejected.

But if the papers in this volume share a common focus on the emergence of new ideas, it is also true that that focus is upon certain specific kinds of new idea. Seven of the 12 chapters of this volume are concerned with the emergence of the most central of all ideas in economics: the notion of the self-regulating nature of a market economy. I refer to the chapter on Mandeville (Chapter 1) and the six chapters on various aspects of the writing of Adam Smith. The most recently written of the chapters on Smith explicitly examines the 'other one' of Smith's two great books, *The Theory of Moral Sentiments*; the other chapters focus primarily, but not exclusively, on the *Wealth of Nations*.

It would be gratuitous for an economist to offer an explanation for his interest in the *Wealth of Nations*. Alfred North Whitehead once said, with pardonable exaggeration, that the history of Western philosophy can be adequately described as a series of footnotes to Plato (A.N. Whitehead, *Process and Reality*). One can say with much less exaggeration that the history of economics over the past 200 years can be adequately characterized as a series of footnotes to Adam Smith – although it must be admitted that the footnotes are getting rather long! It is certainly correct to trace a large part of the 20th century corpus of analytical economics to Book I of the *Wealth of Nations*. But the *Wealth of Nations*, as I discovered, offers the reader much more than that. It is a multi-faceted work, one that deals with a remarkably wide range of issues, and which attempts to provide a grand synthesis of the whole economic universe – and more. The book is, indeed, as Stigler referred to it, a 'stupendous palace erected upon the granite of self-interest'. But it is also, as I came to realize, a palace with many rooms, and even some entire wings, that have been badly neglected. I therefore approached the book, in my first article on Adam Smith ('Institutional Aspects of the *Wealth of Nations*'), from a special angle of vision. For, although the more purely analytical aspects of Book I have been meticulously dissected and analysed, Smith's larger vision of his own contemporary world, and his historical analysis of the economic growth of Europe, have received very little attention. It seemed, therefore, essential to view Smith's new ideas against the backdrop of the larger institutional framework within which economic activity takes place.

As is occasionally the case, opening doors to rooms that had long been shut – or at least neglected – led to some rather surprising findings. The *Wealth of Nations* contains a far richer and more complex examination of human motivation than is apparent in later models of maximizing behaviour in the context of competitive industries. The separate papers reprinted here each explore one or more of these neglected issues – the division of labour (itself one of the most central ideas in the history of economics), paradoxical aspects of Smith's treatment of the role of profits, the influence of consumer tastes on economic growth, and the manner in which the formation of man's moral sentiments influences economic behaviour (this last, of course, involving a tour of Smith's other palace, *The Theory of Moral Sentiments*).

Inevitably, of course, one thing led to another. Smith was very much a man of the 18th century, and it was difficult to re-read the early chapters of the *Wealth of Nations* without a nagging interest in the provenance of such central new ideas as the causes and consequences of the division of labour and the self-regulating behaviour of market economies. In these matters, certainly, Smith owed some sort of debt to Mandeville. Exploring the nature of that debt took me back to that remarkable, if somewhat enigmatic, precursor. After all, long before Smith's birth Mandeville had observed that:

...The whole Superstructure (of Civil Society) is made up of the reciprocal Services, which Men do to each other. How to get these services perform'd by others, when we have Occasion for them, is the grand and almost constant Sollicitude in Life of every individual Person. To expect, that others should serve us for nothing, is unreasonable; therefore all Commerce, that Men can have together, must be a continual bartering of one thing for another (*Fable of the Bees*, vol. II, p. 349).

It is no great intellectual leap, surely, from this formulation to one of the best-known passages in the *Wealth of Nations*, that:

...man has almost constant occasion for the help of his brethren, and it is in vain for him to expect it from their benevolence only. He will be more likely to prevail if he can interest their self-love in his favour, and shew them that it is for their own advantage to do for him what he requires of them...It is not from the benevolence of the butcher, the brewer, or the baker, that we expect our dinner, but from their regard to their own interest. We address ourselves, not to their humanity, but to their self-love, and never talk to them of our own necessities but of their advantages (*Wealth of Nations*, Modern Library Giant, p. 14).

Similarly, although it would be absurd to suggest that Adam Smith could *only* have derived his conception of the economic importance of the division of labour as an engine of economic progress from reading Mandeville, it is certainly true that Mandeville had expressed that insight long before Smith:

Man...naturally loves to imitate what he sees others do, which is the reason that savage People all do the same thing: This hinders them from meliorating their Condition, though they are always wishing for it: But if one will wholly apply himself to the making of Bows and Arrows, whilst another provides Food, a third builds Huts, a fourth makes Garments, and a fifth Utensils, they not only become useful to one another, but the Callings and Employments themselves will in the same Number of Years receive much greater improvements, than if all had been promiscuously follow'd by every one of the Five (*Fable of the Bees*, vol. II, p. 284).

It is hard to resist quoting one other, more elegant, allusion of Mandeville to the division of labour:

What a Noble as well as Beautiful, what a glorious Machine is a First-Rate Man of War, when she is under Sail, well rigg'd, and well mann'd! As in Bulk and Weight it is vastly superior to any other moveable Body of Human Invention, so there is no other that has an equal Variety of differently surprizing Contrivances to boast of. There are many Sets of Hands in the Nation, that, not wanting proper Materials, would be able in less than half a Year to produce, fit out, and navigate a First-Rate: yet it is certain, that this Task would be impracticable, if it was not divided and subdivided into a great Variety of different Labours; and it is as certain, that none of these Labours require any other, than working Men of ordinary Capacities...We often ascribe to the Excellency of Man's Genius, and the Depth of his Penetration, what is in Reality owing to length of Time, and the Experience of many Generations, all of them very little differing from one another in natural Parts and Sagacity (*Fable of the Bees*, vol. II, pp. 141–2).

Mandeville also understood and popularized the critical idea that, in the *absence* of any sort of government regulation, a free market economy would automatically allocate resources in accordance with the needs of the consuming public:

> As it is Folly to set up Trades that are not wanted, so what is next to it is to increase in any one Trade the Numbers beyond what are required. As things are managed with us, it would be preposterous to have as many Brewers as there are Bakers, or as many Woollen-drapers as there are Shoe-makers. This Proportion as to Numbers in every Trade finds itself, and is never better kept than when no body meddles or interferes with it (*Fable of the Bees*, vol. I, pp. 299–300).

Like the earlier papers in this volume, the four papers on Babbage, Marx and Schumpeter are each concerned with the exploration and formulation of new ideas. But these ideas share a common focal point: they are concerned with aspects of technological change, with particular attention to the economic sources, as well as to the consequences, of such change.

My interest in these three authors has its origin in my own preoccupation with the subject of technological change. Babbage, Marx and Schumpeter each made seminal contributions to the understanding of the role played by technological change in economic growth. Babbage's contributions have been almost completely over-looked, although his extraordinary anticipation of modern computer technology is now amply acknowledged. In fact it is interesting to note that, as explained in Chapter 8, Babbage's contribution to economics was largely a result of his frustrated attempts to produce a workable computer.

My analysis of Babbage's book, *On the Economy of Machinery and Manufactures*, is intimately linked to my earlier papers on Adam Smith, which devote considerable attention to the economic role of the division of labour. Babbage wrote more than 50 years after Adam Smith. The interval of time between the early 1770s and early 1830s were precisely the decades that witnessed what later generations came to call the Industrial Revolution. Babbage's book did what Smith's could not possibly have done: it introduced the factory into the realm of economic analysis. Babbage's book is immensely valuable for its detailed description of the British factory *circa* 1830. But on the foundation of his descriptive account he offered the first analytical treatment of the economies associated with increasing returns to scale and a highly original improvement upon Adam Smith's time-honoured treatment of the division of labour.

In each of these insights, but especially the second, Babbage exercised a profound influence on Marx. Indeed, it would not be too much to say that Marx's most severe criticisms of capitalism turn upon the consequences of the extensive division of labour that that economic system had uniquely brought into the world.

Thus, the writings of the two 19th century figures, Babbage and Marx, represent, in certain essential respects, a further and deeper exploration of issues that had been examined by Smith and (even earlier) by Mandeville in the 18th century. Both Babbage and Marx were confronting a world that had undergone dramatic changes, not least in technology and the organization of work, since the publication of the *Wealth of Nations*. Marx's discussion of the dynamic roles of both technology and science turn upon his historical analysis of the emergence of capitalist institutions after 1500 and particularly in the century or so preceding 1850.

Schumpeter, of course, drew heavily, sometimes in a deliberately paradoxical fashion, upon Marx. Indeed, the first four chapters of the book that is the primary focus of my paper on Schumpeter, *Capitalism, Socialism and Democracy*, provides a profound evaluation and appreciation of Marx's more purely scholarly contributions. And what unites Schumpeter to Marx is precisely the central theme of each of the papers that make up this volume: the attempt to understand the dynamic aspects of capitalist institutions.

MANDEVILLE AND LAISSEZ-FAIRE

By Nathan Rosenberg

There is nothing so universally sincere upon Earth, as the Love which all Creatures, that are capable of any, bear to themselves.[1]

It is a well-established tradition in dealing with the development of economic thought in the XVIIIth century to make a brief obeisance to Bernard Mandeville as some sort of "precursor" of Adam Smith, laissez-faire, and all that. According to one's personal tastes, it is also the usual practice to select for quotation some choice tidbits from *The Fable of the Bees,* paying little or no attention to Mandeville's extensive prose commentaries, and then to proceed to other things. This treatment of Mandeville as an important ideological forerunner of Adam Smith and spokesman for laissez-faire has been forcefully presented by F. B. Kaye in the introduction to his definitive edition of *The Fable of the Bees.* Kaye argues there that

In the *Fable* Mandeville maintains, and maintains explicitly, the theory at present known as the *laissez-faire* theory, which dominated modern economic thought for a hundred years and is still a potent force. . . . *The Fable of the Bees,* I believe, was one of the chief literary sources of the doctrine of *laissez-faire.*[2]

Kaye's point of view has been widely disseminated [3] (frequently without Kaye's qualifications and without his stress upon Mandeville's philosophical individualism). Mandeville's deliberately paradoxical subtitle, "Private Vices, Publick Benefits," has been frequently cited as representing an embodiment of the newly-emerging laissez-faire philosophy.

Although the view has thus been accorded wide currency that Mandeville adhered to, and espoused, a fundamentally laissez-faire ideology, it is a position which has been strongly opposed by no less an authority than Professor Viner:

[1] Bernard Mandeville, *The Fable of the Bees* (2 vols., Oxford, 1924), ed. F. B. Kaye, I, 200. *The Fable of the Bees* will subsequently be cited as *Fable.*

[2] *Fable,* I, cxxxix–cxl.

[3] For example, A. Chalk, "The Rise of Economic Individualism," *Journal of Political Economy* (August 1951), 347: " . . . there is much justification for F. B. Kaye's assertion that Mandeville's *Fable of the Bees* is the first *systematic* presentation of the laissez-faire philosophy." In a footnote, Chalk adds: "In the *Fable,* Mandeville applies the principle of self-interest to virtually all spheres of economic activity. The unifying thread is, of course, natural law, for the beneficent social effects of the pursuit of self-interest flow 'naturally' and spontaneously from the operation of a laissez-faire system." Cf. also article on "Mandeville" in *Encyclopedia of the Social Sciences,* X, 93, 94.

Many scholars, including economists who should know better, regard Mandeville as a pioneer expounder of laissez-faire individualism in the economic field and as such as an anticipator of Adam Smith. . . . It is a common misinterpretation of Mandeville . . . to read his motto, "Private Vices, Publick Benefits," as a laissez-faire motto, postulating the natural or spontaneous harmony between individual interests and the public good. The motto as it appeared on title pages of *The Fable of the Bees* was elliptical. In his text, Mandeville repeatedly stated that it was by "the skilful Management of the clever Politician" that private vices could be made to serve the public good, thus ridding the formula of any implication of laissez-faire.[4]

Viner argues, then, that Mandeville was not, as Kaye and numerous economists had asserted, an advocate of laissez-faire. Although he strikes a cautionary note on the hazards of applying ". . . to 18th century writers modern ideas as to the dividing line between 'interventionists' and exponents of 'liberalism' or of 'laissez-faire,' "[5] Professor Viner seems content to permit Mandeville to be identified as an exponent of state intervention.[6]

It is the purpose of this paper to explore and, it is hoped, to resolve the problems posed by these apparently conflicting interpretations of Mandeville's work. What actions does Mandeville regard as appropriate to "the skilful Management of the clever Politician"?

A convenient place to start, and one which will serve also to clear the ground for subsequent discussion, is Mandeville's treatment of foreign trade. Mandeville was clearly a Mercantilist in the specific sense of being intensely concerned with the importance of regulating a country's trade balance with the rest of the world for the purpose of assuring an excess, in value terms, of exports over imports.

[4] Jacob Viner, Introd. to Bernard Mandeville, *A Letter to Dion* (Augustan Reprint Society, Berkeley, Cal., 1953), 11, 13–14. Reprinted in Jacob Viner, *The Long View and the Short* (Glencoe, Ill., 1958), 332–42. Cf. also Viner's review of Schumpeter's *History of Economic Analysis* (*American Economic Review* [Dec. 1954]), 904, ftn. 7. (Also reprinted in Jacob Viner, *The Long View and the Short*, 343–65.) Although Professor Viner deals with Mandeville only very briefly in his *Studies in the Theory of International Trade* (N. Y., 1937), he seems at that time to have adhered to the interpretation of Mandeville which he has more recently criticized: "More important, in preparing the way for Adam Smith, was Mandeville's more elaborate reasoning in support of individualism and laissez-faire, resting on his famous argument that 'private vices' such as 'avarice' and luxury were 'public benefits' " (99). This is cited so that members of the economics profession who regard themselves as proper objects of Professor Viner's gentle rebuke to "economists who should know better," may know that they are at least members of a company sufficiently distinguished to include an earlier Viner.

[5] Viner, *A Letter to Dion*, 12.

[6] " . . . Helvetius as an apostle of state intervention was not only not departing from Mandeville but was echoing him even as to language. Helvetius said that motives of personal temporal interest sufficed for the formation of a good society, provided they were 'maniés avec adresse par un législateur habile.' " *Ibid.*, 15.

Every Government ought to be thoroughly acquainted with, and stedfastly to pursue the Interest of the Country. Good Politicians by dextrous Management, laying heavy Impositions on some Goods, or totally prohibiting them, and lowering the Duties on others, may always turn and divert the Course of Trade which way they please . . . above all, they'll keep a watchful Eye over the Balance of Trade in general, and never suffer that all the Foreign Commodities together, that are imported in one Year, shall exceed in Value what of their own Growth or Manufacture is in the same exported to others.[7]

Although Mandeville thus completely embraced the central policy prescription of mercantilism, it is worth noting that he seems to have been brought to this position at least in some measure as a result of his preoccupation with the problem of luxury, and as a result of his attempt to demonstrate that a taste for luxury was not necessarily economically harmful. Mandeville's most important discussions of the necessity of controlling foreign trade, in order to assure a favorable balance, occur in contexts where he is attempting to prove that national impoverishment need not inevitably follow from the development of a taste for luxury goods. Typically, he seems to be saying that so long as we exert the appropriate controls over our imports of foreign luxury goods, and keep a watchful eye on the overall foreign trade balance, we need never worry that we shall be impoverished by such tastes.

. . . What I have insisted on the most, and repeated more than once, is the great Regard that is to be had to the Balance of Trade, and the Care the Legislature ought to take that the Yearly Imports never exceed the Exports; and where this is observed, and the other things I spoke of are not neglected, I still continue to assert that no Foreign Luxury can undo a Country. . . .[8]

Although Mandeville, moreover, was free of many of the grosser forms of Mercantilist errors (he did not, e.g. ever identify or confuse a country's wealth or income with its money supply),[9] he may un-

---

[7] *Fable*, I, 115–16. Mandeville adds, significantly: "Note, that I speak now of the Interest of those Nations that have no Gold or Silver of their own Growth, otherwise this Maxim need not to be so much insisted on" (116). Cf. also I, 249.

[8] *Fable*, I, 249. The passage occurs in a brief addendum which Mandeville attached to later editions of the *Fable*. Cf. also *Fable*, I, 108–16 and *A Letter to Dion*, 41–45.

[9] Spain, indeed, Mandeville regards as having been ruined partly by "too much money." " . . . by *too much Money*, the making of Colonies and other Mismanagements, of which it was the occasion, Spain is from a fruitful and well-peopled Country, with all its mighty Titles and Possessions, made a barren and empty Thoroughfare, thro' which Gold and Silver pass from America to the rest of the World; and the Nation, from a rich, acute, diligent and laborious, become slow, idle, proud and beggarly People; so much for Spain" (*Fable*, I, 196). On a more

questionably be categorized as a Mercantilist in the sense that he recommended that the government ought to intervene in the normal market processes, with the use of a variety of regulatory devices, for the purpose of assuring the maintenance of a "favorable" balance of trade.

It should be understood that the subsequent discussion, except where otherwise noted, deals with Mandeville's views respecting the domestic economy alone, divorced from its trade nexus with the rest of the world.

It will be argued here that Mandeville, when he is not dealing specifically with matters pertaining to foreign trade, presents a fairly well-articulated conception of the rôle of government in economic and social affairs which is not adequately encompassed by such terms as "mercantilism," "interventionism," or "laissez-faire," at least in their more generally-accepted connotations. However, the mere demonstration that Mandeville's intellectual product was, in some important respects, *differentiated* from these groups would be, by itself, of limited interest. It will be further suggested that, if interpreted sympathetically, Mandeville's writings contain a treatment of the process of social change and a conception of the rôle of government which were in important respects more sophisticated and certainly much more interesting than the ones comprehended in the intellectual tradition of laissez-faire.

This conception is due, primarily, to Mandeville's evolutionary treatment of social development and human institutions.[10] Although much of Mandeville's discussion of the origin and growth of human society is essentially allegorical and not to be regarded as an historical account, it manifests what Kaye calls "his precocious feeling for evolution." [11] Human institutions are not to be regarded as the product of human ingenuity, much less the result of a single mind. They are, rather, the fruits of a long and gradual growth process. The results of this evolution are not only contrivances beyond the ingenuity of individuals; once they have evolved, they multiply manyfold the otherwise crude and limited abilities of the individual human agent.

---

positive note, Mandeville states: " . . . let the Value of Gold and Silver either rise or fall, the Enjoyment of all Societies will ever depend upon the Fruits of the Earth, and the Labour of the People; both which joined together are a more certain, a more inexhaustible, and a more real Treasure, than the Gold of Brazil, or the Silver of Potosi" (*Fable*, I, 197–198).

[10] This component of Mandeville's thought was clearly recognized by Kaye (*Fable*, I, Introduction, lxiv–lxvi) but, even though he accorded it explicit treatment, he did not adequately relate it to the main body of Mandeville's economic ideas. It was partly from the failure to do so that Kaye was able to remain satisfied with his treatment of Mandeville as an early exponent of the doctrine of laissez-faire.   [11] *Fable*, Introduction, lxv.

To Men who never turn'd their Thoughts that way, it certainly is almost inconceivable to what prodigious Height, from next to nothing, some Arts may be and have been raised by human Industry and Application, by the uninterrupted Labour, and joint Experience of many Ages, tho' none but Men of ordinary Capacity should ever be employ'd in them. What a Noble as well as Beautiful, what a glorious Machine is a First-Rate Man of War, when she is under Sail, well rigg'd and well mann'd! As in Bulk and Weight it is vastly superior to any other moveable Body of human Invention, so there is no other that has an equal Variety of differently surprizing Contrivances to boast of. There are many Sets of Hands in the Nation, that, not wanting proper Materials, would be able in less than half a Year to produce, fit out, and navigate a First-Rate: yet it is certain, that this Task would be impracticable, if it was not divided and subdivided into a great Variety of different Labours; and it is as certain, that none of these Labours require any other, than working Men of ordinary Capacities.

From this it is concluded

That we often ascribe to the Excellency of Man's Genius, and the Depth of his Penetration, what is in Reality owing to length of Time, and the Experience of many Generations, all of them very little differing from one another in natural Parts and Sagacity.[12]

Mandeville's evolutionary perspective permeates all of his thinking. Man's greatest accomplishments have come about through this process of slow and almost imperceptible development over many generations. They are the product, not of inspiration (either human or divine) but of the collective experience of the human race. Even language and the faculty of speech, Mandeville argues, have come into the world "By slow degrees, as all other Arts and Sciences have done, and length of time; Agriculture, Physick, Astronomy, Architecture, Painting, &c."[13] It is within this context of Mandeville's conception of evolutionary development that we must consider what is the best-known ingredient of his social analysis and his chief claim to notoriety: i.e. his tireless emphasis on the central rôle of man's egotism and self-regarding qualities in creating a smoothly-functioning social system. Man is a compound of passions (desires, appetites) which have been implanted in him by nature, and his actions at any time are to be explained in terms of those of his appetites—fear, anger, hunger, lust, pride, envy, avarice—which happen to be uppermost. " . . .the Sociableness of Man arises only from these Two things, *viz.* The multiplicity of his Desires, and the continual Opposition he

12 *Fable*, II, 141–2. Cf. also *Fable*, II, 186–7: " . . . the Works of Art and human Invention are all very lame and defective, and most of them pitifully mean at first: Our Knowledge is advanced by slow Degrees, and some Arts and Sciences require the Experience of many Ages, before they can be brought to any tolerable Perfection.   13 *Fable*, II, 287.

meets with in his Endeavours to gratify them" (*Fable*, I, 344). The growth of human society is to be seen as an extensive historical process whereby human relationships have been so contrived and manipulated that man's pursuit of his self-interest is rendered at least consistent with the larger needs of society.

> . . . no Societies could have sprung from the Amiable Virtues and Loving Qualities of Man, but on the contrary . . . all of them must have had their Origin from his Wants, his Imperfections, and the variety of his Appetites: We shall find likewise that the more their Pride and Vanity are display'd and all their Desires enlarg'd, the more capable they must be of being rais'd into large and vastly numerous Societies. . . .
>
> I hope the Reader knows that by Society I understand a Body Politick, in which Man either subdued by Superior Force, or by Persuasion drawn from his Savage State, is become a Disciplin'd Creature, that can find his own Ends in Labouring for others, and where under one Head or other Form of Government each Member is render'd Subservient to the Whole, and all of them by cunning Management are made to Act as one.[14]

When Mandeville states, in the closing sentence of *A Search into the Nature of Society*, that "Private Vices by the dextrous Management of a skilful Politician may be turned into Publick Benefits," he is not so much stating an interventionist policy maxim as attempting to generalize about a central aspect in man's past progress as a social animal. In the context of this essay he is saying that the nature and development of civilized institutions are owing primarily to man's vices—i.e. his self-seeking behavior, his pride, vanity and cupidity.[15] "Dextrous Management" is not to be taken as the advocacy of a policy of continuous government intervention in domestic market processes; rather, it is a way of stating that the welfare of society has been most advanced by the introduction and diffusion of laws and institutions which best utilize man's basic passions and which channel his energies into socially-useful activities. "Private Vices, Publick Benefits" is indeed highly elliptical because it does not indicate the nature of the mechanism by which this beneficent social transformation is made to take place. However, even to say, as Mandeville does, that it is through " . . . the dextrous Management of a skilful Politician," is a

---

[14] *Fable*, I, 346–47.

[15] In the penultimate paragraph of *A Search into the Nature of Society*, Mandeville states: " . . . I flatter my self to have demonstrated that, neither the Friendly Qualities and kind Affections that are natural to Man, nor the real Virtues he is capable of acquiring by Reason and Self-Denial, are the Foundation of Society; but that what we call Evil in this World, Moral as well as Natural, is the grand Principle that makes us sociable Creatures, the solid Basis, the Life and Support of all Trades and Employments without Exception: That there we must look for the true Origin of all Arts and Sciences, and that the Moment Evil ceases, the Society must be spoiled, if not totally dissolved" (*Fable*, I, 369).

highly inept summary in that it really mis-states the historical rôle which Mandeville's own analysis accords to the politician.

A continuous thread running throughout all of Mandeville's work is that (a) man is a bundle of very specific passions and appetites which dominate his behavior, and that to pretend otherwise is sheer hypocrisy,[16] and (b) the function of government is to establish an environment of such a nature that the individual's attempt to gratify his passions will result in actions which are meritorious from the point of view of the goals of the state. It is at this juncture that we arrive at the essence of the conflicting interpretations of Mandeville. The traditional categories of interventionism and laissez-faire are inadequate to convey the position of someone who wishes the government to intervene in the affairs of the domestic economy, but only in order that it may establish a social and legal framework within which the interaction of self-seeking egos will result in an orderly satisfaction of man's economic needs. In this sense most commentators on Mandeville have taken hold of an authentic piece of his analysis but have misconstrued the part for the whole.

Mandeville is emphatically not *advocating* interventionism as a long-run practice of government, in the sense that he believes that government should be endowed with the power to make *arbitrary* interventions in normal market processes. Mandeville was, indeed, an interventionist, as Viner insists. But he was a rather unique sort of interventionist. He intended that the ultimate result of these interventions would be the creation of a society which would "run itself"—i.e. the work of the politician is not to repress man's egoistic impulses and action, but to provide the channels or grooves along which these impulses may be asserted. A social framework which has been appropriately contrived will do this automatically, but the development of such a framework—although it is the primary task of the politician—is a task of extraordinary delicacy and complexity.

Whoever would civilize Men, and establish them into a Body Politick, must be thoroughly acquainted with all the Passions and Appetites, Strength and Weaknesses of their Frame, and understand how to turn their greatest Frailties to the Advantage of the Publick.[17]

---

[16] Although Mandeville is astute enough to perceive that a certain amount of hypocrisy is indispensable in a society characterized by extensive economic interdependence: " . . . it is impossible we could be sociable Creatures without Hypocrisy . . . In all Civil Societies Men are taught insensibly to be Hypocrites from their Cradle, no body dares to own that he gets by Publick Calamities, or even by the Loss of Private Persons. The Sexton would be stoned should he wish openly for the Death of the Parishioners, tho' every body knew that he had nothing else to live upon" (*Fable*, I, 349). The several paragraphs following, pp. 349–354, are strongly recommended as a masterful bit of social psychologizing.

[17] *Fable*, I, 208. Elsewhere he states: "The Power and Sagacity as well as Labour

. . . all Lawgivers have two main Points to consider, at setting out; first, what things will procure Happiness to the Society under their Care; secondly, what Passions and Properties there are in Man's Nature, that may either promote or obstruct this Happiness.[18]

When Mandeville's spokesman. Cleomenes, is asked by Horatio, in the Sixth Dialogue, ". . . what is it at last, that raises opulent Cities and Powerful Nations from the smallest Beginnings?" Cleomenes answers in an illuminating fashion:

All the Ground Work, that is required to aggrandise Nations, you have seen in the *Fable of the Bees*. All sound Politicks, and the whole Art of governing, are entirely built upon the Knowledge of human Nature. The great Business in general of a Politician is to promote, and, if he can, reward all good and useful Actions on the one hand; and on the other, to punish, or at least discourage, every thing that is destructive or hurtful to Society.[19]

The function of the politician. then, is to establish appropriate "rules of the game," to structure the system of rewards and punishments in such a way that individuals, in pursuit of their private interests, will be induced to perform socially useful acts. This in turn, however, required that a truly extraordinary number of restraints be imposed upon human behavior since man's avarice and envy will otherwise suggest innumerable techniques whereby he may profit through purely predatory acts at the expense of his unfortunate neighbor.[20]

Would you be convinc'd of these Truths, do but employ yourself for a Month or two, in surveying and minutely examining into every Art and Science, every Trade, Handicraft and Occupation, that are profess'd and follow'd in such a City as *London;* and all the Laws, Prohibitions, Ordinances and Restrictions, that have been found absolutely necessary, to hinder both private Men and Bodies corporate, in so many different Stations, first from interfering with the Publick Peace and Welfare; secondly, from openly wronging and secretly over-reaching, or any other way in-

---

and Care of the Politician in civilizing the Society, has been no where more conspicuous, than in the happy Contrivance of playing our Passions against one another" (*Fable*, I, 145). Also: ". . . it was not any Heathen Religion or other Idolatrous Superstition, that first put Man upon crossing his Appetites and subduing his dearest Inclinations, but the skillful Management of wary Politicians; and the nearer we search into human Nature, the more we shall be convinced, that the Moral Virtues are the Political Offspring which Flattery begot upon Pride" (*Fable*, I, 51). Cf. also I, 46–47, and *An Enquiry into the Origin of Honour*, 20.

[18] *Fable*, II, 275.   [19] *Ibid.*, 320–21.

[20] Cf. Adam Smith, *Wealth of Nations* (Modern Library Edition): "Such, it seems, is the natural insolence of man, that he almost always disdains to use the good instrument, except when he cannot or dare not use the bad one" (751). Cf. also Nathan Rosenberg, "Some Institutional Aspects of the *Wealth of Nations*," *The Journal of Political Economy* (December 1960), 557–70.

juring, one another: If you will give yourself this Trouble, you will find the Number of Clauses and Proviso's, to govern a large flourishing City well, to be prodigious beyond Imagination; and yet every one of them tending to the same Purpose, the curbing, restraining and disappointing the inordinate Passions, and hurtful Frailties of Man. You will find moreover, which is still more to be admired, the greater part of the Articles, in this vast Multitude of Regulations, when well understood, to be the Result of consummate Wisdom.[21]

Cleomenes immediately adds that, among the regulations he refers to, ". . . there are very few, that are the Work of one Man, or of one Generation; the greatest part of them are the Product, the joynt Labour of several Ages."[22] The evolutionist conception, emphasized above, is even further underscored when Cleomenes, in the next sentence, urges Horatio to recall the shipbuilding analogy (discussed above) of the Third Dialogue.

Mandeville's discussion of the manner in which the social framework of the economy evolves, and the rôle of government in initiating alterations. makes abundantly clear how inadequate, for describing his system at least, is the firmly-established dichotomy between interventionism and laissez-faire [23] (or, for that matter, Elie Halévy's distinction between an artificial identification of interest and a natural identification of interest).[24] For a society where each individual's pursuit of his self-interest is made to harmonize with the interests of other individuals—such a society is, itself, the product not only of historical evolution: it is also, in a very meaningful sense, the *creation* of wise governments. The "dextrous Management" of such governments refers, not to interventionism in the sense in which this term is opposed to laissez-faire; it refers to the creation of a framework of wise laws. Mandeville, in fact, elucidates this meaning while employing precisely the terminology which provides one of the chief bases for his classification as an interventionist:

Horatio. According to your System, it [the art of governing] should be little more, than guarding against human Nature.

Cleomenes. But it is a great while, before that Nature can be rightly understood; and it is the Work of Ages to find out the true Use of the Pas-

[21] *Fable*, II, 321.   [22] *Fable*, II, 321–22.

[23] In his *An Essay on Charity*, Mandeville states a proposition which sounds very much like a later well-known maxim of laissez-faire: "It is the Business of the Publick to supply the Defects of the Society, and take that in hand first which is most neglected by private Persons" (*Fable*, I, 321). Mandeville, however, merely regards it as an essential function of government to remedy these "Defects." His statement does not define the *limits*, or impose a restriction, upon the legitimate activities of government, as would have been the case had he inserted the strategic word "only" into his sentence.

[24] Halévy, *The Growth of Philosophic Radicalism* (New York, 1949), 15–18.

sions, and to raise a Politician, that can make every Frailty of the Members add Strength to the whole Body, and by dextrous Management turn *private Vices into publick Benefits.*

Horatio. It must be a great Advantage to an Age, when many extraordinary Persons are born in it.

Cleomenes. It is not Genius, so much as Experience, that helps men to good Laws . . . the wisest Laws of human Invention are generally owing to the Evasions of bad Men, whose Cunning had eluded the Force of former Ordinances, that had been made with less Caution.[25]

Once the appropriate system of laws has been developed, society will virtually run itself, driven almost entirely by the energy of individual egoisms. In other words, once the wisdom accrued from human experience and the understanding of human nature is embodied in an appropriate system of laws and regulations, the intervention of government in the day to day processes of economic activity will be minimized. Even the need for intelligence in office-holders will be minimal, since the system Mandeville visualizes is one where intelligence is, in effect, built into the institutional structure.[26] Such offices, therefore, need to be supplied only with mediocre abilities in order to function satisfactorily.[27]

In attempting to explain the functioning and administration of a "well-ordered" city or state, Mandeville has frequent recourse to mechanical analogies. In all cases he means to convey the impression of precise and systematic division of function, interdependence, automaticity, and predictability of outcome regardless of the nature of the human materials involved. Referring to the astonishing human effort which must have gone into the development of musical clocks, "that are made to play several Tunes with great Exactness," Cleomenes suggests that

[25] *Fable,* II, 319.

[26] "In all Business that belongs to the *Exchequer,* the Constitution does nine parts in ten; and has taken effectual Care, that the happy Person, whom the King shall be pleas'd to favour with the Superintendency of it, should never be greatly tired or perplex'd with his Office" (*Fable,* II, 325).

[27] " . . . it is the Interest of every Nation to have their Home Government, and every Branch of the Civil Administration, so wisely contriv'd, that every Man of midling Capacity and Reputation may be fit for any of the highest Posts" (*Fable,* II, 323). In discussing the "present grandeur" of the Dutch, Mandeville insists that " . . . what they would ascribe to the Virtue and Honesty of Ministers, is wholly due to their strict Regulations, concerning the management of the publick Treasure, from which their admirable Form of Government will not suffer them to depart; and indeed one good Man may take another's Word, if they so agree, but a whole Nation ought never to trust to any Honesty, but what is built upon Necessity; for unhappy is the People, and their Constitution will be ever precarious, whose Welfare must depend upon the Virtues and Consciences of Ministers and Politicians" (*Fable,* I, 190). Cf. also *Fable,* II, 335.

There is something analogous to this in the Government of a flourishing City, that has lasted uninterrupted for several Ages: There is no Part of the wholesome Regulations, belonging to it, even the most trifling and minute, about which great Pains and Consideration have not been employ'd, as well as Length of Time; and if you will look into the History and Antiquity of any such City, you will find that the Changes, Repeals, Additions and Amendments, that have been made in and to the Laws and Ordinances by which it is ruled, are in Number prodigious: But that when once they are brought to as much Perfection, as Art and human Wisdom can carry them, the whole Machine may be made to play of itself, with as little Skill, as is required to wind up a Clock; and the Government of a large City, once put into good Order, the Magistrates only following their Noses, will continue to go right for a great while, tho' there was not a wise Man in it. . . . [28]

This (and similar mechanical analogies) really expresses the nub of Mandeville's case.[29] Mandeville was searching for a system where arbitrary exertions of government power would be minimized. But this in turn required for its realization a social and legal framework which would induce people, out of a concern only for their own interests (and however they chose to define these interests) to perform acts of a socially-useful sort.[30] To be sure, this framework contains innumerable prohibitions, coercions, and constraints, but they are entirely predictable because they are embodied in public statutes and therefore they provide a basis for rational calculation and systematic goal-directed behavior. Mandeville believed that the most vital aspect of any society—its success or failure generally—depends upon the skill with which it is able to direct men's passions toward the achievement of goals defined by a larger collectivity. He is (as is not, with Mandeville, always the case) entirely serious when he states, in the Preface to the Fable of the Bees, that "Laws and Government are to the Political Bodies of Civil Societies, what the Vital Spirits and Life it self are to the Natural Bodies of Animated Creatures" (Fable, I, 3). And, if the present interpretation is correct, the responsibility for creating the most appropriate legal and political framework is peculiarly the task of the "skilful Politician."

[28] Fable, II, 322–23. Cf. also the knitting-frame simile, 322, and the reference to the weighted roasting spits, 325.

[29] And also provides, incidentally, some measure of the analytical gulf separating Mandeville from, say, Cantillon or Hume. With respect to economics, Mandeville had a fine intuition; but, at crucial points, he typically reasons by analogy instead of analysis.

[30] " . . . The whole Superstructure (of Civil Society) is made up of the reciprocal Services, which Men do to each other. How to get these Services perform'd by others, when we have Occasion for them, is the grand and almost constant Sollicitude in Life of every individual Person. To expect, that others should serve us for nothing, is unreasonable; therefore all Commerce, that Men can have together, must be a continual bartering of one thing for another" (Fable, II, 349).

Mandeville's own choice of language is also partly to blame for exaggerating the interventionist implications of his argument. His frequent references to the work of the ("cunning," "wary," "skilful," "clever") politician seem to imply conscious and deliberate interventionist actions on the part of particular individuals at specific points in historical time. In fact, his language represents an unfortunate way of telescoping what he regards as an essentially evolutionary process—unfortunate because the whole essence of the evolutionary aspect is blotted out by a terminological usage which fails utterly to convey his meaning. Mandeville's real meaning, however, is clarified in an important passage in his later work. *The Origin of Honour* (published in 1732):

> *Horatio.* But, how are you sure, that this [the origin of honour] was the Work of Moralists and Politicians, as you seem to insinuate?
> *Cleomenes.* I give those Names promiscuously to All that, having studied Human Nature, have endeavour'd to civilize Men, and render them more and more tractable, either for the Ease of Governours and Magistrates, or else for the Temporal Happiness of Society in general. I think of all Inventions of this Sort . . . that they are the joint Labour of Many. Human Wisdom is the Child of Time. It was not the Contrivance of one Man, nor could it have been the Business of a few Years, to establish a Notion, by which a rational Creature is kept in Awe for Fear of it Self, and an Idol is set up, that shall be its own Worshiper.[31]

Mandeville conceives, then, of the development of civilization as having involved a continuous and gradual evolution of human institutions in order to accommodate them most effectively to an intractable human nature.[32] When, however, he reasons about the current organ-

---

[31] *The Origin of Honour*, 40–41.

[32] In *An Enquiry into the Origin of Honour*, Cleomenes indicates his agreement with Horatio when the latter states: "It is not in the Power then, you think, of Politicians to contradict the Passions, or deny the Existence of them, but that, when once they have allow'd them to be just and natural, they may guide Men in the Indulgence of them, as they please." Cleomenes then goes on to cite the institution of marriage as an example of the way in which legislators guide men in the indulgence of their passions, thereby forestalling the " . . . innumerable Mischiefs that would ensue . . . " were the relations between the sexes regulated only by "caprice" and "unruly fancy" (*The Origin of Honour*, 28–29). In *A Letter to Dion*, after discussing with approval the regulation of foreign trade, Mandeville offers his readers " . . . another Instance, how palpable and gross Vices may be, and are turn'd into Publick Benefits. It is the Business of all Law-givers to watch over the Publick Welfare, and, in order to procure that, to submit to any Inconveniency, any Evil, to prevent a much greater, if it is impossible to avoid that greater Evil at a cheaper Rate. Thus the Law, taking into Consideration the daily encrease of Rogues and Villains, has enacted, that if a Felon, before he is convicted himself, will impeach two or more of his Accomplices, or any other Malefactors, so that they are convicted of a Capital Crime, he shall be pardon'd and dismiss'd

ization of human society, he deliberately jumps from those aspects which immediately concern him, to the raw data of human nature (as he conceives it), thereby skipping the historical process by which the institutions developed, and substituting a functionalist type of explanation.[33] When concerned with the rôle or function of particular institutions in the human scheme of things, what is important is to demonstrate how these institutions serve a purpose by guiding men in the indulgence of specific passions. But, for such occasions, a genetic account of their origin and development is not important, even if the historical information were available. Since Mandeville's primary interests were with contemporary and not historical problems, he used the phrase " . . . the dextrous Management of the skilful Politician" most often as a convenient shorthand method for summarizing an essentially evolutionary process. However, even where the phrase appears as part of an explicitly normative assertion—dealing with actions government *ought* to take—his recommendations are usually (with the important exception of foreign trade) not of a sort which may properly be regarded as interventionist. We should distinguish here between:

1. Legislation which defines the legal and institutional framework within which economic action takes place (Sherman Anti-trust Act);
2. Legislation which attempts to achieve a specific end by government edict or coercion or by compelling people to behave in a manner which is not consistent with their economic interests as determined by market forces (Edict of Diocletian).

---

with a Reward in Money. There is no Doubt but this is a good and wise Law; for without such an Expedient, the Country would swarm with Robbers and Highwaymen Ten-times more than it does; for by this Means we are not only deliver'd from a greater Number of Villains, than we could expect to be from any other; but it likewise stops the Growth of them, breaks their Gangs, and hinders them from trusting One another." The moral which Mandeville draws—including the terminology with which he draws it—directly confirms the interpretation which is here being placed upon his work: "This shews the usefulness of such a Law, and at the same Time the Wisdom of the Politician, by whose skilful Management the Private Vices of the Worst of Men are made to turn to a Publick Benefit" (*A Letter to Dion*, 42–43, 45).

[33] "The restless Industry of Man to supply his Wants, and his constant Endeavours to meliorate his Condition upon Earth, have produced and brought to Perfection many useful Arts and Sciences, of which the Beginnings are of uncertain Aera's, and to which we can assign no other Causes, than human Sagacity in general, and the joynt Labour of many Ages. . . . When I have a Mind to dive into the Origin of any Maxim or political Invention, for the Use of Society in general, I don't trouble my Head with enquiring after the Time or Country, in which it was first heard of, nor what others have wrote or said about it; but I go directly to the Fountain Head, human Nature itself, and look for the Frailty or Defect in Man, that is remedy'd or supply'd by that Invention. . . ." (*Fable*, II, 128). Cf. also Fable, II, 271.

On this basis, *most* of Mandeville's recommendations dealing with the domestic economy fall into the first category, and the logic of his argument, as developed in this paper, points overwhelmingly to such an interpretation. Mandeville's primary interest was not in interfering with the processes of the market place but in assuring that such processes worked out to socially-desirable ends. His conception of what was socially-desirable—indeed his whole conception of social welfare—was extraordinarily limited, but that takes us beyond the scope of the present paper.

Purdue University.

[2]

Reprinted for private circulation from
THE JOURNAL OF POLITICAL ECONOMY
Vol. LXVIII, No. 6, December 1960
Copyright 1960 by the University of Chicago
PRINTED IN U.S.A.

SOME INSTITUTIONAL ASPECTS OF THE *WEALTH OF NATIONS*

NATHAN ROSENBERG
University of Pennsylvania

PERHAPS as a result of the increasingly formal nature of economics as an academic discipline, the institutional content and preoccupations of Adam Smith's *Wealth of Nations* have suffered prolonged neglect. The following syllogistic restatement, by Wesley Mitchell, may be taken as representative of contemporary formulations of Smith's central argument:

First, every individual desires to increase his own wealth; second, every individual in his local situation can judge better than a distant statesman what use of his labor and capital is most profitable; third, the wealth of the nation is the aggregate of the wealth of its citizens; therefore, the wealth of the nation will increase most rapidly if every individual is left free to conduct his own affairs as he sees fit.[1]

The view which will be presented here is not that this syllogism is wrong, as an interpretation of Smith's views, but that it is uninteresting. By jumping directly from the conception of man as a rational creature to the policy recommendation of laissez faire and all that, it completely short-circuits much of the real substance of Smith's work. By visualizing the human agent as engaged in the effort to maximize a single, unambiguous magnitude, two aspects of Smith's book and the crucial importance of the interplay between them are ignored: (1) his much more elaborate conception of the *conflicting* forces which impel the human agent to action and, as a direct result, (2)

his sustained inquiry into the ultimate impact, in terms of human action and its welfare consequences, of different kinds of institutional arrangements. It is the purpose of the present paper to examine the interrelationships between these two sets of forces.

We begin, then, by adding what Smith regarded as certain essential components of human behavior to the traditional image of the relentless pursuit of material gain.

In addition to the well-known "constant, uniform and uninterrupted effort of every man to better his condition," Smith attached great importance to the belief that the generality of mankind is intractably slothful and prone to indolence. A major counterbalance to the desire for and the pursuit of wealth, therefore, is a love of ease and inactivity. "It is the interest of every man to live as much at his ease as he can. . . ."[2]

A critical corollary of this position is that, although it is the desire for wealth which prods and lures mankind to put forth his greatest efforts, the *attainment* and possession of wealth are regarded by Smith as almost universally corrupting. For, once such wealth has been acquired, man naturally gives vent to his desire for ease. "The indolence and vanity of the rich"[3] is fully as important a force in Smith's system as is the desire for riches

---

[1] Wesley Mitchell, *The Backward Art of Spending Money*, Augustus M. Kelley, Inc., New York, 1950, p. 85; see also his *Lecture Notes on Types of Economic Theory*, Augustus M. Kelley, Inc., New York, 1949, Vol. I, chap. 5.

[2] Adam Smith, *The Wealth of Nations*, p. 718. Subsequently referred to as *"Wealth."* All references are to the Cannan edition which was reissued in the Modern Library Series (New York: Random House, 1937).

[3] *Wealth*, p. 683.

557

15

itself. For "a man of a large revenue, whatever may be his profession, thinks he ought to live like other men of large revenues; and to spend a great part of his time in festivity, in vanity, and in dissipation."[4]

Thus the considerable wealth of the large landlord virtually disqualifies him from supervising the efficient operation of his estate. His background and opulence render him incapable of devoting unremitting attention to details, of making those marginal calculations which are so essential to efficiency.[5] Elsewhere, in speaking of landlords, Smith refers to "that indolence, which is the natural effect of the ease and security of their situation."[6]

Perhaps even more disastrous, because of its effects on capital accumulation, is the effect of high profits upon the business class:

> The high rate of profit seems every where to destroy that parsimony which in other circumstances is natural to the character of the merchant. When profits are high, that sober virtue seems to be superfluous, and expensive luxury to suit better the affluence of his situation.[7]

Although he does not spell it out, there seems to be some rate of profits which may be regarded as optimum from the point of view of achieving the maximum rate of economic growth. Higher profits are clearly regarded as desirable up to some level, since they constitute both the major source and the major incentive for the accumulation of capital. Beyond this unspecified optimum, however, "parsimony . . . that sober virtue seems to be superfluous." Thus Smith opposes monopoly not only because it results in resource misallocation. Monopoly has the equally insidious effect of retarding capital accumulation, since

easily earned profits result in prodigality.[8] Indeed, as will be seen below, the conflicting forces which motivate man to act really establish an optimum level of income in all economic activities.

Finally, and most important, Smith regards it as a strategic component of the human personality that man is naturally deceitful and unscrupulous and will quite willingly employ predatory practices so long as such practices are available to him. "Such, it seems, is the natural insolence of man, that he almost always disdains to use the good instrument, except when he cannot or dare not use the bad one."[9]

Given these human characteristics, it is plain that the mere absence of external restraints and the freedom to pursue self-interest do not suffice, in Smith's view, to establish social harmony or to protect society from "the passionate confidence of interested falsehood."[10] What are required, above all, are institutional mechanisms which *compel* man, in his "natural insolence," "to use the good instrument."

What the usual emphasis on self-interest and individual freedom overlooks is that such self-interest can be pursued in innumerable antisocial ways. It is not sufficient to answer that Smith assumed a competitive framework in his analysis and policy recommendations, because such a framework is not sufficiently specific. Atomistic competition, absence of collusion, and mobility of resources are not nearly sufficient to establish the linkage between unhampered pursuit of self-interest and social well-

---

[4] *Ibid.*, p. 766.   [6] *Ibid.*, p. 249.
[5] *Ibid.*, pp. 363–64.   [7] *Ibid.*, p. 578.

[8] *Ibid.*, pp. 578–79.
[9] *Ibid.*, p. 751. Smith's generally low estimate of humanity is subjected to an entertaining, tongue-in-cheek, treatment in a recent article by Arthur H. Cole, "Puzzles of the 'Wealth of Nations,'" *Canadian Journal of Economics and Political Science*, XXIV (February, 1958), 1–8.
[10] *Wealth*, p. 463.

being. Smith himself clearly realized this. Indeed, large portions of his *Wealth of Nations* are specifically devoted to analyzing the nature of the appropriate institutional framework.

Failure to stress the relationship between Smith's broader conception of human nature and the institutional order with which he was so much preoccupied leads to the creation of unnecessary problems of interpretation and "reconciliation." Thus we have recently been told that

Smith's reliance on moral sentiments as prerequisites of any workable system of competition has often been lost sight of and even denied by later generations of economists who preferred to popularize Smith's reference to the invisible hand as evidence of his glorification of selfishness. Nothing could be further from the truth. It is unthinkable that a moral philosopher of the stature of Adam Smith, who published *The Theory of Moral Sentiments* in 1759, would have abandoned his conceptions of the moral laws governing human behavior in 1776 when he published *The Wealth of Nations*, without making such a change of view explicit. It is, therefore, imperative that *The Wealth of Nations* be read in conjunction with the earlier *Theory of Moral Sentiments* in order to understand that Smith presupposes the existence of a natural moral law as a result of which the prudent man was believed to be anxious to improve himself only in fair ways, i.e., without doing injustice to others.[11]

It will be shown below that such an interpretation is not only totally incorrect but does a considerable injustice to the subtlety and sophistication of Smith's argument.

[11] K. William Kapp, *The Social Costs of Private Enterprise* (Cambridge, Mass.: Harvard University Press, 1950), pp. 28–29. Smith's general skepticism and reluctance to attach too much force to the unalloyed operation of humanitarian motives, even where it might appear most appropriate, is neatly conveyed in the following quotation: "The late resolution of the Quakers in Pennsylvania to set at liberty all their negro slaves, may satisfy us that their number cannot be very great. Had they made any considerable part of their property, such a resolution could never have been agreed to" (*Wealth*, p. 366).

A neglected theme running through virtually all of the *Wealth of Nations* is Smith's attempt to define, in very specific terms, the details of the institutional structure which will best harmonize the individual's pursuit of his selfish interests with the broader interests of society. Far from assuming a "spontaneous" identity of interests (in the mere absence of government restrictions) or of being "blind to social conflicts,"[12] Smith was obsessed with the urge to go beyond the ordinary market-structure definition of competition and to evaluate the effectiveness of different institutional forms in *enforcing* this identity.

The ideal institutional order for Smith is one which places the individual under just the proper amount of psychic tension. The individual applies himself with maximum industry and efficiency when the reward for effort is neither too low (slaves, apprentices) nor too great (monopolists, large landowners).[13] However, more complicated than the *intensity*

[12] "A sunny optimism radiates from Smith's writing. He had no keen sense for social disharmonies, for interest conflicts. . . . On the whole, it is true to say that he was blind to social conflicts. The world is for him harmonious. Enlightened self-interest ultimately increases social happiness" (Gunnar Myrdal, *The Political Element in the Development of Economic Theory* [London: Routledge & Kegan Paul, Ltd., 1953], p. 107).

[13] The manifest impossibility of acquiring and enjoying wealth is, of course, completely stultifying to economic efficiency: "The experience of all ages and nations, I believe, demonstrates that the work done by slaves, though it appears to cost only their maintenance, is in the end the dearest of any. A person who can acquire no property, can have no other interest but to eat as much, and to labour as little as possible. Whatever work he does beyond what is sufficient to purchase his own maintenance, can be squeezed out of him by violence only, and not by any interest of his own" (*Wealth*, p. 365).

On the other hand, as already cited: "A man of a large revenue, whatever may be his profession, thinks he ought to live like other men of large revenues; and to spend a great part of his time in festivity, in vanity, and in dissipation" (*ibid.*, p. 766).

dimension of individual effort is the matter of the *direction* into which this effort is channeled. Smith is, in effect, searching for the appropriate definition of an institutional order which will eliminate zero-sum (or even negative-sum) games. It is the function of institutional arrangements to cut off all avenues (and they are many) along which wealth may be pursued without contributing to the welfare of society. Such a goal in practice requires a careful balancing of incentive, of provision of opportunity to enlarge one's income, against the need to minimize the opportunities for abuse, i.e., possibilities for increasing one's income in an antisocial fashion.

A central, unifying theme in Smith's *Wealth of Nations*, then, is his critique of human institutions on the basis of whether or not they are so contrived as to frustrate man's baser impulses ("natural insolence") and antisocial proclivities and to make possible the pursuit of self-interest *only* in a socially beneficial fashion. Indeed, it will become apparent below that Smith's basic argument applies to the whole spectrum of social contrivances and is not restricted to economic affairs. The question is, in each case, whether institutions do, or do not, harness man's selfish interests to the general welfare. This is, of course, the basis of Smith's critique of mercantilism.

The violence of Smith's polemic against mercantilism lay in the fact that it enabled merchants to better their condition in a manner which did not contribute to the nation's economic welfare. As a result of the dispensation of monopoly grants, of the arbitrary bestowal of "extraordinary privileges" and "extraordinary restraints" upon different sectors of industry by the government, the individual merchant was able to enrich himself without at the same time enriching the nation. For, as Smith clearly recognizes, the pursuit of one's economic self-interest is not necessarily confined to the economic arena. When it spills over into the political arena, it leads to actions which detract from, rather than add to, the economic welfare of society. By contrast, the competitive order which Smith advocated was an institutional arrangement which was characterized, negatively, by the absence of all special privilege and sources of market influence and, positively, by the all-pervasive and uninhibited pressures of the market place. The price system, as Smith saw it, was an intensely coercive mechanism. Its decisive superiority as a way of organizing economic life lay in the fact that, *when it was surrounded by the appropriate institutions*, it tied the dynamic and powerful motive force of self-interest to the general welfare. Its free operation would, in most cases, leave the individual producer no alternative but to pursue his economic interests in a manner conducive to the national welfare.[14]

The secondary literature on Adam Smith has devoted considerable attention to the ways in which the establishment of a free-market network will promote economic efficiency. But the emphasis has been primarily on the allocative efficiency of the free market and too little on the ways in which appropriate institutions contribute to the productivity of the human agent as a factor of production—a matter of supreme importance to Smith. Appropriate institutions increase both the *motivation* and the

---

[14] For Smith's own qualifications of this proposition see Jacob Viner, "Adam Smith and Laissez-Faire," chap. v of J. M. Clark *et al.*, *Adam Smith, 1776–1926: Lectures To Commemorate the Sesquicentennial of the Publication of "The Wealth of Nations"* (Chicago: University of Chicago Press, 1928). I wish to acknowledge my intellectual indebtedness to Viner's masterly analysis of Smith.

capacity of the human agent, whereas inappropriate institutions detract from these things.

Thus Smith opposes apprenticeship laws not only because they impede the mobility of labor between industries but also because they constitute institutional arrangements which pervert the incentive to industry and hard work. During his apprenticeship the young man perceives (correctly) that there is no connection between his effort and his reward (as would exist, e.g., under piecework), and habits of slothfulness and laziness are therefore encouraged:

The institution of long apprenticeships has no tendency to form young people to industry. A journeyman who works by the piece is likely to be industrious, because he derives a benefit from every exertion of his industry. An apprentice is likely to be idle, and almost always is so, because he has no immediate interest to be otherwise. . . . A young man naturally conceives an aversion to labour, when for a long time he receives no benefit from it. . . . But a young man would practise with much more diligence and attention, if from the beginning he wrought as a journeyman, being paid in proportion to the little work which he could execute, and paying in his turn for the materials which he might sometimes spoil through awkwardness and inexperience.[15]

Smith had much to say, of course, about the whole complex of institutions surrounding the ownership and cultivation of the land. His condemnation of such feudal relics as the laws of entail and primogeniture, which impeded the free marketability and therefore the optimum employment of land, is well known. Here, too, however, his search is for the most appropriate institutional scheme. Indeed, all of Smith's historical discussion of systems of land tenure (especially Book III, chap. 2) constitutes a highly interesting account of how specific legal and traditional arrangements in

[15] *Wealth*, pp. 122–23.

Europe have impeded economic progress by failing to provide proper and necessary incentives to landlord and tenant.[16]

The excessive wealth of the great landlord renders him incapable of efficient operation of his estate.[17] However, so long as large estates continue to exist, their most efficient mode of operation poses a serious problem. To place the operation of the land in the hands of a hired agent would be to sever completely the linkage between self-interest and social welfare which the union of property ownership and self-management ordinarily provides. Under such an arrangement,

the country . . . would be filled with idle and profligate bailiffs, whose abusive management would soon degrade the cultivation, and reduce the annual produce of the land, to the diminution, not only of the revenue of their masters, but of the most important part of that of the whole society.[18]

The larger the unit of ownership under a single proprietor, the greater the abuses we may expect from the "negligent, expensive, and oppressive management of his factors and agents."[19] As a logical extension of this argument, Smith observes that

the crown lands of Great Britain do not at present afford the fourth part of the rent, which could probably be drawn from them if they were the property of private persons. If the crown lands were more extensive, it is probable they would be still worse managed.[20]

[16] For a recent treatment of the same problem, bearing numerous parallels to Smith's argument, see United Nations, *Land Reform: Defects in Agrarian Structure as Obstacles to Economic Development* (New York: United Nations, Department of Economic Affairs, 1951).

[17] *Wealth*, pp. 363–64.

[18] *Ibid.*, p. 784.

[19] *Ibid.*, p. 775.

[20] *Loc. cit.* So strongly did Smith feel about the importance of maintaining the union between ownership and management that he actually suggested a

Where lands were tenant-operated, Smith attached great importance to all arrangements, either legal or customary, which assured a close relationship between personal diligence and reward. Thus Smith regards long leases and security against arbitrary eviction as decisive in accounting for English achievements, which he felt contrasted so favorably with those of her Continental neighbors:

> There is, I believe, no-where in Europe, except in England, any instance of the tenant building upon the land of which he had no lease, and trusting that the honour of his landlord would take no advantage of so important an improvement. Those laws and customs so favourable to the yeomanry, have perhaps contributed more to the present grandeur of England, than all their boasted regulations of commerce taken together.[21]

The ideal unit of agricultural organization, of course, is the small proprietorship, which represents a fusion of all the Smithian virtues:

> A small proprietor . . . who knows every part of his little territory, who views it all with the affection which property, especially small property, naturally inspires, and who upon that account takes pleasure not only in cultivating but in adorning it, is generally of all improvers the most industrious, the most intelligent, and the most successful.[22]

Within this context, Smith's well-known opposition to the joint-stock company should occasion no surprise, nor should it be treated, as it occasionally is, as a quaint ("pre-industrial") archaism

on his part. Whatever advantages the corporate form of organization might bring, Smith regarded the offsetting disadvantages as decisive. The divorce of ownership and management and the consequent loss of incentive to diligence and efficiency are precisely the same objections that he raises to the management of large estates by persons other than the owners:

> The trade of a joint stock company is always managed by a court of directors. This court, indeed, is frequently subject, in many respects, to the controul of a general court of proprietors. But the greater part of those proprietors seldom pretend to understand any thing of the business of the company; and when the spirit of faction happens not to prevail among them, give themselves no trouble about it, but receive contentedly such half yearly or yearly dividend, as the directors think proper to make to them.[23]

Moreover, all the ordinary incentives to economize, naturally existing in the owner-operated firm, are lost upon the managers of a joint-stock company. Smith makes it perfectly clear that he would object to the adequacy of recent attempts to measure the effectiveness of competitive forces by the use of industry (or product) concentration ratios. For he regards bigness itself, in the *absolute* and not only the relative sense, as objectionable. Joint-stock companies destroy the incentive to efficiency *within* the individual firm:

> The directors of such companies, however, being the managers rather of other people's money than of their own, it cannot well be ex-

---

form of discriminatory taxation, contrived in such a manner "that the landlord should be encouraged to cultivate a part of his own land" (*ibid.*, pp. 783–84).

   21 *Ibid.*, pp. 368–69. Elsewhere, Smith observes: "Some leases prescribe to the tenant a certain mode of cultivation, and a certain succession of crops during the whole continuance of the lease." With typical sarcasm he attributes this arrangement to "the landlord's conceit of his own superior knowledge (a conceit in most cases very ill founded)" (p. 783).

   22 *Ibid.*, p. 392. Notice, however, that Smith regards it as an important virtue of the cultivating landlord that he can afford to bear the costs of experimentation. "The landlord can afford to try experiments, and is generally disposed to do so. His unsuccessful experiments occasion only a moderate loss to himself. His successful ones contribute to the improvement and better cultivation of the whole country" (*ibid.*, p. 784).

   23 *Ibid.*, p. 699.

ASPECTS OF THE *WEALTH OF NATIONS* 563

pected, that they should watch over it with the same anxious vigilance with which the partners in a private copartnery frequently watch over their own. Like the stewards of a rich man, they are apt to consider attention to small matters as not for their master's honour, and very easily give themselves a dispensation from having it. Negligence and profusion, therefore, must always prevail, more or less, in the management of the affairs of such a company.[24]

If an "unremitting exertion of vigilance and attention . . . cannot long be expected from the directors of a joint stock company,"[25] the mercantile projects of princes hold out even smaller prospects of success. Such projects

have scarce ever succeeded. The profusion with which the affairs of princes are always managed, renders it almost impossible that they should. The agents of a prince regard the wealth of their master as inexhaustible; are careless at which price they buy; are careless at what price they sell; are careless at what expence they transport his goods from one place to another. Those agents frequently live with the profusion of princes, and sometimes too, in spite of that profusion, and by a proper method of making up their accounts, acquire the fortunes of princes.[26]

Thus Smith is constantly searching out the impact of specific institutional forms upon the human actor. Given his basic conception of human motivations and propensities, the specific kinds of behavior which we may expect of any individual will depend on the way the institutions surrounding him are structured, for these determine the alternatives open to him and establish the system of rewards and penalties within which he is compelled to operate. Indeed, Smith not only directs some very harsh remarks at human hypocrisy but clearly implies that, once the institutional framework is specified, human behavior becomes highly predictable. After

[24] *Ibid.*, p. 700.
[25] *Ibid.*, p. 713.
[26] *Ibid.*, p. 771.

an extensive criticism of the self-seeking behavior of the servants of the East India Company, he states:

I mean not, however, by any thing which I have here said, to throw any odious imputation upon the general character of the servants of the East India Company, and much less upon that of any particular persons. It is the *system* of government, *the situation in which they are placed*, that I mean to censure; not the character of those who have acted in it. *They acted as their situation naturally directed*, and they who have clamoured the loudest against them would, probably, not have acted better themselves.[27]

Although it would occur to few people to look to Smith for guidance in the conduct of government business, there is much useful instruction in such matters in the *Wealth of Nations* (Book V). The general lesson which has always been drawn from Smith—especially by those who have clearly neglected to read him (or Viner[28])—has concerned the very limited number of functions which a government can "appropriately" perform. Of much greater interest for our present purposes are the rules laid down or implied by Smith as to how the government ought to organize the conduct of its affairs, for here Smith touches, at great length, upon the subject matter of this paper.

The guiding principle in the organization of public affairs may be stated briefly: "Public services are never better performed than when their reward comes only in consequence of their being performed, and is proportioned to the diligence employed in performing them."[29] But this statement is neither so obvious

[27] *Ibid.*, pp. 605–6 (italics mine). The importance of institutional determinants of human behavior is reinforced, in Smith's view, by his belief that natural, inborn differences among men are not very significant and are typically exaggerated (see *ibid.*, pp. 15–16).

[28] Viner, *op. cit.*

[29] *Wealth*, p. 678.

nor so platitudinous as it may sound, for the establishment of the optimum arrangements in accordance with this principle is an extraordinarily difficult task and even today (perhaps one should say "especially today") is seriously neglected. Although reward should be "proportioned to the diligence employed," care must be taken that such diligence can be exerted only in socially beneficial directions. Here again it is the direction, rather than the mere intensity, of human effort that is crucially important. For, as Smith points out, in legal proceedings the income of attorneys and clerks of court had indeed been proportioned to their diligence. But, unfortunately, this diligence had been defined and measured for remunerative purposes in a too strictly quantitative sense, i.e., in terms of the number of pages of their written output. As a result,

in order to increase their payment, the attornies and clerks have contrived to multiply words beyond all necessity, to the corruption of the law language of, I believe, every court of justice in Europe. A like temptation might perhaps occasion a like corruption in the form of law proceedings.[30]

The administration of justice is, indeed, rife with examples of the difficulties involved in devising techniques which effectively link the pursuit of self-interest with the public welfare. Although present arrangements leave much to be desired, anything which tends to reduce the financial interest of the lawyer in the case of his client is studiously to be avoided. "Lawyers and attornies, at least, must always be paid by the parties; and, if they were not, they would perform their duty still worse than they actually perform it."[31]

Yet the administration of justice in the broader sense ought *never* to be conducted primarily with respect to financial

considerations, most especially where the sovereign himself exercises judicial authority. For this establishes a highly improper liaison with self-interest which leads to the flagrant abuse of justice, rather than its promotion:

This scheme of making the administration of justice subservient to the purposes of revenue, could scarce fail to be productive of several very gross abuses. The person, who applied for justice with a large present in his hand, was likely to get something more than justice; while he, who applied for it with a small one, was likely to get something less. Justice too might frequently be delayed, in order that this present might be repeated. The amercement, besides, of the person complained of, might frequently suggest a very strong reason for finding him in the wrong, even when he had not really been so.[32]

The exact methods devised for the remuneration of judges are, therefore, of considerable importance. Fixed salaries, while limiting possibilities for corruption, are likely to lead to indolence and neglect, whereas allowing the judges to

[30] *Ibid.*, p. 680. Had the Russians read their Smith with nearly the same diligence as they did their Marx, they might not now be so plagued with problems perfectly analogous to, but far more serious than, "the conveyances of a verbose attorney."

"Orders from above have an entirely different effect from that desired by the planners themselves. Thus they plan output in tons in many ministries (including heavy machine-building and iron and steel) so that the factories concentrate on the heavier goods within each item of the assortment (product-mix) specified in the plan. They plan output of textiles by length and not area, so that factories produce narrower cloths than their looms will take in order to boost their output figures. They plan geological surveys in metres drilled and not in tons of minerals discovered, so that you can fulfil the plan by doing unnecessary drilling. The output of each factory is planned in wholesale prices as well as in physical terms; and as wholesale prices include the cost of raw materials, factories concentrate on those items which use more raw materials and less labour, again in order to boost their output figures" (R. W. Davies, "Industrial Planning Reconsidered," *Soviet Studies*, April, 1957, p. 428).

[31] *Wealth*, p. 677.

[32] *Ibid.*, p. 675.

establish and to collect fees, out of which they are to derive their incomes, increases the possibility that the pursuit of self-interest will lead to corrupt practices. Since, at the same time, it is desirable that the law courts should defray the expenses of their operation and that the judiciary should be completely independent of the executive branch, Smith proposes a carefully contrived system whereby fees are independently determined and standardized, means of payment precisely defined and publicly recorded, and payment to the judges withheld until proceedings are completed. Under these circumstances, Smith is hopeful, judges will have practically no alternative but to mete out justice in a fair and expeditious manner.[33]

The strong feelings which Smith harbored against "that insidious and crafty animal, vulgarly called a statesman or politician," are too well known to require elaboration. They represented the *fons et origo* of the many perversions and extravagances which Smith identified with "the Mercantile System." More important, however, is the fact that Smith regards politicians and government officials as a class of men peculiarly insu-

lated not only from the ordinary pressures of the market but from any other institutionalized compulsion which engages the pursuit of their selfish interests with the public welfare. At the same time, the opportunities and devices typically available for enriching themselves directly at the expense of the public he regards as myriad. Just as in the case of the servants of the East India Company, however, it must be emphasized that Smith condemns not politicians per se but the institutional framework within which politicians typically find themselves.

On the question of the functions which may appropriately be undertaken by governments, Smith makes several highly interesting observations, indicating that his antigovernment bias was, in substantial measure, a reflection of the currently limited possibilities for engaging the "interested diligence" of public officials upon the efficient operation of government undertakings. For example, Smith cites approvingly the mercantile projects carried out by small European governments. His invidious comparisons with the government of England turn, not on a matter of principle, but upon the almost certain incapacity of the British government to engage successfully in similar undertakings, in contrast with the established efficiency of the (small) governments of Venice and Amsterdam:

[33] *Ibid.*, pp. 677–81. The system of paying fees to courts of law, Smith argues, has led in the past to competition among different courts of justice which had highly beneficial consequences. The competition for litigation led not only to an expansion in the jurisdiction of courts originally set up for specific purposes, such as the court of exchequer, but also, as a direct consequence, to a swift and impartial justice. Even more interesting is his suggestion that such intercourt competition was a dynamic force in changing the law itself and in leading to the emergence of new legal concepts, such as the highly important writ of ejectment. Smith reports that "the artificial and fictitious writ of ejectment, the most effectual remedy for an unjust outer or dispossession of land," was invented by the courts of law to regain a considerable amount of litigation which had been temporarily lost, in this competitive process, to the court of chancery (*ibid.*, p. 679).

The orderly, vigilant, and parsimonious administration of such aristocracies as those of Venice and Amsterdam, is extremely proper, it appears from experience, for the management of a mercantile project of this kind. But whether such a government as that of England; which, whatever may be its virtues, has never been famous for good oeconomy; which, in time of peace, has generally conducted itself with the slothful and negligent profusion that is perhaps natural to monarchies; and in time of war has constantly acted with all the thoughtless extravagance that democracies are apt to fall into; could be safely trusted with the management of such a project, must at least be a good deal more doubtful.[34]

Similarly, although cautioning that much of the information available concerning events in Asia was derived from such unreliable sources as the accounts of "stupid and lying missionaries," Smith concedes that roads and canals may be operated by Asian governments with a high degree of efficiency. This is because, in such places as China and Indostan, the primary source of revenue to the sovereign is derived from a land-tax or land-rent. Under these circumstances, it is in the direct interest of the sovereign to provide and maintain the most efficient possible network of transportation facilities.[35] It is highly improbable, however, "during the present state of things," that any European government could provide such transport facilities with any degree of efficiency because their self-interests are not similarly engaged by their sources of revenue:

> The revenue of the sovereign does not, in any part of Europe, arise chiefly from a land-tax or land-rent. In all the great kingdoms of Europe, perhaps, the greater part of it may ultimately depend upon the produce of the land: But that dependency is neither so immediate, nor so evident. In Europe, therefore, the sovereign does not feel himself so directly called upon to promote the increase, both in quantity and value, of the produce of the land, or, by maintaining good roads and canals, to provide the most extensive market for that produce.[36]

What is involved here, therefore, is not only the matter of administrative

competence or efficiency but also the absence of institutional arrangements so structured as to engage the motive and interests of those concerned.

Smith's shrewd perception of the impact of different organizational arrangements upon the individual pursuit of wealth appears in the distinction that he draws between the operation of roads and canals. Canals, he argues, may more properly be left in private hands than roads. This is because the interested diligence of the canal-owner requires the canal to be maintained, or it will become impassable through neglect and therefore cease entirely to be a source of revenue. Highways, on the other hand, deteriorate by degrees and, although entirely neglected, may still remain passable. If private persons are allowed to collect such tolls, the roads will therefore suffer considerable neglect, since such persons will lack the personal incentive to maintain them.[37]

---

[34] *Ibid.*, p. 770. Of course, Smith insists that, wherever possible and appropriate, the administration of smaller (local) units of government is to be preferred to that of larger, national units (*ibid.*, p. 689).

[35] *Ibid.*, p. 688; see also pp. 789–90.

[36] *Ibid.*, pp. 688–89.

[37] *Ibid.*, p. 684. In a discussion of the appropriate investment criteria for underdeveloped countries, Albert Hirschman recently made a proposal whose inner logic was strikingly similar to that underlying Smith's distinction between the operation of roads and canals: "Priority should be given to investments, industries, and technical processes which either hardly require maintenance or *must* have maintenance because its absence carries with it a very high penalty, i.e., leads to accidents or immediate breakdown rather than to slow deterioration in the quantity and quality of output. The fact that the performance of the airlines in Columbia is excellent, that of the railroads mediocre, and that of the roads outright poor can be explained in terms of this criterion: nonmaintenance would lead to certain disaster in the case of airplanes, but roads can be left to deteriorate for a long time before they finally disappear, and railroads occupy a somewhat intermediate position from this viewpoint." (Albert Hirschman, "Economics and Investment Planning: Reflections Based on Experience in Columbia," in *Investment Criteria and Economic Growth* (Cambridge, Mass.: Center for International Studies, Massachusetts Institute of Technology), p. 48; see also Albert Hirschman, *The Strategy of Economic Development* (New Haven, Conn.: Yale University Press, 1958), pp. 139–43.

Smith's search for an institutional scheme which will establish and enforce an identity of interests between the public and private spheres even carries over into his discussion of the nation's military establishment. After an extended discussion of the changing technology of warfare and its consequences for the organization of a nation's military establishment, he concludes: "It is only by means of a standing army . . . that the civilization of any country can be perpetuated, or even preserved for any considerable time."[38] The obvious threat which such a standing army poses to republican principles, "wherever the interest of the general and that of the principal officers are not necessarily connected with the support of the constitution of the state,"[39] is to be remedied by insuring that military leadership is recruited only from among those classes whose self-interest is indissolubly linked with the support of the existing government. Thus,

where the sovereign is himself the general, and the principal nobility and gentry of the country the chief officers of the army; where the military force is placed under the command of those who have the greatest interest in the support of the civil authority, because they have themselves the greatest share of that authority, a standing army can never be dangerous to liberty.[40]

Smith's further exploration of this general theme is richly developed in his discussion of religious and educational institutions (Book V, chap. 1, Arts. 2d and 3d). Although Smith raises strong social and political objections to the accumulation of wealth and power by ecclesiastical institutions, he argues that such accumulation almost certainly de-

stroys their effectiveness as "institutions for the instruction of people of all ages" as well. For members of the clergy are likely to be most zealous and industrious as teachers of religious doctrine if they "depend altogether for their subsistence upon the voluntary contributions of their hearers."[41] If they are independently endowed, if their interested diligence, in other words, is not made dependent on public assessment of the effectiveness of their performance, they are likely to become negligent and slothful in the fulfilment of their duties. It is this situation which prompted Smith to make such frequent disparaging references to clergy of "ancient and established systems . . . reposing themselves upon their benefices" and to the "contemptuous and arrogant airs" displayed by "the proud dignitaries of opulent and well-endowed churches," etc.[42]

But, although Smith is opposed to the "independent provision" of the clergy, he does not advocate the alternative of leaving them to the free pursuit of their interested diligence. For the extreme tensions under which the clergy would then be placed would tempt them to adopt reprehensible practices which they might otherwise not choose, were the compulsions less great. Such a policy would lead to deceitful appeals to a naïve, credulous, and superstitious public and wholesale exploitation of the gullibility of the latter—in effect, unfair ecclesiastical

[38] *Wealth*, p. 667.

[39] *Ibid.*, p. 667.

[40] *Ibid.*, pp. 667–68.

[41] *Ibid.*, p. 740.

[42] *Ibid.*, pp. 741 and 762. A further consequence of large endowments and benefices, to which Smith attached considerable importance, is that, by their competitive attractions, they draw superior talents out of universities and into the church. "After the church of Rome, that of England is by far the richest and best endowed church in Christendom. In England, accordingly, the church is continually draining the universities of all their best and ablest members" (*ibid.*, p. 763; see also pp. 762–64).

practices.[43] Thus the special circumstances surrounding the usual functions of the clergy lead Smith to amend somewhat his general maxim: "In every profession, the exertion of the greater part of those who exercise it, is always in proportion to the necessity they are under of making that exertion."[44] The difficulty here is that extreme necessity is not only likely to maximize effort and to overcome the natural indolence of the clergy but to influence the direction of that effort in socially disagreeable ways. Here again Smith's concern is not only with the maximization of effort but with the more subtle dimensions of human behavior.

It is of considerable interest to the argument of this paper to note that, although Smith is highly critical of almost every religious order with which he deals, he does single out at least one important exception. Reference is made to the very high praise indeed which Smith accords to the Presbyterian clergy:

There is scarce perhaps to be found anywhere in Europe a more learned, decent, independent, and respectable set of men, than the greater part of the presbyterian clergy of Holland, Geneva, Switzerland, and Scotland.[45]

And, further:

The most opulent church in Christendom does not maintain better the uniformity of faith, the fervour of devotion, the spirit of order, regularity, and austere morals in the great body of the people, than this very poorly endowed church of Scotland.[46]

One may, if one wishes, dismiss this major exception as originating in a source of bias too obvious to be worth recording.

But this would be doing much less than justice to the scope of Smith's argument and to the fact that this judgment is consistent, at least in Smith's eyes, with criteria which he develops and employs elsewhere. Smith seems to feel that the mode of payment devised for the Presbyterian clergy struck just that optimum balance between underpayment, which drove the mendicant orders to that excessive and misplaced zeal which Smith likened to a plundering army,[47] and overpayment from large independent endowments, which was so often responsible for indolence, negligence, and "contemptuous and arrogant airs." The consistency of Smith's judgment and the generality of his argument are perfectly clear in the closing paragraph of the section devoted to the clergy:

The proper performance of every service seems to require that its pay or recompence should be, as exactly as possible, proportioned to the nature of the service. If any service is very much under-paid, it is very apt to suffer by the meanness and incapacity of the greater part of those who are employed in it. If it is very much over-paid, it is apt to suffer, perhaps, still more by their negligence and idleness. A man of a large revenue, whatever may be his profession, thinks he ought to live like other men of large revenues; and to spend a great part of his time in festivity, in vanity, and in dissipation. But in a clergyman this train of life not only consumes the time which ought to be employed in the duties of his function, but in the eyes of the common people destroys almost entirely that sanctity of character which can alone enable him to perform those duties with proper weight and authority.[48]

Smith's devastating remarks respecting the state of education are often treated as a mere *curiosum*. In fact, however, Smith's critique of educational in-

---

[43] See *ibid.*, pp. 742–43, for the extended quotation from Hume's *History of England* which Smith approvingly inserts.

[44] *Wealth*, p. 717.

[45] *Ibid.*, p. 762.

[46] *Ibid.*, p. 765.

[47] *Ibid.*, p. 742: "The mendicant orders derive their whole subsistence from (voluntary) oblations. It is with them, as with the hussars and light infantry of some armies: no plunder, no pay."

[48] *Ibid.*, p. 766.

stitutions— especially universities—is entirely consistent with the general principles which have been referred to in this paper. Because of special privileges and independent endowments, England's great universities in particular lack the appropriate institutional mechanisms which link the pursuit of self-interest on the part of the faculty to the need to perform satisfactorily their professional duties. This is especially the case where the colleges are not only heavily endowed[49] but where also (*mirabile dictu!*) the teachers themselves constitute the governing body.[50] Under such a self-perpetuating arrangement the incomes of teachers bear virtually no relation to their proficiency as either scholars or pedagogues. This sham is intensified in those cases where class attendance is made obligatory and students are unable to exercise their consumer sovereignty by awarding their fees to instructors of greatest competence. In those cases where the instructor derives his entire income from endowments, the connection between effort and reward is completely ruptured, and the situation is hopeless. For even if the teacher is naturally energetic and constitutionally incapable of a life of total quiescence, his energies will be channeled into directions *other* than that of scholarship, since the marginal private gains in such pursuits have been effectively set at zero.[51]

The result is, inevitably, a total and shameful neglect of learning.[52]

The situation, mercifully, is not so bad in the public schools, which "are much less corrupted than the universities." The principal reason for the difference, as might be expected, is that "the reward of the schoolmaster in most cases depends principally, in some cases almost entirely, upon the fees or honoraries of his scholars."[53]

The central argument of this paper may be restated as follows: Smith's *Wealth of Nations* provided the first systematic guide to the manner in which the price mechanism allocated resources in a free-market economy, and the book has been justly celebrated for this unique achievement.[54] At the same time, however, Smith was very much preoccupied with establishing the conditions under which this market mechanism would operate most effectively. His conception of human behavior allowed for the free operation of certain impulses, motivations, and behavior patterns which were calculated to thwart, rather

---

[49] "The endowments of schools and colleges have necessarily diminished more or less the necessity of application in the teachers. Their subsistence, so far as it arises from their salaries, is evidently derived from a fund altogether independent of their success and reputation in their particular professions" (*ibid.*, p. 717).

[50] Perhaps it should be added that, in Smith's opinion, the control of a university by some "extraneous jurisdiction" (bishop, governor, minister of state) was likely to be ignorant and capricious in nature—as in the French universities (*ibid.*, pp. 718–19).

[51] "If he is naturally active and a lover of labour, it is his interest to employ that activity in any way, from which he can derive some advantage, rather than in the performance of his duty, from which he can derive none" (*ibid.*, p. 718).

[52] "In the university of Oxford, the greater part of the public professors have, for these many years, given up altogether even the pretence of teaching" (*ibid.*, p. 718). And, more generally: "The discipline of colleges and universities is in general contrived, not for the benefit of the students, but for the interest, or more properly speaking, for the ease of the masters. Its object is, in all cases, to maintain the authority of the master, and whether he neglects or performs his duty, to oblige the students in all cases to behave to him as if he performed it with the greatest diligence and ability" (*ibid.*, p. 720).

[53] *Ibid.*, p. 721.

[54] Cf., however, the reservations expressed by Schumpeter, to whom nothing, except Walras' *Elements*, appears to have been sacred (J. A. Schumpeter, *History of Economic Analysis* [New York: Oxford University Press, 1954], pp. 184–86).

than to reinforce, the beneficent operation of market forces, and Smith was
therefore very much concerned with providing an exact, detailed specification of
an optimal institutional structure. Later
generations of economists have virtually
ignored this aspect of Smith's analysis
both by oversimplifying his conception
of human behavior and by merely invok-
ing, without examination, a competitive
economy. The result has been a neglect of
some of the most fruitful and suggestive
aspects of Smith's analysis and a distor-
tion of the broader implications of his
argument. The present paper represents
a partial attempt to restore this balance.

Recent concern among economists

with problems of economic development
and with specific areas of government
policy formulation suggests a resurgence
of interest in the incidence of different
institutional forms upon economic behavior.[55] Although the *Wealth of Nations*
is certainly not the last word on this subject, its analytical framework still constitutes a most useful point of departure.

[55] Cf., for example, W. A. Lewis, *The Theory of
Economic Growth* (Homewood, Ill.: Richard D.
Irwin, Inc., 1955), esp. chap. iii, and the masterly
analysis of the American patent system in Fritz
Machlup, *An Economic Review of the Patent System*
(Study No. 15 of the Subcommittee on Patents,
Trademarks and Copyrights of the Committee on
the Judiciary, U.S. Senate [Washington: Govern-
ment Printing Office, 1958]).

Adam Smith on the Division of Labour: Two Views or One?

By Nathan Rosenberg[1]

Adam Smith's treatment of the division of labour has intrigued readers and commentators for many years. On the one hand it provided a masterful analysis of the gains from specialization and exchange upon which, it is no exaggeration to say, the discipline of economics was nurtured. On the other hand, Smith's apparent afterthoughts of Book V, where he refers to the deleterious effects of the division of labour upon the work force, constitute a major source of inspiration for the socialist critique of capitalist institutions, as Marx himself acknowledged. For Smith states here, in part:

> In the progress of the division of labour, the employment of the far greater part of those who live by labour, that is, the great body of the people, comes to be confined to a few very simple operations, frequently to one or two. But the understandings of the greater part of men are necessarily formed by their ordinary employments. The man whose whole life is spent in performing a few simple operations, of which the effects too are, perhaps, always the same, or very nearly the same, has no occasion to exert his understanding, or to exercise his invention in finding out expedients for removing difficulties which never occur. He naturally loses, therefore, the habit of such exertion, and generally becomes as stupid and ignorant as it is possible for a human creature to become. . . . His dexterity at his own particular trade seems . . . to be acquired at the expense of his intellectual, social, and martial virtues. But in every improved and civilised society this is the state into which the labouring poor, that is, the great body of the people, must necessarily fall, unless government takes some pains to prevent it.[2]

The apparent contradiction between the views of Book I and Book V has often been commented upon. Marx observes in *Capital* that Adam Smith " . . . opens his work with an apotheosis on the division of labour. Afterwards, in the last book which treats of the sources of public revenue, he occasionally repeats the denunciations of the division of labour made by his teacher, A. Ferguson."[3] More recently, in a reappraisal of this subject, Dr. E. G. West presents a confrontation of " Adam Smith's Two Views on the Division of Labour " which

---

[1] The author is indebted to his colleague, June Flanders, for helpful suggestions.
[2] Adam Smith, *Wealth of Nations*, Modern Library edition, edited by Edwin Cannan, pp. 734–5. All subsequent references are to this edition.
[3] Karl Marx, *Capital*, Foreign Languages Publishing House, Moscow, 1961, p. 123. Marx's curious notion, that Adam Smith was heavily indebted to Adam Ferguson in his analysis of the consequences of division of labour, will be dealt with in a later footnote.

127

A

he regards as " contradictory ", " incompatible ", and involving a
" striking inconsistency ".[1] Since the issues involved are intrinsically
important in addition to playing a seminal role both in the development of economic thought and in the critique of capitalist institutions
and capitalist development, I propose to re-examine Smith's treatment
of division of labour primarily as it relates to one central issue : the
determinants of inventive activity. I will show that Smith's treatment
of this problem is, in certain respects, considerably more complex
and interesting than it has previously been made out to be. Furthermore,
I hope to demonstrate that his analysis is free of the inconsistencies
and contradictions which have been attributed to it. The issues at
stake are of considerable importance, since Smith's long-term prognosis
for capitalism is centred upon its capacity for generating technical
change and thus substantially raising *per capita* income. This capacity,
in turn, is made by Smith to depend overwhelmingly—indeed one may
almost say exclusively—upon the division of labour and the consequences flowing from it. As Schumpeter has stated, " . . . nobody,
either before or after A. Smith, ever thought of putting such a burden
upon division of labor. With A. Smith it is practically the only factor
in economic progress."[2]

A difficulty which most commentators seem to encounter with
Smith's views on division of labour results from interpreting the discussion in Book I to mean that invention is the sole product of workers'
intelligence.[3] Then, having shown by quotation from Book V that
Smith believed that workers become increasingly " stupid and
ignorant " as a result of division of labour, the inference is drawn
that Smith is involved in a contradiction. This view of Smith is inadequate and misleading on several important counts.

We need, first, to enlarge the scope of our discussion by recognizing
that Smith looks upon inventive activity as a process which has several
dimensions. Increasing division of labour encourages invention in a
variety of ways. It does this, first of all, by sharpening the attention
of the worker and focusing it more forcefully than before upon a
narrow range of processes. By narrowing down the range the worker
is enabled to lavish greater care as well as curiosity upon his work.
His mind is subjected to fewer distractions. In the absence of the need
to make frequent readjustments by moving from one sort of activity
to another, the worker proceeds in a spirit of " vigorous application ".[4]

---

[1] E. G. West, " Adam Smith's Two Views on the Division of Labour ", *Economica*,
February 1964, pp. 23–32.
[2] Joseph A. Schumpeter, *History of Economic Analysis*, New York, 1954, p. 187.
[3] In his opening paragraph, for example, West states : " The reader is first
reminded of the discussion in Book I of the economic effects of the division of labour,
and of its favourable moral and intellectual effects on the workers " (*West, loc. cit.,*
p. 23). And later : " The argument of Book I clearly suggests that the division of
labour enhances man's mental stature as it increases the quantity of goods produced " (p. 25).
[4] *Wealth of Nations*, pp. 8–9.

> The division of labour no doubt first gave occasion to the invention of machines. If a man's business in life is the performance of two or three things, the bent of his mind will be to find out the cleverest way of doing it; but when the force of his mind is divided it cannot be expected that he should be so successful.[1]

The worker's perception of mechanical deficiencies and of possibilities for improving the efficiency of an operation is heightened by the unrelieved intensity in the focus of his attention. Smith's apocryphal story of the young boy who, anxious to get off and give vent to his youthful exuberance with his playfellows, invented a device which opened and closed the valves of a steam engine without his assistance, is surely compelling evidence that Smith regarded the invention as a consequence of a narrow focusing of interest and attention rather than of a mature or developed intelligence.

A further important aspect of Smith's view of inventive activity, as his story of the boy and the steam engine makes clear, is motivation. One of the major themes of the *Wealth of Nations*, of course, is its exhaustive examination of the manner in which institutional arrangements structure the decision-making of the individual, sometimes in a manner which harmonizes private interest and social interest, and sometimes in a manner which disrupts them.[2] Smith has a great deal to say, for example, on the impact of different systems of land ownership on the introduction of agricultural improvements. Although his reference here is primarily to capital formation, rather than invention, the importance of motivation in stimulating certain types of economic behaviour shows up clearly, and is applicable to the issue of the determinants of invention and innovation as well.

On the one hand the large landowner is corrupted by his easy and luxuriant style of life:

> To improve land with profit, like all other commercial projects, requires an exact attention to small savings and small gains, of which a man born to a great fortune, even though naturally frugal, is very seldom

---

[1] *Lectures on Justice, Police, Revenue and Arms delivered in the University of Glasgow by Adam Smith*, edited by Edwin Cannan, 1896, p. 167 (subsequently referred to as *Lectures*). Cf. also *Wealth of Nations*, pp. 9–10, and an early draft of the *Wealth of Nations*, which appears in W. R. Scott, *Adam Smith as Student and Professor*, Glasgow 1937, p. 336 (subsequently referred to as *Early Draft*). West recognizes the effect of increasing division of labour in performing these functions. My objection to his treatment is in his insistence that the progressive division of labour increases intelligence as well as alertness. " It is, however, in the third proposition, that invention and mechanization are encouraged by the division of labour, where we find Smith's most philosophical and conclusive case for favourable effects upon intelligence and alertness." West, *op. cit.*, p. 25. I find no evidence, either in the quotations cited by West, or in my own reading of Book I of the *Wealth of Nations* or elsewhere in Smith's writings, to support the interpretation that increasing division of labour improves either the worker's intelligence or understanding. Dexterity, certainly; alertness, yes; intelligence, no.

[2] This problem has been examined in some detail in Nathan Rosenberg, " Some Institutional Aspects of the *Wealth of Nations* ", *Journal of Political Economy*, December 1960, pp. 557–70.

capable. The situation of such a person naturally disposes him to attend rather to ornament which pleases his fancy than to profit for which he has so little occasion.[1]

On the other hand, the varying forms of tenantry had, historically, discouraged improvement on the part of the cultivator. " It could never . . . be the interest even of this last species of cultivators [metayers] to lay out, in the further improvement of the land, any part of the little stock which they might save from their own share of the produce, because the lord, who laid out nothing, was to get one-half of whatever it produced."[2]

Where a system of farmers developed, as in England, with legal protections and security of tenure, considerable improvements might be undertaken.[3] For the motivation of the farmer is strengthened by the reasonable assurance that he will himself enjoy the fruits of his own initiative, ingenuity and industry. In fact, " after small proprietors . . . rich and great farmers are, in every country, the principal improvers ".[4] Small proprietors are, however, unsurpassed.

A small proprietor . . . who knows every part of his little territory, who views it all with the affection which property, especially small property, naturally inspires, and who upon that account takes pleasure not only in cultivating but in adorning it, is generally of all improvers the most industrious, the most intelligent, and the most successful.[5]

Perhaps the most extreme example of the impairment of the incentive to invent is the case of slavery. For here the individual is deprived of all possibility of " bettering his condition " and has scarcely any motive for improving his productivity. " A person who can acquire no property, can have no other interest but to eat as much, and to labour as little as possible."[6] Interestingly enough, Smith seems to have vacillated a good deal on the precise handling of this issue. In the *Early Draft* he tentatively attributes an invention to a slave.

Some miserable slave, condemned to grind corn between two stones by the meer strength of his arms, pretty much in the same manner as painters bray their colours at present, was probably the first who thought

---

[1] *Wealth of Nations*, p. 364. In *Lectures* Smith had stated (p. 228): " Great and ancient families have seldom either stock or inclination to improve their estates, except a small piece of pleasure-ground about their house."

[2] *Wealth of Nations*, p. 367.

[3] " . . . The yeomanry of England are rendered as secure, as independent, and as respectable as law can make them ". *Ibid.*, p. 394.

[4] *Ibid.*, p. 371.

[5] *Ibid.*, p. 392. Elsewhere Smith heaps praise upon successful merchants who have turned country gentlemen. " Merchants are commonly ambitious of becoming country gentlemen, and when they do, they are generally the best of all improvers " (p. 384). For the successful merchant has been subjected to the rigours and discipline of commercial life and has acquired the values and habits essential to the successful introduction of improvements. " The habits . . . of order, oeconomy and attention, to which mercantile business naturally forms a merchant, render him fitter to execute, with profit and success, any project of improvement " (p. 385).

[6] *Ibid.*, p. 365. Cf. *Lectures*, p. 225: " When lands . . . are cultivated by slaves, they cannot be greatly improven, as they have no motive to industry."

of supporting the upper stone by a spindle and of turning it round by a crank or handle which moved horizontally, according to what seems to have been the original, rude form of hand mills. . . .[1]

In the *Lectures*, however, he at one point repeats the " probable " attribution of the upper spindle to a slave[2] while later in the volume he asserts that " . . . slaves . . . can have no motive to labour but the dread of punishment, and can never invent any machines for facilitating their business ".[3] Finally, in the *Wealth of Nations*, although Smith does not much modify his basic scepticism toward slaves, he hedges his statement, in characteristic Smithian fashion, with qualifying phrases: " Slaves . . . are *very seldom* inventive; and all the *most important* improvements, either in machinery, or in the arrangement and distribution of work, which facilitate and abridge labour, have been the discoveries of freemen."[4]

This quotation suggests our next point, which is of considerable importance to Smith's understanding of the relationship between division of labour and invention. Adam Smith clearly recognised the existence of a hierarchy of inventions involving varying degrees of complexity, and requiring differing amounts of technical competence, analytical sophistication and creative and synthesizing intellect. Similarly, he distinguished between the ingenuity required to produce any particular invention on the one hand, and to modify it, improve it, or to apply it to new uses on the other. Interestingly enough, Smith's most detailed treatment is in the *Early Draft;* less appears in the *Lectures* and in the *Wealth of Nations.*[5] With the only slight exception of his treatment of slavery, however, there is no internal evidence that Smith altered his position between the *Early Draft* and the *Wealth of Nations.*

It should be noticed, first of all, that although Smith's attempt to reconstruct the past with respect to the invention of machines takes the form, in his exposition, of conjectural history, he nevertheless shows a clear awareness of the evolutionary process in the development of

---

[1] *Early Draft*, pp. 336–37.

[2] " Some miserable slave who had perhaps been employed for a long time in grinding corn between two stones, probably first found out the method of supporting the upper stone by a spindle ". *Lectures*, p. 167.

[3] *Ibid.*, p. 231. Smith was surely a bit unreasonable concerning the motivation of a slave to undertake inventions. When the only consequence is to reduce his master's costs, the slave may be assumed to be uninterested ; but when the invention improves the conditions of work in some respect, surely the slave has such a motive. It is obviously in the personal interest of the slave to devise inventions which eliminate the most irksome and backbreaking varieties of work typically performed by slaves—such as the early methods of grinding corn. See *Early Draft*, pp. 336–37.

[4] *Wealth of Nations*, p. 648. Emphasis added. The quotation continues : " Should a slave propose any improvement of this kind, his master would be very apt to consider the proposal as the suggestion of laziness, and of a desire to save his own labour at the master's expense. The poor slave, instead of reward, would probably meet with much abuse, perhaps with some punishment. In the manufactures carried on by slaves, therefore, more labour must generally have been employed to execute the same quantity of work, than in those carried on by freemen."

[5] The most relevant passages are pp. 336–8 of the *Early Draft*, pp. 167–8 of the *Lectures*, and pp. 9–10 of the *Wealth of Nations*.

human artifacts. After surveying some of the basic inventions in agriculture and in grinding mills, he states: " These different improvements were probably not all of them the inventions of one man, but the successive discoveries of time and experience, and of the ingenuity of many different artists." Also: " We have not, nor cannot have, any complete history of the invention of machines, because most of them are at first imperfect, and receive gradual improvements and increase of powers from those who use them."[1]

At the rudest and lowest level, some simple inventions were, as indicated earlier, within the capacity of a common slave to invent. In the past many inventions of not too great complexity were made by common workmen. " A great part of the machines made use of in those manufactures in which labour is most subdivided, were originally the inventions of common workmen, who, being each of them employed in some very simple operation, naturally turned their thoughts towards finding out easier and readier methods of performing it."[2]

Reverting to the operation of the grinding mill, Smith is prepared to concede that the simpler inventions (he cites the feeder and shoe) might have been developed by the miller himself. However, the more complex inventions were probably beyond the limited vision and capacity of the miller. Here Smith suggests that such sophisticated innovations as the cogwheel and the trundle were probably the work of millwrights. For these inventions " . . . bear the most evident marks of the ingenuity of a very intelligent artist ". Smith shows here[3] an awareness of the vital role to be played by the capital-goods industries as a source of technological change. Such possibilities, he argues, however, are limited by the size of the market for capital goods which, in turn, determines when (and whether) capital-goods production can be undertaken as a specialized trade. " All the improvements in machinery . . . have by no means been the inventions of those who had occasion to use the machines. Many improvements have been made by the ingenuity of the makers of the machines, when to make them became the business of a peculiar trade. . . ."[4]

---

[1] *Early Draft*, p. 337, and *Lectures*, p. 167. Smith's evolutionist position here is strongly reminiscent of Mandeville: " . . . We often ascribe to the Excellency of Man's Genius, and the Depth of his Penetration, what is in Reality owing to length of Time, and the Experience of many Generations, all of them very little differing from one another in natural Parts and Sagacity ". *Fable of the Bees*, ed. F. B. Kaye, 1924, volume II, p. 142. Also " . . . the Works of Art and human Invention are all very lame and defective, and most of them pitifully mean at first: Our knowledge is advanced by slow Degrees, and some Arts and Sciences require the Experience of many Ages, before they can be brought to any tolerable Perfection ". *Ibid.*, pp. 186–7. For further discussion of Mandeville's evolutionist views of social development, see Nathan Rosenberg, " Mandeville and Laissez-faire ", *Journal of the History of Ideas*, April–June 1963, pp. 183–96.

[2] *Wealth of Nations*, p. 9.

[3] *Early Draft*, p. 337. Smith's preoccupation with technological change in milling operations is shared by Marx, who states that " the whole history of the development of machinery can be traced in the history of the corn mill ". *Capital*, p. 348.

[4] *Wealth of Nations*, p. 10.

Continuing up the scale of complexity and sophistication, invention at the highest levels involves acts of insight, creative synthesis, and the capacity to draw upon diverse fields of knowledge. The most important inventions of all are the works of philosophers, who perceive and exploit new relationships and natural phenomena to human advantage.[1] A philosopher or " meer man of speculation " is

> one of these people whose trade it is, not to do any thing but to observe every thing, and who are upon that account capable of combining together the powers of the most opposite and distant objects. To apply in the most advantageous manner those powers, which are allready known and which have already been applyed to a particular purpose, does not exceed the capacity of an ingenious artist. But to think of the application of new powers, which are altogether unknown, and which have never before been applied to any similar purpose, belongs to those only who have a greater range of thought and more extensive views of things than naturally fall to the share of a meer artist.[2]

The loftiest pinnacles of inventive activity, then, are occupied by philosophers, and the less rarefied heights are inhabited by artists whose activities involve less novelty and creative insight and who engage also in improving upon the inventions of more illustrious men.

> It was a real philosopher only who could invent the fire engine,[3] and first form the idea of producing so great an effect, by a power in nature which had never before been thought of. Many inferior artists, employed in the fabric of this wonderful machine may after wards discover more happy methods of applying that power than those first made use of by its illustrious inventor. It must have been a philosopher who, in the same manner first invented, those now common and therefore disregarded, machines, wind and water mills. Many inferior artists may have afterwards improved them.[4]

In short, the " capacity to invent " cannot be assessed or measured in absolute terms; the concept is meaningful only in relation to the complexity of the existing technology and the degree of creative imagination required in order for new " breakthroughs " to occur. Presumably, then, even if the alertness and intellectual capacity of the common labourer remained constant, or increased somewhat, it would be inadequate to perform the increasingly complicated intellectual feats required of an inventor in a technically progressive society.

[1] In his " History of Astronomy " Smith defines philosophy as " . . . the science of the connecting principles of nature . . . as in those sounds, which to the greater part of men seem perfectly agreeable to measure and harmony, the nicer ear of a musician will discover a want, both of the most exact time, and of the most perfect coincidence: so the more practised thought of a philosopher, who has spent his whole life in the study of the connecting principles of nature, will often feel an interval betwixt two objects, which, to more careless observers, seem very strictly conjoined." Adam Smith, " History of Astronomy ", in *Essays on Philosophical Subjects*, pp. 19 and 20. It is this ability to perceive gaps and to formulate problems which, for Smith, constitutes the critical step in scientific inquiry and also in the discovery and application of useful knowledge.
[2] *Early Draft*, pp. 337–8.
[3] i.e., steam engine.
[4] *Early Draft*, p. 338. Cf. also *Lectures*, pp. 167–8.

A strategic determinant, within Smith's framework, of the *capacity* to invent is now clear. Major inventions involve the ability to draw upon diverse areas of human knowledge and experience and to combine them in a unique fashion to serve some specific purpose. The ideal intellectual equipment for such synthesis is possessed by " . . . philosophers or men of speculation, whose trade it is not to do any thing, but to observe every thing; and who, upon that account, are often capable of combining together the powers of the most distant and dissimilar objects ".[1] This is, of course. precisely the talent which workmen become progressively *less* capable of exerting as the increasing division of labour continually narrows the range of the worker's activities (and therefore, since " . . . the understandings of the greater part of men are necessarily formed by their ordinary employments ",[2] of his comprehension). Although, therefore, division of labour strengthens the force of a worker's attention upon a narrow range of activities and perhaps as a result increases his capacity for instituting small improvements, it is likely to disable him completely for the task of undertaking major inventions which involve drawing upon ranges of knowledge and experience to which he is less and less likely to be exposed. Originally. therefore, when production involved a relatively simple technology, increasing division of labour, by sharpening and concentrating the focus of a worker's attention, made it easier for him to invent and to institute non-fundamental improvements within the existing technology. As technology becomes increasingly complex, however, and as the solutions to problems require the ability to draw upon sources of knowledge and experience from a wide range of areas or disciplines, the worker is likely to be increasingly inadequate because of the exceedingly narrow repertory of materials from which he can draw.

But though Smith visualized the worker as becoming increasingly stupid and ignorant as a result of further division of labour. there is no reason to believe that this was necessarily inconsistent or incompatible with the possibilities for continuing technical progress and invention. This, in fact, brings us to a major point of this article. Smith looked upon the growing division of labour as a process which had not only an historical but necessarily also an important social dimension. Therefore, to concentrate solely on the impact of the division of labour upon the working class leads to the adoption of a very partial and misleading view of the economic and social consequence of division of labour. This can be seen most forcefully if we look at the changing structure of the social division of labour as a society moves from a primitive to a civilized condition.

The movement from a primitive to a civilized society is characterized by an enormous proliferation in the number of productive activities performed in society. In a primitive—i.e., unspecialized—economy each worker is, in general, obliged to perform a significant fraction

[1] *Wealth of Nations*, p. 10.   [2] *Ibid.*, p. 734.

of the total number of activities. As society progresses toward a more civilized state the number of separate activities grows prodigiously but the number performed by each individual worker declines. In an advanced society, then, there are many more activities going on in the economy but the individual worker is confined to a very narrow range. While the structure of the social division of labour becomes more complex, the individual worker's rôle becomes more simple. In the extreme case, and in contemporary jargon, the individual worker becomes the cheapest non-linear servo-mechanism. This was the prospect over which Smith (and later Marx) was so much exercised.[1] There are, however, important forces working in the opposite direction, for the collective intelligence of society grows *as a result of the very process* which causes the understanding of the " inferiour ranks of people " to become increasingly defective.[2] For the increased productivity resulting from specialization and division of labour is evident too in those trades which are concerned with the production of new knowledge.

[1] " The knowledge, the judgment, and the will, which, though in ever so small a degree, are practised by the independent peasant or handicraftsman, in the same way as the savage makes the whole art of war consist in the exercise of his personal cunning—these faculties are now required only for the workshop as a whole. Intelligence in production expands in one direction, because it vanishes in many others. What is lost by the detail labourers, is concentrated in the capital that employs them. It is a result of the division of labour in manufactures that the labourer is brought face to face with the intellectual potencies of the material process of production, as the property of another, and as a ruling power. This separation begins in simple co-operation, where the capitalist represents to the single workman, the oneness and the will of the associated labour. It is developed in manufacture which cuts down the labourer into a detail labourer. It is completed in modern industry, which makes science a productive force distinct from labour and presses it into the service of capital ". Karl Marx, *Capital*, p. 361.

[2] Adam Ferguson had some striking observations on this same process : " It may even be doubted, whether the measure of national capacity increases with the advancement of arts. Many mechanical arts, indeed, require no capacity; they succeed best under a total suppression of sentiment and reason ; and ignorance is the mother of industry as well as of superstition. Reflection and fancy are subject to err ; but a habit of moving the hand, or the foot, is independent of either. Manufactures, accordingly, prosper most where the mind is least consulted, and where the workshop may, without any great effort of imagination, be considered as an engine, the parts of which are men. . . . But if many parts in the practice of every art, and in the detail of every department, require no abilities, or actually tend to contract and to limit the views of the mind, there are others which lead to general reflections, and to enlargement of thought. Even in manufacture, the genious of the master, perhaps, is cultivated, while that of the inferior workman lies waste. . . . The practitioner of every art and profession may afford matter of general speculation to the man of science; and thinking itself, in this age of separations, may become a peculiar craft." Adam Ferguson, *An Essay on the History of Civil Society*, sixth edition, London, 1793, pp. 305–6. In his discussion of the division of labour in *Capital*, Marx suggests (p. 362) that Adam Smith learned about " the disadvantageous effects of division of labour " from Ferguson, and that he merely " reproduces " Ferguson in Book V of the *Wealth of Nations*. Earlier (p. 354) Marx even refers to " A. Ferguson, the master of Adam Smith ". Presumably Marx had in mind the fact that the first edition of Ferguson's *An Essay on the History of Civil Society* was published in 1767, nine years before the *Wealth of Nations*. The discovery of the 1763 *Lectures*, however, sufficiently establishes Smith's priority in this matter. Cf. also Karl Marx, *The Poverty of Philosophy*, Foreign Languages Publishing House, Moscow, no date, pp. 129–30.

In the progress of society, philosophy or speculation becomes, like every other employment, the principal or sole trade and occupation of a particular class of citizens. Like every other employment too, it is sub-divided into a great number of different branches, each of which affords occupation to a peculiar tribe or class of philosophers; and this subdivision of employment in philosophy, as well as in every other business, improves dexterity, and saves time. Each individual becomes more expert in his own peculiar branch, more work is done upon the whole, and the quantity of science is considerably increased by it.[1]

We can express this in an admittedly over-simplified chronological sequence. In all societies antecedent to the development of an extensive division of labour in manufactures, the level of knowledge and understanding of the majority of the population is "considerable", but the dispersion is small, and there are few individuals with attainments and abilities far above the average.

In such a society indeed, no man can well acquire that improved and refined understanding, which a few men sometimes possess in a more civilized state. Though in a rude society there is a good deal of variety in the occupations of every individual, there is not a great deal in those of the whole society. Every man does, or is capable of doing, almost every thing which any other man does, or is capable of doing. Every man has a considerable degree of knowledge, ingenuity, and invention; but scarce any man has a great degree. The degree, however, which is commonly possessed, is generally sufficient for conducting the whole simple business of the society.[2]

In an advanced society with an extensive division of labour, however, the intellectual attainments of the "labouring poor" are hopelessly stultified and corrupted by the monotony and uniformity of the work process. On the other hand, such a society is made up of an endlessly variegated number of such activities, and although the worker's own personal assignment may be unchallenging and lacking in significant opportunities, the sum total of the occupations in society presents extraordinary opportunities for the detached and contemplative philosophers.[3] Although then the *modal* level of understanding is very

---

[1] *Wealth of Nations*, p. 10. Smith had expressed this same view as far back as the writing of the *Early Draft* (p. 338): " Philosophy or speculation, in the progress of society, naturally becomes, like every other employment, the sole occupation of a particular class of citizens. Like every other trade it is subdivided into many different branches, and we have mechanical, chemical, astronomical, physical, metaphysical, moral, political, commercial and critical philosophers. In philosophy, as in every other business, this subdivision of employment improves dexterity and saves time. Each individual is more expert at his particular branch. More work is done upon the whole and the quantity of science is considerably increased by it." More succinctly, Smith stated a few pages later (p. 344): " In opulent and commercial societies . . . to think or to reason comes to be, like every other employment, a particular business, which is carried on by a very few people, who furnish the public with all the thought and reason possessed by the vast multitudes that labour."
[2] *Wealth of Nations*, p. 735.
[3] At this point Smith parts company with Mandeville who, characteristically, is reluctant to attribute a beneficent social rôle to the man of pure knowledge;

low, the *highest* levels of scientific attainment permitted by the extensive specialization in the production of knowledge are quite remarkable. The *collective* intelligence of the civilized society, then, is very great and presents unique and unprecedented opportunities for further technical progress.

> In a civilized state . . . though there is little variety in the occupations of the greater part of individuals, there is an almost infinite variety in those of the whole society. These varied occupations present an almost infinite variety of objects to the contemplation of those few, who, being attached to no particular occupation themselves, have leisure and inclination to examine the occupations of other people. The contemplation of so great a variety of objects necessarily exercises their minds in endless comparisons and combinations, and renders their understandings, in an extraordinary degree, both acute and comprehensive.[1]

We can now complete our analysis by calling attention to two further points, both of which reinforce the interpretation of Smith presented here. First of all, the more extreme debilitating consequences of the division of labour do not make themselves felt upon those employed in agriculture. This is owing to the fact that the dependence of agriculture upon the changing of the seasons imposes constraints upon the extent to which division of labour can be carried in that sector.[2] Precisely because the division of labour has failed to make the extensive inroads upon agricultural practices that it did upon manufacturing, Smith insists that the understanding of the inhabitants of the countryside is superior to that of their counterparts in manufacturing. Indeed, " after what are called the fine arts, and the liberal professions . . . there is perhaps no trade which requires so great a variety of knowledge and experience ".[3] Smith contrasts invidiously the knowledge, judgment and experience required in the common mechanic trades with that required in agriculture. Furthermore, " not only the art of the farmer, the general direction of the operations of husbandry, but many inferior branches of country labour, require much more skill and experience than the greater part of mechanic trades ".[4] Smith clearly believes that the agricultural worker avoids the " drowsy stupidity " of his urban cousins because the changing requirements of his work are continually imposing demands upon his judgment and

---

" . . . They are very seldom the same Sort of People, those that invent Arts, and Improvements in them, and those that enquire into the Reason of Things: this latter is most commonly practis'd by such, as are idle and indolent, that are fond of Retirement, hate Business, and take delight in Speculation: whereas none succeed oftener in the first, than active, stirring, and laborious Men, such as will put their Hand to the Plough, try Experiments, and give all their Attention to what they are about ". Mandeville, *op. cit.*, vol. II, p. 144.

[1] *Wealth of Nations*, pp. 735–6.
[2] *Ibid.*, p. 6; *Lectures*, p. 164; *Early Draft*, pp. 329–30.
[3] *Wealth of Nations*, p. 126.
[4] *Ibid.*, p. 127.

discretion, and therefore keeping alive those mental capacities which the urban worker eventually loses through sheer desuetude.[1] Even

> the common ploughman, though generally regarded as the pattern of stupidity and ignorance, is seldom defective in this judgment and discretion. He is less accustomed, indeed, to social intercourse than the mechanic who lives in a town. His voice and language are more uncouth and more difficult to be understood by those who are not used to them. His understanding, however, being accustomed to consider a greater variety of objects, is generally much superior to that of the other, whose whole attention from morning till night is commonly occupied in performing one or two very simple operations. How much the lower ranks of people in the country are really superior to those of the town, is well known to every man whom either business or curiosity has led to converse much with both.[2]

Our final point is that Smith sees the upper ranks of society as a group which is thoroughly insulated from the ravages of the division of labour. Whereas the agricultural population is exempted from the worst ravages of division of labour by inherent limits upon the extent to which such division can be carried in agriculture, people " of some rank or fortune " are exempted by virtue of the simple fact that they are not compelled to earn their livelihoods through prolonged drudgery and exertions at relatively menial activities.

> The employments . . . in which people of some rank or fortune spend the greater part of their lives, are not, like those of the common people, simple and uniform. They are almost all of them extremely complicated, and such as exercise the head more than the hands. The understandings of those who are engaged in such employments can seldom grow torpid for want of exercise. The employments of people of some rank and fortune, besides, are seldom such as harass them from morning to night. They generally have a good deal of leisure, during which they may perfect themselves in every branch either of useful or ornamental knowledge of which they may have laid the foundation, or for which they may have acquired some taste in the earlier part of life.[3]

It is clear, then, that although the division of labour has potentially disastrous effects upon the moral and intellectual qualities of the labour force, and although Smith was seriously concerned with these

---

[1] Smith may well have been prejudiced against urban life, as West has suggested, but it should now be clear that it is not necessary to resort to such a *deus ex machina* in order to account for Smith's views. West states: " . . . it seems likely that Smith's complaint of moral and intellectual degeneration was directed more against town life as such than against the factory which was only one aspect of it " (West p. 30). In the light of the interpretation set forward here, it seems much easier to regard Smith's complaints as a logical consequence of the differential incidence of division of labour upon rural and urban populations. Furthermore, of course, Smith objects to towns because, in large measure as a result of geographic concentration, the spirit of monopoly and restraints upon the competitive process develop much more readily in urban than in rural areas. See *Wealth of Nations*, pp. 126–7.

[2] *Ibid.*, p. 127.

[3] *Ibid.*, pp. 736–7.

effects, he did not fear that such developments would constitute a serious impediment to continued technological change.[1]

Thus Smith shows an acute perception of the social and human as well as the economic consequences of the division of labour in society. Whatever merit or demerit his analysis may have (it is my opinion that it has considerable merit) it is certainly free of serious contradictions. The main thrust of his analysis, as I have argued, is that, as a direct result of increasing division of labour, the creativity of society as a whole grows while that of the labouring poor (" . . . that is, the great body of the people ") declines. Marx was deeply appreciative of the nice dialectic of Smith's analysis, and certainly learned a good deal from it, although he referred scornfully to Smith's modest proposals for educating the workers as consisting only of the administration of " homoeopathic doses ".[2] Be that as it may, there are many who would contend that the broader aspects of the process with which Smith was attempting to come to grips—the causes and the consequences of technical progress—still constitute some of the most serious problems of industrializing societies.

Purdue University,
Lafayette, Indiana.

---

[1] Smith, perhaps somewhat optimistically, regarded philosophical inquiries as a natural development among leisured classes of societies which had achieved some minimum degree of order, stability and wealth. " Those of liberal fortunes, whose attention is not much occupied either with business or with pleasure, can fill up the void of their imagination, which is thus disengaged from the ordinary affairs of life, no other way than by attending to that train of events which passes around them. While the great objects of nature thus pass in review before them, many things occur in an order to which they have not been accustomed. Their imagination, which accompanies with ease and delight the regular progress of nature, is stopped and embarrassed by those seeming incoherences; they excite their wonder and seem to require some chain of intermediate events, which, by connecting them with something that has gone before, may thus render the whole course of the universe consistent and of a piece. Wonder, therefore, and not any expectation of advantage from its discoveries, is the first principle which prompts mankind to the study of Philosophy, of that science which pretends to lay open the concealed connexions that unite the various appearances of nature; and they pursue this study for its own sake, as an original pleasure or good in itself, without regarding its tendency to procure them the means of many other pleasures ". " History of Astronomy ", *op. cit.*, pp. 33–4.

[2] *Capital*, p. 362.

4

Adam Smith, Consumer Tastes, and Economic Growth

Nathan Rosenberg*

Purdue University

Adam Smith's neglect of demand in explaining the determination of natural price is well known. But is it also true, as it is often inferred or assumed, that demand forces play no important role in the *Wealth of Nations*? As an *analytical* matter, the traditional interpretation is certainly a defensible one. If one confines oneself to the theory of value, the pickings are distinctly lean in that book. But, of course, only a rather small fraction of Smith's major work is explicitly concerned with the theory of value. If one is interested also in inquiring into the nature and causes of the wealth of nations—and it is at least arguable that Smith possessed such an interest —it is possible that demand-side forces may be utilized in an important way. In describing and accounting for the process of economic growth as it occurred in Europe, does Smith rely heavily on demand forces as explanatory variables? Granted his limited use of demand within an analytical context, are such forces important within the framework of *historical generalizations* concerning economic growth?

This paper will attempt to furnish an affirmative answer to the last question. It will be argued that the taste and preference structure of consumers—or at least certain *classes* of consumers—is indispensable to Smith's explanation of the process of economic growth. More specifically, it will be shown that (1) the composition of demand and (2) the impact of the availability of new commodities upon household behavior have, historically, been critical determinants of the "progress of opulence in different nations."[1]

It will be argued further that Smith has a fairly well integrated view of

---

* The author wishes to acknowledge the benefit which he has derived from discussions with James Lorimer.

[1] Book III of the *Wealth of Nations* is titled "Of the Different Progress of Opulence in Different Nations." On the contents of Book III Schumpeter stated: "It did not attract the attention it seems to merit. In its somewhat dry and uninspired wisdom, it might have made an excellent starting point of a historical sociology of economic life that was never written" (Schumpeter, 1954, p. 187).

361

the nature and formation of human tastes and the manner and direction in which human wants develop over time. This view is an essential part of his conception of economic growth. It is not, however, expressed in a single place, and therefore it will be necessary to draw upon various sources to achieve the desired synthesis—in particular, to supplement Smith's statement in various portions of the *Wealth of Nations* with materials from the earlier *Theory of Moral Sentiments*.

In examining the role played by demand in Smith's view of development, it will be helpful to concentrate our attention on the economic surplus generated by different societies in different stages of development. For economic growth is regarded as essentially a matter of the size of the surplus at any moment in time and the manner in which it is disposed of. As we will see, certain aspects of consumer tastes are regarded by Smith as affecting all of these factors in a decisive way.

All of the earliest forms of society were, of course, preoccupied with the acquisition of food. "Among savage and barbarous nations, a hundredth or little more than a hundredth part of the labour of the whole year, will be sufficient to provide them with such cloathing and lodging as satisfy the greater part of the people. All the other ninety-nine parts are frequently no more than enough to provide them with food" (Smith, 1937, p. 163). Adam Smith distinguishes two stages prior to a settled agricultural society: (1) "hunters, the lowest and rudest state of society, such as we find it among the native tribes of North America" and (2) "nations of shepherds, a more advanced state of society, such as we find it among the Tartars and Arabs" (Smith, 1937, p. 653). The next more advanced stage is "a nation of mere husbandmen," one where plants have been domesticated and a settled agriculture is carried on, but where there is "little foreign commerce, and no other manufactures but those coarse and household ones which almost every private family prepares for its own use" (Smith, 1937, p. 655). Subsequent stages, to which (and only to which) Smith applies the term "civilized society," possess more extensive commerce, including foreign commerce, and a more extensive manufacturing sector, within which there exists an elaborate specialization of function among workmen (Smith, 1937, pp. 656–57).

Since "subsistence is, in the nature of things, prior to conveniency and luxury" (Smith, 1937, p. 357), the growth of the non-agricultural sector is dependent upon improvements in productivity in agriculture. "When by the improvement and cultivation of land the labour of one family can provide food for two, the labour of half the society becomes sufficient to provide food for the whole. The other half, therefore, or at least the greater part of them, can be employed in providing other things, or in satisfying the other wants and fancies of mankind" (Smith, 1937, p. 163). It is the growth in agricultural productivity, then, which makes possible urban society and the productive activities which are uniquely associated with

cities.[2] A surplus above subsistence needs emerges at very early stages in
the development of societies. Although a nation of hunters provides only
a "precarious subsistence" and "universal poverty," a nation of shepherds
can produce a very substantial surplus above subsistence requirements.[3]
From this early stage onward, therefore, the disposition of the surplus becomes a matter of primary importance. This in turn raises the question of
the distribution of income and the manner in which above-subsistence
incomes are disposed of.

In a society of shepherds the range of commodities available for consumption is severely circumscribed. In the absence of the goods produced
by a more advanced state of the arts and manufactures (whether domes-
tically produced or made available through foreign trade), there are very
few opportunities for expenditures on personal consumption. The result is
that the wealthy acquire numerous dependents and retainers who rely for
their subsistence entirely upon their masters:

> A Tartar chief, the increase of whose herds and flocks is
> sufficient to maintain a thousand men, cannot well employ that
> increase in any other way than in maintaining a thousand men.
> The rude state of his society does not afford him any manu-
> factured produce, any trinkets or baubles of any kind, for which
> he can exchange that part of his rude produce which is over and
> above his own consumption. The thousand men whom he thus
> maintains, depending entirely upon him for their subsistence,
> must obey his orders in war, and submit to his jurisdiction in
> peace. He is necessarily both their general and their judge, and
> his chieftainship is the necessary effect of the superiority of his
> fortune (Smith, 1937, p. 671; cf. Smith, 1956, pp. 15–16).

This point is, in fact, a general one applicable to all societies which do
not have available to them the products of a more advanced and refined
manufacturing.[4] The opportunity cost to the rich of supporting the poor is,
at the margin, quite literally zero, and therefore the hospitality of the rich

---

[2] "The cultivation and improvement of the country...which affords subsistence,
must, necessarily, be prior to the increase of the town, which furnishes only the means
of conveniency and luxury. It is the surplus produce of the country only, or what is
over and above the maintenance of the cultivators, that constitutes the subsistence of
the town, which can therefore increase only with the increase of this surplus produce"
(Smith, 1937, p. 357).

[3] Smith in fact attributes the establishment of regular government to the in-
equalities of property which emerge among shepherd societies. "The appropriation
of herds and flocks which introduced an inequality of fortune, was that which first
gave rise to regular government. Till there be property there can be no government,
the very end of which is to secure wealth, and to defend the rich from the poor"
(Smith, 1956, p. 15).

[4] All large countries, in fact, have some minimal amount of manufacturing. See
Smith's qualification (Smith, 1937, p. 381).

"seems to be common in all nations to whom commerce and manufactures are little known" (Smith, 1937, p. 386):

> In a country which has neither foreign commerce, nor any of the finer manufactures, a great proprietor, having nothing for which he can exchange the greater part of the produce of his lands which is over and above the maintenance of the cultivators, consumes the whole in rustic hospitality at home. If this surplus produce is sufficient to maintain a hundred or a thousand men, he can make use of it in no other way than by maintaining a hundred or a thousand men. He is at all times, therefore, surrounded with a multitude of retainers and dependants, who having no equivalent to give in return for their maintenance, but being fed entirely by his bounty, must obey him, for the same reason that soldiers must obey the prince who pays them. Before the extension of commerce and manufactures in Europe, the hospitality of the rich and the great, from the sovereign down to the smallest baron, exceeded every thing which in the present times we can easily form a notion of (Smith, 1937, p. 385).

In order to appreciate Smith's further argument, it is important to understand an aspect of his interpretation of human behavior. Smith believed that, in all but the most primitive societies, "the necessities and conveniencies of the body" were easily provided for (Smith, 1817, p. 343; see also Smith, 1956, p. 160). In more advanced societies, the striving in the economic arena takes place not to procure goods which cater to human needs in any utilitarian sense; for the goods acquired by the rich are of "frivolous utility" and provide, at best, "trifling conveniencies."[5] The effort involved in their acquisition certainly cannot be justified in terms of the direct utility they afford. Indeed, in speaking of the decision of the poor man's son to pursue wealth, Smith says: "To obtain the conveniencies which these [wealth and greatness] afford, he submits in the first year, nay in the first month of his application, to more fatigue of body, and more uneasiness of mind, than he could have suffered through the whole of his life from the want of them" (Smith, 1817, p. 291).[6]

---

[5] "The poor man's son, whom Heaven in its anger has visited with ambition" finds, after a lifetime of "unrelenting industry" that "wealth and greatness are mere trinkets of frivolous utility, no more adapted for procuring ease of body or tranquility of mind, than the tweezer-cases of the lover of toys; and, like them too, more troublesome to the person who carries them about with him than all the advantages they can afford him are commodious. *There is no other real difference between them, except that the conveniencies of the one are somewhat more observable than those of the other*" (Smith, 1817, pp. 290–92 [*emphasis added*]). In old age, "power and riches appear then to be, what they are, enormous and operose machines contrived to produce a few trifling conveniencies to the body" (Smith, 1817, p. 293; see also pp. 236–37).

[6] Also: "It is not ease or pleasure, but always honour, of one kind or another, though frequently an honour very ill understood, that the ambitious man really pursues" (Smith, 1817, p. 100).

What then is the object pursued by mankind if it is not the pleasure, comfort, and ease afforded by the acquisition of a large stock of worldly goods? Briefly, the recognition and admiration of our fellow human beings. "To deserve, to acquire, and to enjoy, the respect and admiration of mankind, are the great objects of ambition and emulation" (Smith, 1817, pp. 94–95).[7]

Although this respect and admiration should properly be attained through studying to be wise and practicing to be virtuous, "the great mob of mankind" is not adequately equipped to discern and appreciate wisdom and virtue and indiscriminately accords its respect and admiration to the rich and powerful.[8] Hence arises a corruption of the moral sentiments,[9] and hence the pursuit of riches is primarily actuated not by the enjoyment of riches itself but by the recognition and distinction which the possession and display of wealth affords:[10]

> It is chiefly from this regard to the sentiments of mankind, that we pursue riches and avoid poverty. For to what purpose is all the toil and bustle of this world? What is the end of avarice and ambition, of the pursuit of wealth, or power, and pre-eminence? Is it to supply the necessities of nature? The wages of the meanest labourer can supply them. We see that they afford him food and clothing, the comfort of a house, and of a family. If we examine his economy with rigour, we should find that he spends a great part of them upon conveniencies, which may be regarded as superfluities, and that, upon extraordinary occasions, he can give something even to vanity and distinction. What then is the cause of our aversion to his situation, and why should those who have been educated in the higher ranks of life, regard

[7] The importance of the pursuit of rank, and the unimportance of satisfying bodily needs, is expressed even more forcefully later on: "Though it is in order to supply the necessities and conveniencies of the body, that the advantages of external fortune are originally recommended to us, yet we cannot live long in the world without perceiving that the respect of our equals, our credit and rank in the society we live in, depend very much upon the degree in which we possess, or are supposed to possess these advantages. The desire of becoming the proper objects of this respect, of deserving and obtaining this credit and rank among our equals, is perhaps, the strongest of all our desires, and our anxiety to obtain the advantages of fortune is, accordingly, much more excited and irritated by this desire, than by that of supplying all the necessities and conveniencies of the body, which are always very easily supplied" (Smith, 1817, p. 343).

[8] "We frequently see the respectful attentions of the world more strongly directed towards the rich and the great, than towards the wise and the virtuous" (Smith, 1817, p. 94).

[9] Chapter III, Part I, of the *Theory of Moral Sentiments* is titled "Of the Corruption of Our Moral Sentiments, Which Is Occasioned by This Disposition To Admire the Rich and the Great, and To Despise or Neglect Persons of Poor and Mean Condition."

[10] "With the greater part of rich people, the chief enjoyment of riches consists in the parade of riches" (Smith, 1937, p. 172; cf. Smith, 1817, p. 77).

it as worse than death, to be reduced to live, even without labour, upon the same simple fare with him, to dwell under the same lowly roof, and to be clothed in the same humble attire? Do they imagine that their stomach is better, or their sleep sounder, in a palace than in a cottage? The contrary has been so often observed, and, indeed, is so very obvious, though it had never been observed, that there is nobody ignorant of it. From whence, then, arises that emulation which runs through all the different ranks of men, and what are the advantages which we propose by that great purpose of human life which we call bettering our condition? To be observed, to be attended to, to be taken notice of with sympathy, complacency, and approbation, are all the advantages which we can propose to derive from it. It is the vanity, not the ease, or the pleasure, which interests us. But vanity is always founded upon the belief of our being the object of attention and approbation. The rich man glories in his riches, because he feels that they naturally draw upon him the attention of the world, and that mankind are disposed to go along with him in all those agreeable emotions with which the advantages of his situation so readily inspire him. At the thought of this, his heart seems to swell and dilate itself within him, and he is fonder of his wealth, upon this account, than for all the other advantages it procures him (Smith, 1817, pp. 77–78).[11]

Furthermore:

Nature has wisely judged that the distinction of ranks, the peace and order of society, would rest more securely upon the plain and palpable difference of birth and fortune, than upon the invisible and often uncertain difference of wisdom and virtue. The undistinguishing eyes of the great mob of mankind can well enough perceive the former: it is with difficulty that the nice discernment of the wise and the virtuous can sometimes distinguish the latter (Smith, 1817, p. 366).

Thus, the behavior of upper income receivers must be understood in terms of their pursuit of rank and distinction, and this underlies Smith's

---

[11] Later Smith states: "And thus, place, that great object which divides the wives of aldermen, is the end of half the labours of human life; and is the cause of all the tumult and bustle, all the rapine and injustice, which avarice and ambition have introduced into this world. People of sense, it is said, indeed despise place; that is, they despise sitting at the head of the table, and are indifferent who it is that is pointed out to the company by that frivolous circumstance, which the smallest advantage is capable of overbalancing. But rank, distinction, pre-eminence, no man despises, unless he is either raised very much above, or sunk very much below, the ordinary standard of human nature" (Smith, 1817, p. 90).

continuous reference, in the *Wealth of Nations*, to the vanity of the rich in attempting to account for the pattern of their consumption expenditures.[12]

In a society where the finer manufactures are not available, opportunities for cultivating one's vanity are necessarily limited. In the absence of such commodities, large rental incomes are employed in hospitality, in the maintenance of a large group of retainers, and in acts of bounty to one's tenants. In spite of these acts of generosity, however, the typical behavior of large landowners as late as the time of European feudalism was reasonably frugal. Large landowners were not extravagant, and it was even common for them to save. This was true not only of the nobility but of the sovereign himself, who frequently accumulated treasure. "In countries where a rich man can spend his revenue in no other way than by maintaining as many people as it can maintain, he is not apt to run out, and his benevolence it seems is seldom so violent as to attempt to maintain more than he can afford" (Smith, 1937, p. 391; cf. also pp. 414, 859–60).

All this was, however, transformed by the growth of commerce and manufactures, which brought an enormous enlargement of the commodity universe. Although the finer manufactures have sometimes grown up out of the "gradual refinement of those household and coarser manufactures which must at all times be carried on even in the poorest and rudest countries" (Smith, 1937, p. 382), foreign trade has, historically, played a crucial role in European countries:

> The inhabitants of trading cities, by importing the improved manufactures and expensive luxuries of richer countries, afforded some food to the vanity of the great proprietors, who eagerly purchased them with great quantities of the rude produce of their own lands. The commerce of a great part of Europe in those times, accordingly, consisted chiefly in the exchange of their own rude, for the manufactured produce of more civilized nations. Thus the wool of England used to be exchanged for the wines of France, and the fine cloths of Flanders, in the same manner as the corn of Poland is at this day exchanged for the wines and brandies of France, and for the silks and velvets of France and Italy.
>
> A taste for the finer and more improved manufactures, was in this manner introduced by foreign commerce into countries where no such works were carried on (Smith, 1937, p. 380).

[12] "To be pleased with...groundless applause is a proof of the most superficial levity and weakness. It is what is properly called vanity" (Smith, 1817, p. 186). And later: "He is guilty of vanity who desires praise for qualities which are either not praiseworthy in any degree, or not in that degree in which he expects to be praised for them, who sets his character upon the frivolous ornaments of dress and equipage, or upon the equally frivolous accomplishments of ordinary behaviour" (Smith, 1817, p. 501).

In making available a wide range of goods with which a great proprietor could gratify his "most childish vanity," a "revolution of the greatest importance to the public happiness" was brought about (Smith, 1937, p. 391). For the resulting alteration in expenditure flows, reflecting the tastes of (non-capitalist) upper income groups when confronted with an enlarged range of consumer goods, was directly responsible for events of major significance. These include, in addition to an accelerated rate of growth of output, the gradual erosion of the political power of the landowning classes and the decline of feudal institutions generally, the accelerated growth of capitalist institutions, and a large-scale shift in the composition of resource use and output.

The expansion in the range of alternatives for the disposition of the economic surplus had the immediate effects of (1) shifting the composition of consumer expenditure flows away from services and toward goods; (2) shifting upward the consumption functions of large property owners, who previously lived within their incomes because of the limited scope afforded for the exercise of personal vanity; and (3) less obvious, but at least as important, the strength of the desire for these new goods provided a motive for efficient cultivation which was previously lacking. The increased incentive provided by the availability of new goods led to the elimination of known inefficiencies which had previously been tolerated and to legal and institutional changes which, by strengthening economic incentives, Smith regarded as indispensable to sustained economic growth.

The transformation in the consumption expenditures of the wealthy which is wrought by the availability of finer manufactured goods in a previously agricultural society is, Smith appears to believe, highly predictable. For he argues that all members of higher income classes in an agricultural society—landlords, clergy, and sovereign—succumb equally, and with the same consequences, to the seductive attractions of these new goods. For, although "the desire of food is limited in every man by the narrow capacity of the human stomach," it is also true that "the desire of the conveniencies and ornaments of building, dress, equipage, and household furniture, seems to have no limit or certain boundary" (Smith, 1937, p. 164).[13] As a result,

> What all the violence of the feudal institutions could never have effected, the silent and insensible operation of foreign commerce and manufactures gradually brought about. These gradually furnished the great proprietors with something for which they could exchange the whole surplus produce of their lands, and which they could consume themselves without sharing it either with tenants or retainers. All for ourselves, and nothing for other

[13] Some of the more misleading implications of Smith's dictum concerning the "narrow capacity of the human stomach" are examined in Davis (1954). Somewhat surprisingly, Davis did not call attention to the even stronger statement by Smith on the same subject (in Smith, 1817, pp. 295–96).

people, seems, in every age of the world, to have been the vile maxim of the masters of mankind. As soon, therefore, as they could find a method of consuming the whole value of their rents themselves, they had no disposition to share them with any other persons. For a pair of diamond buckles perhaps, or for something as frivolous and useless, they exchanged the maintenance, or what is the same thing, the price of the maintenance of a thousand men for a year, and with it the whole weight and authority which it could give them. The buckles, however, were to be all their own, and no other human creature was to have any share of them; whereas in the more ancient method of expence they must have shared with at least a thousand people. With the judges that were to determine the preference, this difference was perfectly decisive; and thus, for the gratification of the most childish, the meanest and the most sordid of all vanities, they gradually bartered their whole power and authority (Smith, 1937, pp. 388–89).

The behavior of the clergy on their large landed estates was in no essential way different from that of other substantial landowners.[14] Similarly, the sovereign himself, the greatest single landowner, is subjected to the same forces and responds to them in the same manner.[15]

[14] The large rents and tithes received by the clergy were usually paid in the form of agricultural products. "The quantity exceeded greatly what the clergy could themselves consume; and there were neither arts nor manufactures for the produce of which they could exchange the surplus. The clergy could derive advantage from this immense surplus in no other way than by employing it, as the great barons employed the like surplus of their revenues, in the most profuse hospitality, and in the most extensive charity. Both the hospitality and the charity of the ancient clergy, accordingly, are said to have been very great. They not only maintained almost the whole poor of every kingdom, but many knights and gentlemen had frequently no other means of subsistence than by travelling about from monastery to monastery, under pretence of devotion, but in reality to enjoy the hospitality of the clergy.... The gradual improvements of arts, manufactures, and commerce, the same causes which destroyed the power of the great barons, destroyed in the same manner, through the greater part of Europe, the whole temporal power of the clergy. In the produce of arts, manufactures, and commerce, the clergy, like the great barons, found something for which they could exchange their rude produce, and thereby discovered the means of spending their whole revenues upon their own persons, without giving any considerable share of them to other people. Their charity became gradually less extensive, their hospitality less liberal or less profuse. Their retainers became consequently less numerous, and by degrees dwindled away altogether. The clergy too, like the great barons, wished to get a better rent from their landed estates, in order to spend it, in the same manner, upon the gratification of their own private vanity and folly. But this increase of rent could be got only by granting leases to their tenants, who thereby became in a great measure independent of them" (Smith, 1937, pp. 753–55).

[15] In a society with little commerce and manufactures, "the expence even of a sovereign is not directed by the vanity which delights in the gaudy finery of a court, but is employed in bounty to his tenants, and hospitality to his retainers. But bounty and hospitality very seldom lead to extravagance; though vanity almost always does.... In a commercial country abounding with every sort of expensive luxury, the sovereign, in the same manner as almost all the great proprietors in his dominions,

The intensity of the landlord's desire for "trinkets and baubles" led him gradually to dismiss his retainers and to reduce the number of the tenants on his land "to the number necessary for cultivating it."

> By the removal of the unnecessary mouths, and by exacting from the farmer the full value of the farm, a greater surplus, or what is the same thing, the price of a greater surplus, was obtained for the proprietor, which the merchants and manufacturers soon furnished him with a method of spending upon his own person in the same manner as he had done the rest. The same cause continuing to operate, he was desirous to raise his rents above what his lands, in the actual state of their improvement, could afford. His tenants could agree to this upon one condition only, that they should be secured in their possession, for such a term of years as might give them time to recover with profit whatever they should lay out in the further improvement of the land. The expensive vanity of the landlord made him willing to accept of this condition; and hence the origin of long leases (Smith, 1937, p. 390).

Again the same forces operated, with the same consequences, upon the clergy.[16]

Thus, in addition to its other consequences, the structure of tastes of the major propertied classes when confronted with the introduction of new goods resulted in a substantial increase in the economy's output. Agriculture came to be reorganized in a manner which, for the first time, provided strong incentives to the cultivator to raise output over previous levels.[17]

There is another aspect of men's evaluations of the satisfactions afforded by economic success to which Smith attaches much significance. Although, as we have seen, the satisfactions afforded by great wealth are not substantial, they nevertheless *appear* to be so from the vantage point of those less favorably situated. This is, apparently, a systematic bias in men's expectations. Moreover, this overestimation of the pleasures of wealth is one of the most important features of man's psychological endowment, since it has furnished the propelling force for the greater part of his earthly

---

naturally spends a great part of his revenue in purchasing those luxuries. His own and the neighbouring countries supply him abundantly with all the costly trinkets which compose the splendid, but insignificant pageantry of a court. For the sake of an inferior pageantry of the same kind, his nobles dismiss their retainers, make their tenants independent, and become gradually themselves as insignificant as the greater part of the wealthy burghers in his dominions. The same frivolous passions, which influence their conduct, influence his" (Smith, 1937, pp. 414, 861; see also pp. 859–60).

[16] See n. 14.

[17] The role of legal and institutional factors in conditioning economic behavior is discussed at greater length in Rosenberg (1960).

achievements. It is fortunate for society that most men are incapable of making an accurate appraisal of the satisfactions to be derived from success in the pursuit of wealth.[18]

We must now confront a further implication of Smith's proposition that "some forms of expence...seem to contribute more to the growth of public opulence than others" (Smith, 1937, p. 329). From the point of view of economic growth, Smith's position is not only that a taste for goods is preferable to a taste for services.[19] It is also the case that a taste for durable goods is better than a taste for non-durables:

> A man of fortune...may either spend his revenue in a profuse and sumptuous table, and in maintaining a great number of menial servants, and a multitude of dogs and horses; or contenting himself with a frugal table and few attendants, he may lay out the greater part of it in adorning his house or his country villa, in useful or ornamental buildings, in useful or ornamental furniture, in collecting books, statues, pictures; or in things more frivolous, jewels, baubles, ingenious trinkets of different kinds; or, what is most trifling of all, in amassing a great wardrobe of fine clothes (Smith, 1937, p. 329).

A man who purchases durables is every day adding to the stock of useful assets which will be available in the future.[20] Smith's preference for durables

---

[18] "And it is well that nature imposes upon us in this manner. It is this deception which rouses and keeps in continual motion the industry of mankind. It is this which first prompted them to cultivate the ground, to build houses, to found cities and commonwealths, and to invent and improve all the sciences and arts, which ennoble and embellish human life; which have entirely changed the whole face of the globe, have turned the rude forests of nature into agreeable and fertile plains, and made the trackless and barren ocean a new fund of subsistence, and the great high road of communication to the different nations of the earth. The earth, by these labours of mankind, has been obliged to redouble her natural fertility, and to maintain a greater multitude of inhabitants" (Smith, 1817, p. 295).

[19] Here we confront, from the output side, Smith's distinction between productive and unproductive labor. We have no intention of entering into that tortured and protracted controversy, or defending Smith's rather confused and inconsistent treatment. It will be sufficient to state that, *from the point of view of Smith's interest in economic growth,* there was as much conceptual justification for attempting to distinguish between the two types of labor as there is for classifying expenditures in "consumption" and "investment" categories in the national income accounts.

Notice that educational services are an exception to Smith's general preference for goods over services. Working-class parents, he points out, typically purchase insufficient educational services for their children (Smith, 1956, p. 256; Smith, 1937, pp. 736–37). Although teachers produce a service, it is one which, as he elsewhere recognizes, is capable of being accumulated. In his chapter on capital (Book II, chap. i), he explicitly recognizes that talents and skills acquired through education constitute part of the fixed capital of society (pp. 265–66).

[20] "A stock of clothes may last several years: a stock of furniture half a century or a century: but a stock of houses, well built and properly taken care of, may last many centuries" (Smith, 1937, p. 265; cf. Smith, 1817, pp. 314–15).

is, of course, in a sense an extension of the logic underlying his distinction between productive and unproductive labor. Although the effects of the expenditures of the wealthy on non-durables do not perish quite so quickly as the "declamation of the actor, the harangue of the orator, or the tune of the musician" (which perish "in the very instant" of production) (Smith, 1937, p. 315), they do not add directly to the future stock of useful things. Similarly, nations are better off when "men of fortune" shift their expenditures to durable goods. For the current purchases of the rich in this fashion augment the supply of useful goods at some future date. These goods then become available to the "inferior and middling ranks of people" when they are eventually cast off by the wealthy (Smith, 1937, p. 330).[21] If we look upon economic growth as a matter of accumulating things which will provide a flow of useful services in the future, then it is clear that the greater the durability of an item, the more it approximates the characteristics of an investment good. A growing taste for durables is, therefore, favorable to economic growth.[22]

It is worth noting that Smith treats taste itself as a phenomenon which becomes important only in civilized societies where subsistence is easily acquired. His treatment of the conduct of people in savage societies, which are preoccupied with procuring a bare subsistence, suggests that they are controlled by social values and attitudes which provide as little scope as possible for the expression of personal tastes (Smith, 1817, Part V, chap. ii). Furthermore, in his own discussion of the influence of taste in societies where its exercise is allowed some importance, he is usually concerned with consumer durables—furniture, equipage, clothing, watches, palaces, ear-pickers, etc. This is, of course, consistent with the uniformity of content of food consumption implied by his curious statement that "the desire of food is limited in every man by the narrow capacity of the human stomach."

Moreover, the growing taste for goods as opposed to services is crucial for economic growth because it is responsible for the expansion of the capitalist sector of the economy. In part this was a reflection of the technological fact that material goods required a substantial accumulation of capital for their production, whereas the provision of services typically required little capital. This growing preference, therefore, was responsible for fundamental structural changes in both the economy and society. The

[21] "What was formerly a seat of the family of Seymour, is now an inn upon the Bath road. The marriage-bed of James the First of Great Britain, which his Queen brought with her from Denmark, as a present fit for a sovereign to make to a sovereign, was, a few years ago, the ornament of an ale-house at Dunfermline. In some ancient cities, which either have been long stationary, or have gone somewhat to decay, you will sometimes scarce find a single house which could have been built for its present inhabitants" (Smith, 1937, p. 330).

[22] Cf. Nassau Senior: "The wealth of a Country will much depend on the question, whether the tastes of its inhabitants lead them to prefer objects of slow or of rapid destruction" (Senior, 1951, p. 54).

resulting enlargement of the capitalist sector and a growth in a middle class in turn led to a rise in the share of profits in the national income; with this, of course, went a higher proportion of saving and capital accumulation.[23]

The growth of the capitalist sector was important also because it inculcated other qualities—thrift, discipline, orderliness, honesty, industry—and provided a new model (the abstemious and industrious capitalist) for the old one (the dissolute and profligate landowner). Smith seems to have regarded the mere presence of great wealth as exerting a demoralizing influence on the population.[24] He advances the generalization that, in mercantile and manufacturing towns, the poor will be found to be "in general industrious, sober, and thriving"; whereas, in court towns where the population is supported out of revenue rather than capital, "they are in general idle, dissolute and poor" (Smith, 1937, p. 319).[25]

Finally, the growth of commerce and manufactures produces stability in the political and institutional structure of society and security of expectations on the part of the individual which Smith refers to as "by far the most important of all their effects." Hume is cited as the only writer who had previously noted this relationship. Hume's own treatment of the origin, historical growth, and social consequences of capitalist institutions is both fascinating and complex, but that is another story.[26]

[23] Malthus followed Adam Smith very closely here (see Malthus, 1951, pp. 42–43). For an illuminating discussion of the historical background, contemporary observations, and intellectual antecedents for Smith's treatment of profit as a distinct income category, see Meek (1954).

[24] Even capitalists are so corrupted. When profits are too high, that is, in the absence of competitive conditions, the capitalist behaves, in effect, like a large landowner. "The high rate of profit seems every where to destroy that parsimony which in other circumstances is natural to the character of the merchant. When profits are high, that sober virtue seems to be superfluous, and expensive luxury to suit better the affluence of his situation.... Compare and you will be sensible how differently the conduct and character of merchants are affected by the high and by the low profits of stock.... Light come, light go, says the proverb; and the ordinary tone of expence seems every where to be regulated, not so much according to the real ability of spending as to the supposed facility of getting money to spend" (Smith, 1937, pp. 578–79; see the dissenting opinion of Malthus, 1951, p. 192).

[25] He adds: "The idleness of the greater part of the people who are maintained by the expence of revenue, corrupts, it is probable, the industry of those who ought to be maintained by the employment of capital, and renders it less advantageous to employ a capital there than in other places" (Smith, 1937, p. 320). Smith accounts for the past superiority of Glasgow over Edinburgh in these terms. The corrupting effects of wealth can, apparently, nullify or reverse the effects of earlier progress. "The inhabitants of a large village, it has sometimes been observed, after having made considerable progress in manufactures, have become idle and poor, in consequence of a great lord's having taken up his residence in their neighbourhood" (Smith, 1937, p. 320; see also Rae, 1895, pp. 180–81).

[26] "Commerce and manufactures gradually introduced order and good government and with them, the liberty and security of individuals, among the inhabitants of the country, who had before lived almost in a continual state of war with their neighbours, and of servile dependency upon their superiors. This, though it has been the least observed, is by far the most important of all their effects. Mr. Hume is the only writer who, so far as I know, has hitherto taken notice of it" (Smith, 1937, p. 385).

References

Davis, Joseph S. "Adam Smith and the Human Stomach," *Q.J.E.*, LXVIII, No. 2 (May, 1954), 275–86.

Malthus, T. R. *Principles of Political Economy*. New York: Augustus M. Kelley, 1951.

Meek, Ronald. "Adam Smith and the Classical Concept of Profit," *Scottish J. Polit. Econ.*, I, No. 2 (June, 1954), 138–53.

Rae, John. *Life of Adam Smith*. London: Macmillan Co., 1895.

Rosenberg, Nathan. "Some Institutional Aspects of *The Wealth of Nations*," *J.P.E.*, LXVIII, No. 6 (December, 1960), 557–70.

Schumpeter, Joseph. *History of Economic Analysis*. New York: Oxford University Press, 1954.

Senior, Nassau. *An Outline of the Science of Political Economy*. New York: Augustus M. Kelley, 1951.

Smith, Adam. *The Theory of Moral Sentiments*. Philadelphia: Anthony Finley, 1817.

———. *The Wealth of Nations*. New York: Random House, 1937.

———. *Lectures on Justice, Police, Revenue and Arms*. Edited by Edwin Cannan. New York: Kelley & Millman, 1956.

5

VI

Adam Smith on Profits—Paradox Lost and Regained

NATHAN ROSENBERG*

ADAM Smith's treatment of the business community in general and the entrepreneur in particular is an especially interesting subject.[1] It seemed therefore to be both useful and rewarding to ferret out and to examine Smith's treatment of the role of the entrepreneur in *The Wealth of Nations*.[2] After all, in a book which has been regarded as the *locus classicus* of the *laissez-faire* ideology for 200 years, a book which shook the world by recommending a maximum degree of freedom for business enterprise— in such a book surely the entrepreneur would play a major role. Although this originally seemed like a reasonable expectation, it was not fulfilled. As I should certainly have realized, Smith's analytical distinctions here were inevitably limited by the modest state of capitalist development itself, and the relatively small degree of specialization of function which still pre- vailed in the middle of the eighteenth century. Indeed, Smith had made a significant contribution to analytical economics merely by his forceful recognition of profit on capital as constituting a separate and distinct income category.[3]

I have not, I am happy to report, returned from this brief excursion into intellectual history completely empty-handed. Instead of the story which I had hoped to tell, I want to report upon a rather unexpected paradox which

---

* Professor of Economics, Stanford University.

[1] See Nathan Rosenberg, 'Some Institutional Aspects of *The Wealth of Nations*', *Journal of Political Economy* (December 1960), 557–70.

[2] Adam Smith, *The Wealth of Nations*, ed. Cannan (1937).

[3] On this subject, see the perceptive article by Ronald Meek, 'Adam Smith and the Classical Concept of Profit', *Scottish Journal of Political Economy* (June 1954). Meek states (138–9) that: 'Many of Smith's predecessors had recognized, of course, that those who employed stock in mercantile pursuits generally received a net reward which was pro- portioned not to the effort, if any, which they expended, but rather to the value of the stock employed. In Smith's new model it was recognized that net gains similar in this respect to mercantile profit were now also being earned on capital employed in other economic pursuits, such as agriculture and manufacture. But, even more important, it was also recognized that the *origin* of these net gains was now very different from what it had formerly been. To Smith's predecessors, generally speaking, profit had appeared as "profit upon alienation"—i.e., as the gain from buying things cheap and selling them dear. To Smith, on the other hand, profit began to appear as an income uniquely associated with the use of capital in the employment of wage-labour . . .'

I encountered. I would like, moreover, to try to unravel this paradox. My determination to do so is not confined to a certain taste for intellectual history—although that would be justification enough—but also because the paradox is one which goes to the heart of Adam Smith's *Weltanschauung*.

Stated in somewhat oversimplified terms, my paradox lies in the fact that Adam Smith treated high wages as being unqualifiedly a Good Thing, and high profits as being unqualifiedly a Bad Thing. Why should so eloquent a spokesman for capitalism and *laissez-faire* regard high profits with such a jaundiced eye? Indeed, he closes his chapter on profits with the following devastating barrage:

Our merchants and master-manufacturers complain much of the bad effects of high wages in raising the price and thereby lessening the sale of their goods both at home and abroad. They say nothing concerning the bad effects of high profits. They are silent with regard to the pernicious effects of their own gains. They complain only of those of other people.

(WN I.ix.24)

So fervently did Smith believe these sentiments that the statement actually appears, substantially unchanged, in two different places in *The Wealth of Nations*.[4]

The question of whether high wages were desirable had such an obviously affirmative answer to Smith that he did not even undertake to justify it but rather asserted it with a rhetorical flourish.

Is this improvement in the circumstances of the lower ranks of the people to be regarded as an advantage or as an inconveniency to the society? The answer seems at first sight abundantly plain. Servants, labourers and workmen of different kinds make up the far greater part of every great political society. But what improves the circumstances of the greater part can never be regarded as an inconveniency to the whole. No society can surely be flourishing and happy, of which the far greater part of the members are poor and miserable.

(WN I.viii.36)

If Adam Smith's views here do not strike our egalitarian sensibilities as particularly startling, that is partly because of a drastic shift in attitudes which Smith himself played some role in bringing about. For earlier in the eighteenth century the dominant view was of the social utility of poverty. Smith's predecessors were very much exercised—indeed, some were absolutely obsessed—over the socially undesirable consequences of high or

---

[4] 'Our merchants frequently complain of the high wages of British labour as the cause of their manufactures being undersold in foreign markets; but they are silent about the high profits of stock. They complain of the extravagant gain of other people; but they say nothing of their own. The high profits of British stock, however, may contribute towards raising the price of British manufactures in many cases as much, and in some perhaps more, than the high wages of British labour' (WN IV.vii.c.29). This statement appeared in the first edition of the book, whereas the one in the text above made its appearance in the second edition.

rising wages. It had been a firmly accepted part of the conventional wisdom that high wages would reduce effort, that the working class response to higher wages could be described—in the jargon of a later day—in the form of a backward-sloping labour supply curve. The dominant view was well expressed by Arthur Young, that repository of conventional wisdom, who wrote in his *Farmer's Tour Through the East of England* in 1771 that 'Every one but an idiot knows that the lower classes must be kept poor or they will never be industrious; I do not mean, that the poor of England are to be kept like the poor of France, but, the state of the country considered, they must (like all mankind) be in poverty or they will not work.'[5] Similarly, Sir William Temple, in his *Vindication of Commerce and the Arts*, says categorically of labourers that '. . . the only way to make them temperate and industrious, is to lay them under the necessity of labouring all the time they can spare from meals and sleep, in order to procure the necessaries of life'.[6] Such were the dominant views of Smith's time.[7]

In such a context, Smith's views were both enlightened and advanced. Moreover, they were novel in a respect which needs to be made quite explicit. Not only did Smith believe that high wages were intrinsically desirable because they improved the standard of living of the mass of the population. He also believed—and here he clashed head-on with the prevailing view—that the working class supply of effort was positively sloped, that higher wages called forth greater effort and not less.

The liberal reward of labour . . . increases the industry of the common people. The wages of labour are the encouragement of industry, which, like every other human quality, improves in proportion to the encouragement it receives. A plentiful subsistence increases the bodily strength of the labourer, and the comfortable hope of bettering his condition, and of ending his days perhaps in ease and plenty, animates him to exert that strength to the utmost. Where wages are high, accordingly, we shall always find the workmen more active, diligent, and expeditious, than where they are low.

(WN I.viii.44)

---

[5] Arthur Young, *Farmer's Tour Through the East of England* (1771), iv. 361.

[6] Sir William Temple, *Vindication of Commerce and the Arts* (1786), 534. First published in 1758.

[7] For an excellent scholarly presentation of the mercantilists' attitude toward labour, see Edgar S. Furniss, *The Position of the Labourer in a System of Nationalism* (1957). For a careful study of the transition from the old set of views to the later ones, see A. W. Coats, 'Changing Attitudes to Labour in the Mid-eighteenth Century', *Economic History Review* (1958), 35–51. Coats states (46) that: 'Apart from a few isolated advocates of a "high wage economy", most British economists before 1750 regarded low wages as an essential precondition of the maintenance of a high volume of exports, although the plea that the British workman should enjoy a higher standard of living than that of his continental counterpart represented a tacit admission that successful competition in foreign markets did not require that home wage levels should be equal to or lower than foreign wage levels. By contrast, in the third quarter of the century there was growing support for the view that high wages and rising living standards were not merely compatible with, but were even a necessary concomitant of the prosperity of our domestic and exported manufactures.'

Although Smith concedes that higher wages are likely to induce some workers to reduce the number of hours worked, he is insistent that such workers constitute only a minority of the labour force. Indeed, Smith appears to be genuinely concerned over the opposite possibility, that a system of incentive wages will cause many workers to suffer the deleterious effects of *overwork*. In this respect he is the first economist of whom I am aware for whom this was a major concern.

Some workmen, indeed, when they can earn in four days what will maintain them through the week, will be idle the other three. This, however, is by no means the case with the greater part. Workmen, on the contrary, when they are liberally paid by the piece, are very apt to over-work themselves, and to ruin their health and constitution in a few years. A carpenter in London, and in some other places, is not supposed to last in his utmost vigour above eight years. Something of the same kind happens, in many other trades, in which the workmen are paid by the piece, as they generally are in manufactures, and even in country labour, whenever wages are higher than ordinary.

(WN I.viii.44)

Where workers do, in fact, avail themselves of long intervals of leisure, Smith finds the cause, not in laziness or deficiency of character, but in deeply-rooted physiological causes.

Excessive application during four days of the week, is frequently the real cause of the idleness of the other three, so much and so loudly complained of. Great labour, either of mind or body, continued for several days together, is in most men naturally followed by a great desire of relaxation, which, if not restrained by force or by some strong necessity, is almost irresistible. It is the call of nature, which requires to be relieved by some indulgence, sometimes of ease only, but sometimes too of dissipation and diversion. If it is not complied with, the consequences are often dangerous, and sometimes fatal, and such as almost always, sooner or later, bring on the peculiar infirmity of the trade. If masters would always listen to the dictates of reason and humanity, they have frequently occasion rather to moderate, than to animate the application of many of their workmen.

(WN I.viii.44)

When Smith turns from the examination of the economic behaviour of the capitalist, his attitude shifts from that of compassion and understanding to one of compulsive and cantankerous criticism and suspicion. The long-term interests of capitalists, to begin with, do not coincide with those of society.

the . . . rate of profit does not, like rent and wages, rise with the prosperity, and fall with the declension, of the society. On the contrary, it is naturally low in rich, and high in poor countries, and it is always highest in the countries which are going fastest to ruin. The interest of this third order [i.e. capitalists], therefore, has not the same connexion with the general interest of the society as that of the other two [i.e. landlord and worker].

(WN I.xi.p.10)

As a result, capitalists as a class are simply not to be trusted.

The proposal of any new law or regulation of commerce which comes from this order, ought always to be listened to with great precaution, and ought never to be adopted till after having been long and carefully examined, not only with the most scrupulous, but with the most suspicious attention. It comes from an order of men, whose interest is never exactly the same with that of the public, who have generally an interest to deceive and even to oppress the public and who accordingly have, upon many occasions, both deceived and oppressed it.

(WN I.xi.p.10)

A businessman who had been taught to regard Adam Smith as a capitalist apologist might well be excused for wondering what sort of strange capitalist apologetics this is, and if this is what we are likely to get from our friends, just what may we expect from our enemies? Part of the answer may be stated briefly. High profits which persist are often the result of those private conspiracies against which Smith so eloquently inveighed, or of government dispensations of exclusive privileges.[8] In both cases the result is an impediment to resource mobility upon which the effective functioning of a market economy must be predicated. The alacrity with which business-men have entered into such arrangements in the past and their persistence and ingenuity in subverting the disciplining effects of the market is the main reason that the text of *The Wealth of Nations* abounds in phraseology extremely critical of the business community: 'the sneaking arts of under-ling tradesmen'; the 'mean and malignant expedients' of merchants and manufacturers; the 'clamour and sophistry of merchants and manu-facturers'; the 'interested sophistry of merchants and manufacturers', 'the mean rapacity, the monopolizing spirit of merchants and manu-facturers', traders who argue with 'all the passionate confidence of interested falsehood'.

Smith's criticisms of mercantilism, which take up a large portion of his book, also issue from the same cause. Smith sees mercantilism as the successful attempt of rapacious businessmen to exploit the machinery of government for their own self-aggrandizement. Such efforts really had their historical origin in the exclusive corporative spirit of privileged groups which grew up in medieval towns and cities.

---

[8] Profits must also remain relatively high in some areas to compensate for additional risk or for a disagreeable activity. For example: 'The keeper of an inn or tavern, who is never master of his own house and who is exposed to the brutality of every drunkard, exercises neither a very agreeable nor a very creditable business. But there is scarce any common trade in which a small stock yields so great a profit' (WN I.x.b.4).

Country gentlemen and farmers, dispersed in different parts of the country, cannot so easily combine as merchants and manufacturers, who being collected into towns, and accustomed to that exclusive corporation spirit which prevails in them, naturally endeavour to obtain against all their countrymen, the same exclusive privilege which they generally possess against the inhabitants of their respective towns.

(WN IV.ii.21)

The violence of Smith's polemic against mercantilism lay in the fact that it enabled merchants to better their condition in a manner which did not contribute to the nation's economic welfare. As a result of the dispensation of monopoly grants, of the arbitrary bestowal of 'extraordinary privileges' and 'extraordinary restraints' upon different sectors of industry by the government, the individual merchant was provided with innumerable opportunities to enrich himself without enriching the nation. Even when legislation is passed with an ostensibly legitimate social purpose in view, the opportunities for profit-making are likely to be restructured in such a way as to lead to private enrichment and not social enrichment. Thus, with respect to the herring bounty, Smith sardonically observes: '. . . the bounty to the white herring fishery is a tonnage bounty; and is proportioned to the burden of the ship, not to her diligence or success in the fishery; and it has, I am afraid, been too common for vessels to fit out for the sole purpose of catching, not the fish, but the bounty.'[9]

The more interesting part of the answer to my question, however, lies not in monopolistic barriers or other impediments to the achievement of static efficiency with respect to resource use. Rather, it involves the realm of dynamic change over time, and broader influences shaping human behaviour. For the growth of trade and commerce and, in their wake, manufactures, are of course associated historically with the rise of the capitalist class. This class gradually displaces the landlord class which had previously dominated the European economy and polity, and had squandered society's social surplus by maintaining a large army of retainers and by what Smith calls 'rustic hospitality'. The new goods made available by expanding commerce bring in their wake drastic social and political changes.

But what all the violence of the feudal institutions could never have effected, the silent and insensible operation of foreign commerce and manufactures gradually brought about. These gradually furnished the great proprietors with something for which they could exchange the whole surplus produce of their lands, and which they could consume themselves without sharing it either with tenants or

---

[9] WN IV.v.a.32. Smith adds the following extraordinary bit of accounting: 'In the year 1759, when the bounty was at fifty shillings the ton, the whole buss fishery of Scotland brought in only four barrels of sea sticks. In that year each barrel of sea sticks cost government in bounties alone £113 15s; each barrel of merchantable herrings £159 7s 6d' (ibid.).

retainers. All for ourselves, and nothing for other people, seems, in every age of the world, to have been the vile maxim of the masters of mankind. As soon, therefore, as they could find a method of consuming the whole value of their rents themselves, they had no disposition to share them with any other persons. For a pair of diamond buckles perhaps, or for something as frivolous and useless, they exchanged the maintenance, or what is the same thing, the price of the maintenance of a thousand men for a year, and with it the whole weight and authority which it could give them. The buckles, however, were to be all their own, and no other human creature was to have any share of them; whereas in the more ancient method of expence they must have shared with at least a thousand people. With the judges that were to determine the preference, this difference was perfectly decisive; and thus, for the gratification of the most childish, the meanest and the most sordid of all vanities, they gradually bartered their whole power and authority.[10]

The growth of the commercial sector and the increasing control over income flows by the capitalist class are a critical element in Smith's version of economic growth because, whereas the landlord directed society's surplus resources into frivolous, unproductive activities, the capitalist now directs these resources into productive channels. As Smith puts it, 'It is the stock that is employed for the sake of profit, which puts into motion the greater part of the useful labour of every society.'[11]

Smith's sociological analysis of the rise of capitalism—primarily in Book III of *The Wealth of Nations*—has been strangely neglected, and will, unfortunately, also be neglected here, since it would require a separate paper to treat adequately. A couple of things, however, need to be asserted. By providing a ready market for agricultural products, the growth of commercial and manufacturing towns provides powerful new incentives to the attainment of efficient resource use in agriculture. Furthermore, and for Smith most important, the growth of commerce, by dissolving feudal ties and obligations, makes good government possible for the first time.

[10] WN III.iv.10; see also III.iv.5. For further discussion, see Nathan Rosenberg, 'Adam Smith, Consumer Tastes, and Economic Growth', *Journal of Political Economy* (May/June 1968), 361–74.

[11] WN I.xi.p.10. The structure of feudal society effectively suppressed the possibility of capital accumulation from all classes—albeit in different ways: 'Under the feudal constitution there could be very little accumulation of stock, which will appear from considering the situation of those three orders of men, which made up the whole body of the people: the peasants, the landlords, and the merchants. The peasants had leases which depended upon the caprice of their masters; they could never increase in wealth, because the landlord was ready to squeeze it all from them, and therefore they had no motive to acquire it. As little could the landlords increase their wealth, as they lived so indolent a life, and were involved in perpetual wars. The merchants again were oppressed by all ranks, and were not able to secure the produce of their industry from rapine and violence. Thus there could be little accumulation of wealth at all; but after the fall of the feudal government these obstacles to industry were removed, and the stock of commodities began gradually to increase.' LJ (B) 282–3 ed. Cannan, 220.

. . . (C)ommerce and manufactures gradually introduced order and good govern-ment, and with them, the liberty and security of individuals, among the inhabi-tants of the country, who had before lived almost in a continual state of war with their neighbours, and of servile dependency upon their superiors. This, though it has been the least observed, is by far the most important of their effects.

(WN III.iv.4)

This good government includes the reduction of crime, which Smith associates with the elimination of the personal ties of dependency of feudalism. He asserts in his *Lectures* that 'Nothing tends so much to corrupt mankind as dependency, while independency still increases the honesty of the people'. And he concludes that 'The establishment of com-merce and manufactures, which brings about this independency, is the best police for preventing crimes' (LJ (B), 204–205; ed. Cannan, 155).

Finally, as suggested earlier, the rise of a capitalist class brings an increasing proportion of society's resources—including agriculture itself—under the control of a more efficient class of decision-makers.[12] But it is the dynamic aspect of this point which requires emphasis. The growth of com-merce is instrumental in shaping character, in altering tastes, and in pro-viding new and more powerful incentives. The growth of commerce, by increasing the importance of the capitalist class as compared to large landowners, increases the proportion of those in society devoted to parsi-mony and frugality, 'those who are naturally the most disposed to accumu-late' (WN IV.vii.c.61), as compared to those who live lives of indolence and prodigality.[13] Commerce inculcates habits of orderliness, reliability, pre-

[12] Smith succinctly lays out the differences in attitude and mentality between the mer-chant and landowner: 'The wealth acquired by the inhabitants of cities was frequently employed in purchasing such lands as were to be sold, of which a great part would fre-quently be uncultivated. Merchants are commonly ambitious of becoming country gentle-men, and when they do, they are generally the best of all improvers. A merchant is accustomed to employ his money chiefly in profitable projects, whereas a mere country gentleman is accustomed to employ it chiefly in expence. The one often sees his money go from him and return to him with a profit: the other, when once he parts with it, very seldom expects to see any more of it. Those different habits naturally affect their temper and disposition in every sort of business. A merchant is commonly a bold; a country gentleman, a timid undertaker. The one is not afraid to lay out at once a large capital upon the improvement of his land, when he has a probable prospect of raising the value of it in proportion to the expence. The other, if he has any capital, which is not always the case, seldom ventures to employ it in this manner. If he improves at all, it is commonly not with a capital, but with what he can save out of his annual revenue' (WN III.iv.3).

[13] Adam Smith's close friend, David Hume, had said: '. . . (A)s the spending of a settled revenue is a way of life entirely without occupation, men have so much need of somewhat to fix and engage them, that pleasures, such as they are, will be the pursuit of the greater part of the landholders, and the prodigals among them will always be more numerous than the misers. In a state, therefore, where there is nothing but a landed interest, as there is little frugality, the borrowers must be very numerous, and the rate of interest must hold proportion to it. The difference depends not on the quantity of money, but on the habits and manners which prevail'. David Hume, *Writings on Economics*, ed. Eugene Rotwein (1955), 50.

cision, and painstaking attention to detail. Participation in business enterprise inevitably inculcates certain behaviour patterns—in particular, those of 'order, oeconomy and attention' (WN III.iv.3) Commerce introduces probity and punctuality. But it is important to note that Smith's argument makes these qualities emerge and spread *as a direct response to personal self-interest.*

Whenever commerce is introduced into any country probity and punctuality always accompany it. These virtues in a rude and barbarous country are almost unknown. Of all the nations in Europe, the Dutch, the most commercial, are the most faithful to their word. The English are more so than the Scotch, but much inferior to the Dutch, and in the remote parts of this country they are far less so than in the commercial parts of it. This is not at all to be imputed to national character, as some pretend; there is no reason why an Englishman or a Scotchman should not be as punctual in performing agreements as a Dutchman. It is far more reducible to self-interest, that general principle which regulates the actions of every man, and which leads men to act in a certain manner from views of advantage, and is as deeply implanted in an Englishman as a Dutchman. A dealer is afraid of losing his character, and is scrupulous in observing every engagement. When a person makes perhaps twenty contracts in a day, he cannot gain so much by endeavouring to impose on his neighbours, as the very appearance of a cheat would make him lose. When people seldom deal with one another, we find that they are somewhat disposed to cheat, because they can gain more by a smart trick than they can lose by the injury which it does their character. . . . Wherever dealings are frequent, a man does not expect to gain so much by any one contract, as by probity and punctuality in the whole, and a prudent dealer, who is sensible of his real interest, would rather choose to lose what he has a right to, than give any ground for suspicion. Everything of this kind is odious as it is rare. When the greater part of people are merchants, they always bring probity and punctuality into fashion, and these, therefore, are the principal virtues of a commercial nation.

This discussion of the character-forming aspects of a commercial society now provides the basis for our confrontation with the 'paradox of high profits', with which this paper is concerned. A commercial society needs to be perceived as a set of institutions which, although at one level it may be treated as a collection of legally free individuals engaging in free contractual agreements, at another level is an intensely coercive system. By this I mean that, in order to succeed under a system of competitive capitalism, one needs to develop certain characteristics—the characteristics of order, economy, attention, and probity, with which Smith is concerned and which are the qualities essential for success under the unique pressures imposed upon individual participants in the business arena by capitalist institutions. The capitalist is haunted by the spectre of bankruptcy. 'Bankruptcy is

[14] LJ (B), 326–28, ed. Cannan, 253–5. For Smith's characterization of the 'inconveniences' of a commercial society, see also 328–33, ed. Cannan, 255–59.

perhaps the greatest and most humiliating calamity which can befal an innocent man. The greater part of men, therefore, are sufficiently careful to avoid it. Some, indeed, do not avoid it; as some do not avoid the gallows' (WN II.iii.29). These characteristics, it should be clear, do not come naturally to man. Man does not by nature prefer the active and energetic life to the life of indolence and repose. Indeed, Smith asserts that 'It is the interest of every man to live as much at his ease as he can' (WN V.i.f.7). As a consequence, Smith regards it as axiomatic that 'In every profession, the exertion of the greater part of those who exercise it, is always in proportion to the necessity they are under of making that exertion' (WN V.i.f.4). Landlords '. . . are the only one of the three orders whose revenue costs them neither labour nor care, but comes to them, as it were, of its own accord, and independent of any plan or project of their own' (WN I.xi.p.8). Their characteristic indolence, therefore, is viewed by Smith as '. . . the natural effect of the ease and security of their situation'.[15]

But, while the landed classes live a life of indolence, self-indulgence, and ostentation, they are merely doing what other classes would do if they had the opportunity. For 'A man of a large revenue, *whatever may be his profession*, thinks he ought to live like other men of large revenues; and to spend a great part of his time in festivity, in vanity, and in dissipation.'[16] The great virtue of competitive capitalism, from this point of view, is that the intense pressures of the market place render such behaviour extremely difficult or impossible on the part of the capitalist class. So long as profits are difficult to earn, and so long as competitive pressures keep the rate of profit low, the system itself may be relied upon to force the capitalist to display the traditional virtues of his class. However, high rates of profit, when they persist, constitute evidence that the competitive mechanism is, for whatever reason, not functioning properly. While it is obvious that this has undesirable consequences in terms of resource allocation (WN IV.viii.

[15] WN I.xi.p.8. In speaking of large landed proprietors, Smith remarks: 'To improve land with profit, like all other commercial projects, requires an exact attention to small savings and small gains, of which a man born to a great fortune, even though naturally frugal, is very seldom capable. The situation of such a person naturally disposes him to attend rather to ornament which pleases his fancy, than to profit for which he has so little occasion. The elegance of his dress, of his equipage, of his house, and household furniture, are objects which from his infancy he has been accustomed to have some anxiety about. The turn of mind which this habit naturally forms, follows him when he comes to think of the improvement of land. He embellishes perhaps four or five hundred acres in the neighbourhood of his house, at ten times the expence which the land is worth after all his improvements; and finds that if he was to improve his whole estate in the same manner, and he has little taste for any other, he would be a bankrupt before he had finished the tenth part of it' (WN III.ii.7).

[16] WN V.i.g.42, italics supplied. Similarly, although Smith's statement about landlords who 'love to reap where they never sowed' is frequently cited, it is usually cited minus a critical qualification which Smith attaches. 'As soon as the land of any country has all become private property, the landlords, *like all other men*, love to reap where they never sowed, and demand a rent even for its natural produce' (WN I.vi.8. italics supplied).

c.25), it has not been commonly noticed that such easily earned profits had other undesirable consequences, to which Smith attached enormous importance. For:

... besides all the bad effects to the country in general, which have already been mentioned as necessarily resulting from a high rate of profit; there is one more fatal, perhaps, than all these put together, but which, if we may judge from experience, is inseparably connected with it. The high rate of profit seems every where to destroy that parsimony which in other circumstances is natural to the character of the merchant. When profits are high, that sober virtue seems to be superfluous, and expensive luxury to suit better the affluence of his situation. But the owners of the great mercantile capitals are necessarily the leaders and conductors of the whole industry of every nation, and their example has a much greater influence upon the manners of the whole industrious part of it than that of any other order of men. If his employer is attentive and parsimonious, the workman is very likely to be so too; but if the master is dissolute and disorderly, the servant who shapes his work according to the pattern which his master prescribes to him, will shape his life too according to the example which he sets him. Accumulation is thus prevented in the hands of all those who are naturally the most disposed to accumulate; and the funds destined for the maintenance of productive labour receive no augmentation from the revenue of those who ought naturally to augment them the most. The capital of the country, instead of increasing, gradually dwindles away, and the quantity of productive labour maintained in it grows every day less and less. Have the exorbitant profits of the merchants of Cadiz and Lisbon augmented the capital of Spain and Portugal? Have they alleviated the poverty, have they promoted the industry of those two beggarly countries? Such has been the tone of mercantile expence in those two trading cities, that those exorbitant profits, far from augmenting the general capital of the country, seem scarce to have been sufficient to keep up the capitals upon which they were made. ... Compare the mercantile manners of Cadiz and Lisbon with those of Amsterdam, and you will be sensible how differently the conduct and character of merchants are affected by the high and by the low profits of stock. .... Light come light go, says the proverb; and the ordinary tone of expence seems every where to be regulated, not so much according to the real ability of spending as to the supposed facility of getting money to spend.

(WN IV.vii.c.61)

It is only the force of competition, apparently, which can be relied upon to keep the capitalist from behaving like an extravagant landowner. This is so because a major determinant of economic behaviour is the ease or difficulty involved in the earning of income. While it may be going too far to suggest that, although Smith did not subscribe to a backward sloping supply curve for labour, he *did* subscribe to it for the capitalist, he does believe that a rise in the rate of profit will reduce the quality, if not the supply, of capitalist effort.

It is true that the barbs which Smith directed at the wealthy usually have large landowners as their target. But there is a good historical reason for this. When Smith wrote, in the middle of the eighteenth century, the land-owning classes still thoroughly dominated English society and provided far more conspicuous targets for his attack on great wealth than did the rising class of merchants and manufacturers. But it should be abundantly clear from what has preceded that Smith's sharp invective against the 'indolence and vanity of the rich' (WN V.i.d.5) is not, in principle or intention, con-fined to any single class in society. Rather, these are characteristics which are attached to the possessors of wealth, from whatever source that wealth is derived, because such possession conditions its owners in highly pre-dictable ways.[17]

This brings me to what is both my final point and perhaps a new paradox to replace the one which I have attempted to resolve. I have argued that Smith's hostility to high profits is rooted in his belief that such profits dull the edges of capitalist performance—as in Cadiz and Lisbon—both by dulling his incentive and capacities as an *earner* of income and by destroying his frugality in *disposing* of that income. The trouble—and the paradox—of high profits is that the *attainment* of wealth corrupts the forces leading to the *generation* of wealth—as is obviously the case with the large land-owner. Therefore a recurring theme of the book bearing the title *An Inquiry into the Nature and Causes of the Wealth of Nations* is that, at least on the individual level, the easy attainment of great wealth is likely to destroy the individual's capacity to contribute to the wealth of nations.[18] In this respect, the supreme and essential virtue of competition is that, while it permits the attainment of modest wealth, it places the easy amassing of great wealth virtually beyond reach. It may fairly be said, therefore, that although Adam Smith certainly does not celebrate the social role of the individual capitalist, he does indeed celebrate the role of the capitalist system—or, more pre-cisely, the role of competitive capitalism.

Yet, with all of Smith's preoccupation with the wealth of nations, he also believes that the pursuit of wealth does not take place for the direct gratification or utilitarian purposes provided by an abundance of worldly goods, but rather because the possession of such goods brings their owner the high esteem and approbation of his fellow man.[19] That paradox—and

[17] See Nathan Rosenberg, 'Some Institutional Aspects of *The Wealth of Nations*'.

[18] Smith also noted the inverse correlation between income level and human fertility. 'A half-starved Highland woman frequently bears more than twenty children, while a pam-pered fine lady is often incapable of bearing any, and is generally exhausted by two or three. Barrenness, so frequent among women of fashion, is very rare among those of inferior station. Luxury in the fair sex, while it inflames perhaps the passion for enjoyment, seems always to weaken, and frequently to destroy altogether, the powers of generation' (WN I.viii.37). It is curious that Malthus never examined the important implications of this statement for his theory of population.

[19] '. . . (W)hat are the advantages which we propose by the great purpose of human life which we call bettering our condition? To be observed, to be attended to, to be taken notice

Adam Smith on Profits—Paradox Lost and Regained   389

surely the insistence upon the relative unimportance of the wealth of nations by the author of *The Wealth of Nations* deserves to be called a paradox—has to be pursued through Smith's earlier work, *The Theory of Moral Sentiments*. But that is another story.

of with sympathy, complacency, and approbation, are all the advantages which we can propose to derive from it. It is the vanity, not the ease or the pleasure, which interests us. But vanity is always founded upon the belief of our being the object of attention and approbation. The rich man glories in his riches, because he feels that they naturally draw upon him the attention of the world, and that mankind are disposed to go along with him in all those agreeable emotions with which the advantages of his situation so readily inspire him. At the thought of this, his heart seems to swell and dilate itself within him, and he is fonder of his wealth upon this account, than for all the other advantages it procures him' (TMS I.iii.2.1). Smith makes this point almost aphoristically in *The Wealth of Nations* when he asserts that 'With the greater part of rich people, the chief enjoyment of riches consists in the parade of riches ' . .' (WN I.xi.c.31). See also Nathan Rosenberg, 'Adam Smith, Consumer Tastes, and Economic Growth', especially 364–7.

[6]

Another Advantage of the Division of Labor

Nathan Rosenberg

Stanford University

It is almost unseemly still to be searching out further advantages which Adam Smith attributed to the division of labor. Surely the 200 years which have now elapsed since the publication of the *Wealth of Nations* has been ample time for even the dullest-witted assortment of scholars to ferret out all interesting bits of Adam Smith's discussion of that subject. Nevertheless the purpose of this paper will be to call attention to yet another significant advantage beyond the three which Adam Smith identified in the celebrated first chapter of the *Wealth of Nations*.[1]

The discussion with which I will be concerned did not appear in the *Wealth of Nations* but in a set of lectures on rhetoric and belles lettres which Adam Smith delivered at the University of Glasgow in 1762–63 (Smith 1971). (Smith scholars who might experience some self-mortification at their failure to perceive the significance of this treatment may therefore be reassured that the lectures have been in the public domain for only a few years.) I intend to show that this discussion is not only neatly consistent with and supplementary to the time-honored treatment in the *Wealth of Nations*, but that it also enlarges our understanding of Smith's views in some important respects.

The material with which I am concerned was presented in a lecture on February 7, 1763.[2] In earlier lectures Smith had been concerned with

The author wishes to acknowledge the valuable comments which he received on an earlier draft from Paul David, David Mowery, and George Stigler.

[1] "This great increase of the quantity of work, which, in consequence of the division of labour, the same number of people are capable of performing, is owing to three different circumstances; first, to the increase of dexterity in every particular workman; secondly, to the saving of the time which is commonly lost in passing from one species of work to another; and lastly, to the invention of a great number of machines which facilitate and abridge labour, and enable one man to do the work of many" (Smith 1937, p. 7). For a further discussion of Smith's views on the division of labor, see Rosenberg (1965).

[2] Interestingly enough, these lectures were delivered at about the same time as his *Lectures on Justice, Police, Revenue and Arms* (Smith 1956). On the exact dating of those student lecture notes Cannan concluded: "It is . . . probable that the actual lectures from which the notes were taken were delivered either in the portion of the academical session of 1763–4 which preceded Adam Smith's departure, or in the session of 1762–3, almost certain that they were not delivered before 1761–2, and absolutely certain that they were not delivered before 1760–1" (Smith 1956, p. xx).

[*Journal of Political Economy*, 1976, vol. 84, no. 4, pt. 1]
© 1976 by The University of Chicago. All rights reserved.

demonstrative and deliberative eloquence and in this lecture turned his attention to judicial eloquence. Legal arguments, he asserts, take essentially two forms, either to demonstrate by "abstract reasoning" that something "follows from some statute," or by showing "how it has been supported as law by former practice and similar adjudged causes or precedents" (1971, p. 168). At this juncture Smith points out that neither the Greek nor Roman lawyers had made any use of the second category, which is so widely exploited by modern lawyers, and he undertakes in a digression to explain this failure. His explanation turns upon a more extensive division of labor in modern as compared with ancient times.

A central feature of earlier periods, Smith points out, is that the duties of judge, general, and legislator were commonly performed by the same persons—"at least the two former are very commonly conjoined" (1971, p. 168). In barbarous societies, when men formed the habit of submitting themselves to control by some superior person, they did not generally distinguish between different realms—military, legislative, or judicial. As a result,

> The same persons therefore who judged them in peace, led them also to battle. In this two-fold capacity of judge and general, the first kings and consuls of Rome, and other magistrates, would reckon the judicial part of their office a burthen, rather than that by which they were to obtain honour and glory; that was only to be got by military exploits. They therefore were very bold in passing sentence. They would pay very little regard to the conduct of their predecessors, as this was the least important part of their office. This part was therefore for their ease separated from the other and given to another sort of magistrates. These, as the Judicial was their only office, would be at much greater pains to gain honour and reputation by it. [Smith 1971, p. 168; cf. Smith 1937, pp. 680–81][3]

In this passage Smith thus argues in favor of a more extensive division

---

[3] Of course Smith also recognized that the exercise of the judicial power on the part of the sovereign was likely to lead to many grave abuses, especially when the administration of justice was made "subservient to the purposes of revenue." See Smith (1937), bk. 5, chap. 1, pt. 2, "Of the Expense of Justice," where he observes: "In all barbarous governments, accordingly, in all those ancient governments of Europe in particular, which were founded upon the ruins of the Roman empire, the administration of justice appears for a long time to have been extremely corrupt; far from being quite equal and impartial even under the best monarchs, and altogether profligate under the worst" (p. 676). More generally: "When the judicial is united to the executive power, it is scarcely possible that justice should not frequently be sacrificed to, what is vulgarly called, politics. . . . In order to make every individual feel himself perfectly secure in the possession of every right which belongs to him, it is not only necessary that the judicial should be separated from the executive power, but that it should be rendered as much as possible independent of that power" (p. 681).

of labor by asserting that it is better to have two important social functions divided up among separate individuals rather than having them combined in a single individual. The reasoning underlying the argument will be familiar to all readers of the *Wealth of Nations*. If an individual's attainment of recognition and success is linked to only one of the two activities which he regularly performs, he will have no particular motivation to perform the other activity well. A man who is simultaneously general and judge should not be expected to devote any extensive effort to the latter function if his place in society is determined entirely by his qualities as a military leader. It hardly requires any marginalist calculations to predict that, if the returns to activity A remain very high while those for activity B are effectively set at zero, the latter activity will be either performed in a most perfunctory way or totally neglected. One can almost hear the Adam Smith of the *Wealth of Nations* intoning at this point: "In every profession, the exertion of the greater part of those who exercise it, is always in proportion to the necessity they are under of making that exertion" (1937, p. 717). If there is no necessity or no gain to be derived from the performance of the judicial function, it cannot reasonably be expected that it will be performed well.[4]

From this point of view, therefore, a new division of labor involving the separation of military and judicial functions makes great sense since those who now perform only the judicial function have a powerful incentive to perform it well. Under the old division of labor, by contrast, judicial responsibilities were in the hands of people who lacked the motivation to perform them well. Indeed, this new division of labor is freighted with the greatest of all social consequences. The establishment of a separate judiciary not only creates new and powerful motives for the efficient performance of judicial functions. It also institutionalizes forces which lead to a highly desirable pattern of cumulative social change. For a full-time judiciary

> . . . would be at pains to strengthen their conduct by the authority of their predecessors. When, therefore, there were a few judges appointed, these would be at great pains to vindicate and

---

[4] As Smith states elsewhere about a university teacher who derives his entire income from endowments and is therefore totally independent of any form of remuneration from his pupils: "His interest is, in this case, set as directly in opposition to his duty as it is possible to set it. It is the interest of every man to live as much at his ease as he can; and if his emoluments are to be precisely the same, whether he does, or does not perform some very laborious duty, it is certainly his interest, at least as interest is vulgarly understood, either to neglect it altogether, or, if he is subject to some authority which will not suffer him to do this, to perform it in as careless and slovenly a manner as that authority will permit. If he is naturally active and a lover of labour, it is his interest to employ that activity in any way, from which he can derive some advantage, rather than in the performance of his duty, from which he can derive none" (1937, p. 718).

864

> support their conduct by all possible means. Whatever, therefore, had been practised by other judges would obtain authority with them, and be received in time as law. This is the case in England. The sentences of former cases are greatly regarded, and form what is called the Common Law, which is found to be much more equitable than that which is founded on Statute only, for the same reason as what is founded on practice and experience must be better adapted to particular cases than that which is derived from theory only. [Smith 1971, pp. 168–69]

Once the division of labor has led to the establishment of an independent judiciary, other dynamic forces are set into motion. For, as Smith emphasizes in the *Wealth of Nations*, the pursuit of private self-interest on the part of judges now generates a competitive process the outcome of which is a judicial system far more responsive to individual needs:

> The fees of court seem originally to have been the principal support of the different courts of justice in England. Each court endeavoured to draw to itself as much business as it could, and was, upon that account, willing to take cognizance of many suits which were not originally intended to fall under its jurisdiction . . . each court endeavoured, by superior dispatch and impartiality, to draw to itself as many causes as it could. The present admirable constitution of the courts of justice in England was, perhaps, originally in a great measure, formed by this emulation, which anciently took place between their respective judges; each judge endeavoring to give, in his own court, the speediest and most effectual remedy, which the law would admit, for every sort of injustice. [1937, p. 679; see also 1956, p. 49]

Note that, in this particular case at least, the competitive process (the endeavor of individuals to widen their jurisdiction) works *against* greater specialization. But justice is, in fact, a very peculiar kind of service, and its dispensation cannot be safely left to the marketplace. The freedom of individuals to "purchase" justice may lead to the destruction of justice itself, especially in the all-too-likely circumstances where the sovereign (or judge) treated judicial service as a source of revenue.[5]

---

[5] "This scheme of making the administration of justice subservient to the purposes of revenue, could scarce fail to be productive of several very gross abuses. The person, who applied for justice with a large present in his hand, was likely to get something more than justice; while he, who applied for it with a small one, was likely to get something less. Justice too might frequently be delayed, in order that this present might be repeated. The amercement, besides, of the person complained of, might frequently suggest a very strong reason for finding him in the wrong, even when he had not really been so. That such abuses were far from being uncommon, the ancient history of every country in Europe bears witness" (Smith 1937, p. 675).

For the free operation of market forces may make it possible for affluent litigants to buy favorable decisions from supposedly impartial judges. The problem is that the enforcement of justice requires that its dispensation be linked institutionally to the power of the state,[6] whereas such linkage inevitably creates numerous opportunities and inducements for the corruption of the service itself. It is an extremely delicate matter to organize the administration of justice in such a way that outcomes are not influenced by the desire for increased revenue on the part of either the judge or the sovereign.[7]

There is another aspect of the administration of justice to which Smith also calls attention. Even when the military and judicial functions have been effectively separated, it is further essential that the judicial function not be placed in the hands of large social units. For it is unlikely that an activity will be performed well if individual motivations are not strongly engaged to perform it well. And when individuals share responsibilities within a sufficiently large collectivity, individual incentives are inevitably diffused or even totally dissipated.[8] In judicial proceedings, as elsewhere, it is in society's interests to maintain the closest possible linkage between individual effort and individual reward. To do this properly therefore requires that the actions of single individuals be highly visible:

> These judges, when few in number, will be much more anxious to proceed according to equity than where there is a great number. The blame then is not so easily laid upon any particular person; they are in very little fear of censure; and are out of danger of suffering much by wrong proceedings. Besides that a great number of judges naturally confirm each other, prejudice and inflame each other's passions. We see accordingly that the sentences of the judges in England are greatly more equitable than those of the Parliament of Paris or other Courts which are severed from censure by their number. The House of Commons, when they acted in a Judicial capacity, have not always proceeded with the greatest wisdom, although their proceedings are kept upon record as well as those of the other Courts, and without doubt in imitation of them. [Smith 1971, p. 169][9]

[6] Although there is a form of competition, just described, among existing courts, there is no free entry into the justice trade, which is monopolized by the state.

[7] It is this problem which accounts for Smith's central concern in "Of the Expense of Justice" (n. 3 above).

[8] Is this an eighteenth-century anticipation of the "free rider" problem?

[9] Similar difficulties had plagued the ancient world. "The case was the same with regard to the Areopagus and the Council of Five Hundred at Athens. Their number was too great to restrict them from arbitrary and summary proceedings. They would here pay as little regard to the proceedings of former judges as those did who at the same time possessed the office of general along with that of judge. The praetor at Rome, indeed, often borrowed from the decrees; but then nothing could be quoted as law to him but what

In his judicial digression Smith therefore emphasizes two different kinds of advantages in connection with an increased division of labor. When responsibilities are divided up among different people so that no one possesses both military and judicial obligations, both obligations will be better performed. Judicial responsibilities are performed better because they now constitute someone's sole responsibility, and that person is being judged solely by how well he performs it. When an individual performs more than one function, but his success is based only upon his performance in one of them, he will neglect the one to which his social status is less attached. On the other hand, it is essential that important social functions not be reposed in large social aggregates. A division of labor involving fewness is essential because fewness is a precondition for establishing individual responsibility. Only when individual responsibility (or fault) can be established will individual effort be reliably engaged in ways which will promote society's larger interests.[10] Thus, whereas Adam Smith had described the advantages of the division of labor in the opening chapter of the *Wealth of Nations* in terms of an improvement in human skills and capacities, his treatment in his lectures on rhetoric and belles lettres calls attention to basic improvements in motivation as well.

When law becomes a highly specialized activity, then, subject to an extensive division of labor and administered by small decision-making units, individual motivations and capacities are more deeply and effectively involved in establishing justice and providing the inhabitants of a country with liberty and security. The point is not of secondary or trivial interest to Smith. Indeed, it is tempting to say that no point was *more* interesting to him, because justice is the essential and indispensable cement which binds a society together. Beneficence, as he was at great pains to establish elsewhere, is not enough. "Beneficence . . . is less essential to the existence of society than justice. Society may subsist, though not in the most comfortable state, without beneficence; but the prevalence of injustice must utterly destroy it" (1880, p. 79).

In this vital way, then, is the history of the increasing division of labor

---

was found in his edict, which was put up at the beginning of each year, and in which he declared in what manner he was to regulate his conduct. (This was the custom till the time of the Edictum Perpetuum.) He would have taken it as a great affront to his judgement to have been told that such an one before had done so-and-so. And no part of the former edicts could be quoted but what was transcribed into his, and in his name it was always to be quoted. There was therefore no room for precedents in any Judicial pleadings amongst the Greeks or Romans . . ." (Smith 1971, pp. 169–70).

[10] It is important to recognize here that Smith is dealing with two separate issues: the extent of the division of labor and the size of the appropriate decision-making unit. In his *Lectures on Rhetoric and Belles Lettres*, however, Smith joins these issues by insisting that fewness is necessary to derive the benefits which might be expected to flow from greater division of labor in judicial proceedings. Note that on p. 169 of those lectures (quoted above) he had stated that judges would be "anxious to proceed according to equity" when they were "few in number." This important qualification, as we will see below, is repeated in the next paragraph (1971, p. 170).

in the judicial process inseparably linked to the fulfillment of other goals which constitute the foundations of any truly civilized community. For beneficence, however desirable and meritorious, is never a sufficiently strong force:

> Though Nature... exhorts mankind to acts of beneficence, by the pleasing consciousness of deserved reward, she has not thought it necessary to guard and enforce the practice of it by the terrors of merited punishment in case it should be neglected. It is the ornament which embellishes, not the foundation which supports, the building, and which it was, therefore, sufficient to recommend, but by no means necessary to impose. Justice, on the contrary, is the main pillar that upholds the whole edifice. If it is removed, the great, the immense fabric of human society, that fabric which to raise and support seems in this world, if I may say so, to have been the peculiar and darling care of Nature, must in a moment crumble into atoms. [Smith 1880, p. 79]

Finally, by joining the hitherto separate threads of Smith's treatment of the division of labor and the administration of justice, we arrive at a deeper appreciation of what Smith had in mind when he observed in chapter 4 of book 3 of the *Wealth of Nations* that " . . . commerce and manufactures gradually introduced order and good government, and with them, the liberty and security of individuals, among the inhabitants of the country, who had before lived almost in a continual state of war with their neighbors, and of servile dependency upon their superiors. This, though it has been the least observed, is by far the most important of all their effects (1937, p. 385).[11] Although it is possible to infer some of Smith's meaning when the statement is placed in the larger context of the argument of the *Wealth of Nations* as a whole,[12] we can now make use

[11] In the next sentence Smith adds: "Mr. Hume is the only writer who, so far as I know, has hitherto taken notice of it." The relationship is, of course, a reciprocal one, in that commerce and manufactures can continue to flourish only in a society where justice continues to be properly administered. "Commerce and manufactures can seldom flourish long in any state which does not enjoy a regular administration of justice, in which the people do not feel themselves secure in the possession of their property, in which the faith of contracts is not supported by law, and in which the authority of the state is not supposed to be regularly employed in enforcing the payment of debts from all those who are able to pay" (1937, p. 862).

[12] The development of freedom and justice depended, historically, upon the destruction of the power and authority of the ancient barons of the Middle Ages and the end of the "servile dependency" of their retainers and tenants upon them. Smith spells out in the *Wealth of Nations* (bk. 3, chap. 4) how the rise of commerce destroyed the power of the ancient barons and thereby "gradually introduced order and good government." Along with this went the elimination of the arbitrary exercise of power. "The tenants having in this manner become independent, and the retainers being dismissed, the great proprietors were no longer capable of interrupting the regular execution of justice, or of disturbing the peace of the country" (1937, p. 390; see also 1956, p. 155): "Nothing tends so much to corrupt mankind as dependency, while independency still increases the honesty of the people. The establishment of commerce and manufactures, which brings about this independency, is the best police for preventing crimes" (see also Rosenberg 1968).

of the student's lecture notes to draw the highly significant conclusion to which Smith intended his argument to lead, that ". . . it may be looked upon as one of the most happy parts of the British Constitution, though introduced merely by chance and to ease the men in power, that the office of judging causes is committed into the hands *of a few persons* whose sole employment it is to determine them (1971, p. 170; my emphasis). For increasing wealth has led, in the British case, via an increasing division of labor, to improvements in the administration of justice of the greatest moment for society. It seems appropriate to leave the last word in this matter to Smith himself:

> The separation of the province of distributing justice between man and man from that of conducting affairs and leading armies, is the great advantage which modern times have over ancient, and the foundation of that greater security which we now enjoy, both with regard to liberty, property, and life. It was introduced only by chance to ease the supreme magistrate of the most laborious and the least glorious part of his power, and has never taken place until the increase of refinement and the growth of society have multiplied business immensely. [1971, p. 170; cf. 1937, pp. 680–81]

References

Rosenberg, N. "Adam Smith on the Division of Labour: Two Views or One?" *Economica* 32 (May 1965): 127–39.

————. "Adam Smith, Consumer Tastes, and Economic Growth." *J.P.E.* 76 (May/June 1968): 361–74.

Smith, A. *The Theory of Moral Sentiments*, as reprinted in *Essays Philosophical and Literary*. London: Ward, Lock, 1880.

————. *The Wealth of Nations*. New York: Modern Library, 1937.

————. *Lectures on Justice, Police, Revenue and Arms, Delivered in the University of Glasgow, Reported by a Student in 1763*. Edited by Edwin Cannan. New York: Kelley & Millman, 1956.

————. *Lectures on Rhetoric and Belles Lettres, Delivered in the University of Glasgow, Reported by a Student in 1762–63*. Edited by John M. Lothian. 1963. Carbondale: Southern Illinois Univ. Press, 1971.

7

History of Political Economy 22:1
© 1990 by Duke University Press
CCC 0018–2702/90/$1.50

Adam Smith and the stock of moral capital

Nathan Rosenberg

I

It may come as a surprise to encounter Adam Smith telling his readers that "the wise and virtuous man is at all times willing that his own private interest should be sacrificed to the public interest of his own particular order or society."[1] To someone whose knowledge of Smith has been confined to *The wealth of nations,* such self-sacrificing altruism is distinctly unexpected. The catch, of course, is that the supply of wise and virtuous men is severely limited. Consequently no society could function effectively if its affairs were organized on the (false) assumption that most men possessed wisdom and virtue in abundance.

Adam Smith, an economist and a philosopher as well as a wise and virtuous man, understood the necessity of recourse to solutions of a second-best nature. Speaking of the man of public spirit, he stated: "When he cannot establish the right, he will not disdain to ameliorate the wrong; but like Solon, when he cannot establish the best system of laws, he will endeavour to establish the best that the people can bear."[2]

Does this have some relevance to the formation of the moral sentiments, with which Smith was so much concerned in his first book? In *The theory of moral sentiments* it is fair to say that Smith was as much interested in the process by which the moral sentiments are shaped as he was in the actual content of those sentiments. Can we therefore think of the process by which these sentiments are formed as an investment in personal morality that has larger significance, not only for the individual, but for society as a whole? If this question can be answered in the affirmative, then is it further possible to ask whether a commercial society is a net investor in moral capital—i.e., is it, on balance, enlarging or depleting its stock of moral capital? In particular, does Smith have

Correspondence may be addressed to the author, Department of Economics, Stanford University, Stanford CA 94305.

1. Adam Smith, *The theory of moral sentiments,* ed. D. D. Raphael and A. L. Macfie (Oxford: Oxford University Press, 1976), 235.
    2. Ibid., 233; see also 233–34, 237.

1

2   *History of Political Economy 22:1 (1990)*

a well-articulated set of views on whether a commercializing economy tends to add to its stock of moral capital in a more effective fashion than did earlier societies?

The very question of how a society shapes the moral sentiments of its members takes on a greatly enlarged significance when we read, in the early pages of *The wealth of nations*, that people are very similar when they first enter the world. In Smith's view, inborn differences among men are very small. Their subsequent behavior is therefore very much a matter of the ways in which society shapes their habits and sentiments.[3]

II

To what kinds of forces does a commercializing society give rise that may be expected to add to the stock of moral capital? It is important to try to answer this question because, at the same time, Smith sees some forces at work in commercialization that tend either to *run down* the stock of moral capital or to create conditions that would appear to *require more of it* than did earlier, precommercial societies.

There are two such sets of "depleting" forces, one more familiar, the other less so.

In Book V of *The wealth of nations* Smith pointed to the deleterious effects of the division of labor, whose productivity-increasing benefits had been so central to Book I and, indeed, to the entire structure of Smith's economic argument. It will suffice to recall one devastating indictment:

> In the progress of the division of labour, the employment of the far greater part of those who live by labour, that is, of the great body

3. "The difference of natural talents in different men is, in reality, much less than we are aware of; and the very different genius which appears to distinguish men of different professions, when grown up to maturity, is not upon many occasions so much the cause, as the effect of the division of labour. The difference between the most dissimilar characters, between a philosopher and a common street porter, for example, seems to arise not so much from nature, as from habit, custom, and education. When they came into the world, and for the first six or eight years of their existence, they were, perhaps, very much alike, and neither their parents nor playfellows could perceive any remarkable difference. About that age, or soon after, they come to be employed in very different occupations. The difference of talents comes then to be taken notice of, and widens by degrees, till at last the vanity of the philosopher is willing to acknowledge scarce any resemblance. . . . By nature a philosopher is not in genius and disposition half so different from a street porter, as a mastiff is from a greyhound, or a greyhound from a spaniel, or this last from a shepherd's dog." Adam Smith, *Wealth of nations*, ed. R. H. Campbell, A. S. Skinner, and W. B. Todd (Oxford: Oxford University Press, 1976), 28–30. David Hume held similar views. In his essay "Of the Original Contract" he asked the reader to "consider how nearly equal all men are in their bodily force, and even in their mental powers and faculties, 'ere cultivated by education" (*Essays*, 1748, 291).

The most authoritative modern treatment of the views of Adam Smith, and other classical economists, on how the larger social framework influences human behavior is Warren Samuels, *The classical theory of economic policy* (Cleveland: World, 1966). See especially ch. 2, "The nonlegal forces of social control."

of the people, comes to be confined to a few very simple operations, frequently to one or two. But the understandings of the greater part of men are necessarily formed by their ordinary employments. The man whose whole life is spent in performing a few simple operations, of which the effects too are, perhaps, always the same, or very nearly the same, has no occasion to exert his understanding, or to exercise his invention in finding out expedients for removing difficulties which never occur. He naturally loses, therefore, the habit of such exertion, and generally becomes as stupid and ignorant as it is possible for a human creature to become. The torpor of his mind renders him, not only incapable of relishing or bearing a part in any rational conversation, but of conceiving any generous, noble, or tender sentiment, and consequently of forming any just judgment concerning many even of the ordinary duties of private life. Of the great and extensive interests of his country he is altogether incapable of judging; and unless very particular pains have been taken to render him otherwise, he is equally incapable of defending his country in war. The uniformity of his stationary life naturally corrupts the courage of his mind, and makes him regard with abhorrence the irregular, uncertain, and adventurous life of a soldier. It corrupts even the activity of his body, and renders him incapable of exerting his strength with vigour and perseverance, in any other employment than that to which he has been bred.[4]

The debilitating effects of the extensive division of labor that characterize commercial societies are, in Smith's view, systematic as well as pervasive: "It is remarkable that in every commercial nation the low people are exceedingly stupid. The Dutch vulgar are eminently so, and the English are more so than the Scotch. The rule is general, in towns they are not so intelligent as in the country, nor in a rich country as in a poor one."[5]

The second, less familiar set of forces that threatens to run down the stock of moral capital in commercializing societies is the impact of commercialization upon the family. The family is the social unit within which relations of affection (which "is in reality nothing but habitual sympathy"),[6] mutual support, and benevolence most naturally prevail.[7]

---

4. *Wealth of nations*, 781–82. See also *Lectures on jurisprudence*. ed. R. L. Meek, D. D. Raphael, and P. G. Stein (Oxford: Oxford University Press, 1978). 538–41. I have treated these matters at greater length in "Adam Smith on the division of labour: two views or one?" *Economica* 32 (May 1965): 127–39.

5. *Lectures*, 539.

6. *Moral sentiments*, 220.

7. "Every man, as the Stoics used to say, is first and principally recommended to his own care; and every man is certainly, in every respect, fitter and abler to take care of himself than of any other person. Every man feels his own pleasures and his own pains more sensibly than those of other people. The former are the original sensations; the latter

4   *History of Political Economy 22:1 (1990)*

In primitive forms of society the cohesion and the security provided by the social unit of the family, including the more extended family, are highly functional. In fact Smith regards the primary function of the family in precommercial societies as ensuring the safety of its members, and not the provision of economic support.

> In pastoral countries, and in all countries where the authority of law is not alone sufficient to give perfect security to every member of the state, all the different branches of the same family commonly chuse to live in the same neighbourhood of one another. Their association is frequently necessary for their common defence. They are all, from the highest to the lowest, of more or less importance to one another. Their concord strengthens their necessary association; their discord always weakens, and might destroy it. They have more intercourse with one another, than with the members of any other tribe. The remotest members of the same tribe claim some connection with one another; and, where all other circumstances are equal, expect to be treated with more distinguished attention than is due to those who have no such pretensions. It is not many years ago that, in the Highlands of Scotland, the Chieftain used to consider the poorest man of his clan, as his cousin and relation. The same extensive regard to kindred is said to take place among the Tartars, the Arabs, the Turkomans, and, I believe, among all other nations who are nearly in the same state of society in which the Scots Highlanders were about the beginning of the present century.[8]

In commercial societies, however, the state is capable of providing for the security of its members, and thus the main motive for maintaining the strength of extended family ties is removed. Hence "regard for remote relations becomes, in every country, less and less, according as this state of civilization has been longer and more completely established."[9]

As the family declines in its social importance, it allows certain other activities to be "spun off" and provided elsewhere. This occurs in no

---

the reflected or sympathetic images of those sensations. The former may be said to be the substance; the latter the shadow.

"After himself, the members of his own family, those who usually live in the same house with him, his parents, his children, his brothers and sisters, are naturally the objects of his warmest affections. They are naturally and usually the persons upon whose happiness or misery his conduct must have the greatest influence. He is more habituated to sympathize with them. He knows better how every thing is likely to affect them, and his sympathy with them is more precise and determinate, than it can be with the greater part of other people. It approaches nearer, in short, to what he feels for himself." Ibid., 219.

8. Ibid., 222–23.

9. Ibid., 223.

less central an activity than the education of the young—at least among the higher social classes. Smith is scathing in his denunciation of the growing practice of sending children away from home—and family—for their education, and for thus substituting a man-made institution for a natural one.

> The education of boys at distant great schools, of young men at distant colleges, of young ladies in distant nunneries and boarding-schools, seems, in the higher ranks of life, to have hurt most essentially the domestic morals, and consequently the domestic happiness, both of France and England. Do you wish to educate your children to be dutiful to their parents, to be kind and affectionate to their brothers and sisters? put them under the necessity of being dutiful children, of being kind and affectionate brothers and sisters: educate them in your own house. From their parent's house, they may, with propriety and advantage, go out every day to attend public schools: but let their dwelling be always at home. Respect for you must always impose a very useful restraint upon their conduct; and respect for them may frequently impose no useless restraint upon your own. Surely no acquirement, which can possibly be derived from what is called a public education, can make any sort of compensation for what is almost certainly and necessarily lost by it. Domestic education is the institution of nature; public education, the contrivance of man. It is surely unnecessary to say, which is likely to be the wisest.[10]

III

Thus, if we were drawing up a balance sheet of the assets and liabilities of a commercial society, it is clear that there are substantial liabilities.

---

10. Ibid., 222. Smith was especially critical of the growing practice of sending young men on a continental tour, which he seemed to think was almost uniquely contrived to reduce the stock of moral capital. "In England, it becomes every day more and more the custom to send young people to travel in foreign countries immediately upon their leaving school, and without sending them to any university. Our young people, it is said, generally return home much improved by their travels. A young man who goes abroad at seventeen or eighteen, and returns home at one and twenty, returns three or four years older than he was when he went abroad; and at that age it is very difficult not to improve a good deal in three or four years. In the course of his travels, he generally acquires some knowledge of one or two foreign languages; a knowledge, however, which is seldom sufficient to enable him either to speak or write them with propriety. In other respects, he commonly returns home more conceited, more unprincipled, more dissipated, and more incapable of any serious application either to study or to business, than he could well have become in so short a time, had he lived at home. By travelling so very young, by spending in the most frivolous dissipation the most precious years of his life, at a distance from the inspection and controul of his parents and relations, every useful habit, which the earlier parts of his education might have had some tendency to form in him, instead of being rivetted and confirmed, is almost necessarily either weakened or effaced." *Wealth of nations*, 773–74.

6   *History of Political Economy 22:1 (1990)*

What can be set upon the asset side of the account? If the family, the social unit that is most responsible for the provision of beneficence, declines, is there anything that can possibly weigh in the balance as an offset to that loss? Can the growth of a commercial society provide benefits that balance such onerous and grievous losses?

There are, indeed, important offsets. Most obvious to readers of *The wealth of nations* are the economic offsets.[11] In the context of the analysis of *The theory of moral sentiments,* I interpret Smith's essential answer to my question as follows. Benevolence, and the beneficence that is often associated with it, are important and powerful forces. Moreover, in a striking but neglected passage, Smith actually asserts that beneficence *pays*—i.e., it brings a larger net flow of benefits to the benefactor.

> Of all the persons . . . whom nature points out for our peculiar beneficence, there are none to whom it seems more properly directed than to those whose beneficence we have ourselves already experienced. Nature, which formed men for that mutual kindness, so necessary for their happiness, renders every man the peculiar object of kindness, to the persons to whom he himself has been kind. Though their gratitude should not always correspond to his beneficence, yet the sense of his merit, the sympathetic gratitude of the impartial spectator, will always correspond to it. The general indignation of other people, against the baseness of their ingratitude, will even, sometimes, increase the general sense of his merit. *No benevolent man ever lost altogether the fruits of his benevolence. If he does not always gather them from the persons from whom he ought to have gathered them, he seldom fails to gather them, and with a tenfold increase, from other people.* Kindness is the parent of kindness; and if to be beloved by our brethren be the great object of our ambition, the surest way of obtaining it is, by our conduct to show that we really love them.[12]

Nevertheless, in spite of the power that he here attributes to beneficence, society can exist without it.[13] What it *cannot* exist without is an

11. The kinds of economic benefits that Smith attributes to the division of labor are too well known to require repetition. Nonetheless, not everyone may be familiar with the *size* of the benefits that Smith appeared to attribute to the division of labor. In discussing the desirability of free trade with France, a much larger country than Britain, he pointed out: "Twenty millions of people perhaps in a great society, working as it were to one anothers hands, from the nature of the division of labour before explained would produce *a thousand times* more goods than another society consisting only of two or three millions." *Lectures*, 512 (emphasis added). Thus, at least for some ranges, Smith believed that output grew in proportion to the cube of inputs—a rather remarkable claim.

12. *Moral sentiments*, 225 (emphasis added).

13. Although the gnawing question still persists: Why is there not a great deal *more* of an activity to which the marginal returns are ostensibly so high?

even more cohesive social force: a sense of justice. The point is so central to the argument of this paper, and Smith's views on this matter have been so strangely neglected, that an extensive quotation seems not only permissible but essential.

It is thus that man, who can subsist only in society, was fitted by nature to that situation for which he was made. All the members of human society stand in need of each others assistance, and are likewise exposed to mutual injuries. Where the necessary assistance is reciprocally afforded from love, from gratitude, from friendship, and esteem, the society flourishes and is happy. All the different members of it are bound together by the agreeable bands of love and affection, and are, as it were, thereby drawn to one common centre of mutual good offices.

But though the necessary assistance should not be afforded from such generous and disinterested motives, though among the different members of the society there should be no mutual love and affection, the society, though less happy and agreeable, will not necessarily be dissolved. Society may subsist among different men, as among different merchants, from a sense of its utility, without any mutual love or affection; and though no man in it should owe any obligation, or be bound in gratitude to any other, it may still be upheld by a mercenary exchange of good offices according to an agreed valuation.

Society, however, cannot subsist among those who are at all times ready to hurt and injure one another. The moment that injury begins, the moment that mutual resentment and animosity take place, all the bands of it are broke asunder, and the different members of which it consisted are, as it were, dissipated and scattered abroad by the violence and opposition of their discordant affections. If there is any society among robbers and murderers, they must at least, according to the trite observation, abstain from robbing and murdering one another. Beneficence, therefore, is less essential to the existence of society than justice. Society may subsist, though not in the most comfortable state, without beneficence; but the prevalence of injustice must utterly destroy it.

Though Nature, therefore, exhorts mankind to acts of beneficence, by the pleasing consciousness of deserved reward, she has not thought it necessary to guard and enforce the practice of it by the terrors of merited punishment in case it should be neglected. It is the ornament which embellishes, not the foundation which supports the building, and which it was, therefore, sufficient to recommend, but by no means necessary to impose. Justice, on the contrary, is the main pillar that upholds the whole edifice. If it is removed, the great, the immense fabric of human society, that

8   *History of Political Economy 22:1 (1990)*

fabric which to raise and support seems in this world, if I may say so, to have been the peculiar and darling care of Nature, must in a moment crumble into atoms.[14]

Thus justice, and the security in one's personal and business affairs that goes with it, is the essential binding agent of society. Though a society is always better off with more "mutual love and affection," it is possible to subsist without them.[15] It is not possible to subsist with a "prevalence of injustice."

IV

The critical question for Smith, of course, is whether the growth of commercial societies can be relied upon to expand and to strengthen justice.

Smith's answer to this question is unambiguously in the affirmative. Commercial societies have the distinctive feature that the rule of law prevails within them, and they can provide that security of property and person that precommercial societies could not.[16] Indeed, it is precisely the availability of that security from the state that gave rise to the weakening of family ties. As Smith puts it, "In commercial countries, where the authority of law is always perfectly sufficient to protect the meanest man in the state, the descendants of the same family, having no such motive for keeping together, naturally separate and disperse, as interest or inclination may direct."[17]

The apparatus of government in a commercial society is, in reality, primarily concerned with providing security to its members—security against external as well as internal threats. In fact, in one passage in the student lecture notes Smith seems to regard a rise in government expen-

---

14. *Moral sentiments*, 85–86.

15. Sometimes attitudes that prevail among members of a family can be artificially reproduced outside it. "Among well-disposed people, the necessity or conveniency of mutual accommodation, very frequently produces a friendship not unlike that which takes place among those who are born to live in the same family. Colleagues in office, partners in trade, call one another brothers; and frequently feel towards one another as if they really were so. Their good agreement is an advantage to all; and, if they are tolerably reasonable people, they are naturally disposed to agree. We expect that they should do so; and their disagreement is a sort of a small scandal. The Romans expressed this sort of attachment by the word *necessitudo,* which, from the etymology, seems to denote that it was imposed by the necessity of the situation." Ibid., 223–24. It is unfortunate that Smith did not choose to develop this point further.

16. "Commerce and manufactures can seldom flourish long in any state which does not enjoy a regular administration of justice, in which the people do not feel themselves secure in the possession of their property, in which the faith of contracts is not supported by law, and in which the authority of the state is not supposed to be regularly employed in enforcing the payment of debts from all those who are able to pay. Commerce and manufactures, in short, can seldom flourish in any state in which there is not a certain degree of confidence in the justice of government." *Wealth of nations*, 910.

17. *Moral sentiments*, 197.

ditures as not only unavoidable but desirable, since it is evidence that the society has attained a high degree of affluence (or opulence, to use Smith's preferred word).

We may observe that the government in a civilized country is much more expensive than in a barbarous one; and when we say that one government is more expensive than another, it is the same as if we said that the one country is farther advanced in improvement than another. To say that the government is expensive and the people not oppressed is to say that the people are rich. There are many expences necessary in a civilized country for which there is no occasion in one that is barbarous. Armies, fleets, fortified places and public buildings, judges and officers of the revenue must be supported, and if they be neglected disorder will ensue.[18]

To appreciate fully the role of justice in a commercial society, it is necessary to recall how feudal society effectively destroyed the possibility for capital accumulation and, as a direct result, a more extensive division of labor and economic growth.[19] The structure of feudal society suppressed the possibilities for capital accumulation from each of the three major social classes, although in different ways.

Under the feudal constitution there could be very little accumulation of stock, which will appear from considering the situation of those three orders of men which made up the whole body of the people, the peasants, the landlords, and the merchants. The peasants had leases which depended upon the caprice of their masters. They could never encrease in wealth because the landlord was ready to squeeze it all from them, and therefore they had no motive to acquire it. As little could the landlords encrease their wealth, as they lived so indolent a life and were involved in perpetual wars. The merchants again were oppressed by all ranks, and were not able to secure the produce of their industry from rapine and violence. Thus there could be little accumulation of wealth at all. But after the fall of the feudal government, these obstacles to industry were removed and the stock of commodities began gradually to encrease.[20]

18. *Lectures,* 530–31. Note the preoccupation with the provision of security, broadly defined, in the last sentence.

19. Although despotisms can maintain some degree of stability, they cannot provide genuine security. Indeed, despotism "is more destructive of security and leisure than anarchy itself." Adam Smith, "History of astronomy," in *Essays on philosophical subjects,* ed. W. P. D. Wightman, J. C. Bryce, and I. S. Ross (Oxford: Oxford University Press, 1980), 51.

20. *Lectures,* 520; see also 522–23. Elsewhere Smith describes the violence of feudalism as follows: Under "feudal subordination" the great lords "continued to make war

10   *History of Political Economy 22:1 (1990)*

Of course, the gradual increase that Smith refers to in the last sentence was generated by the emerging capitalist class. The growth of the commercial sector and the increasing control over income flows by the capitalist class are critical elements in Smith's view of economic growth. This is because of the very different behavior that he attributes to different property owners—specifically, landlords versus capitalists. Whereas landlords direct society's surplus resources into frivolous and unproductive activities, the capitalist directs the resources over which he exercises control into economically productive channels: "It is the stock that is employed for the use of profits, which puts into motion the greater part of the useful labor of every society."[21]

The growth of a capitalist class brings an increasing proportion of society's resources—including agriculture itself—under the control of a more efficient class of decision-makers.[22] But it is the dynamic aspect of this point that requires emphasis. The growth of commerce is instrumental in shaping character, in altering tastes, and in providing new and more powerful incentives. The growth of commerce, by increasing the importance of the capitalist class as compared to large landowners, increases the proportion of those in society devoted to parsimony and frugality, "those who are naturally the most disposed to accumulate,"[23] as compared to those who live lives of indolence and prodigality.[24] Com-

---

according to their own discretion, almost continually upon one another, and very frequently upon the king; and the open country still continued to be a scene of violence, rapine, and disorder." *Wealth of nations*, 418. It was only after the decline of the conditions of feudal dependency that "the great proprietors were no longer capable of interrupting the regular execution of justice, or of disturbing the peace of the country." Ibid., 421.

21. *Wealth of nations*, 266.

22. Smith succinctly lays out the differences in attitude and mentality between the merchant and landowner: "the wealth acquired by the inhabitants of cities was frequently employed in purchasing such lands as were to be sold, of which a great part would frequently be uncultivated. Merchants are commonly ambitious of becoming country gentlemen, and when they do, they are generally the best of all improvers. A merchant is accustomed to employ his money chiefly in profitable projects. whereas a mere country gentleman is accustomed to employ it chiefly in expence. The one often sees his money go from him and return to him again with a profit: the other, when once he parts with it, very seldom expects to see any more of it. Those different habits naturally affect their temper and disposition in every sort of business. A merchant is commonly a bold; a country gentleman, a timid undertaker. The one is not afraid to lay out at once a large capital upon the improvement of his land, when he has a probable prospect of raising the value of it in proportion to the expence. The other, if he has any capital, which is not always the case, seldom ventures to employ it in this manner. If he improves at all, it is commonly not with a capital, but with what he can save out of his annual revenue." Ibid., 411.

23. Ibid., 612.

24. Adam Smith's close friend, David Hume, had said: "as the spending of a settled revenue is a way of life entirely without occupation, men have so much need of somewhat to fix and engage them, that pleasures, such as they are, will be the pursuit of the greater part of the landholders, and the prodigals among them will always be more numerous than the misers. In a state, therefore, where there is nothing but a landed interest, as there is little frugality, the borrowers must be very numerous, and the rate of interest must hold

merce inculcates habits of orderliness, reliability, precision, and pains-taking attention to detail. Participation in business enterprise inevitably inculcates certain behavior patterns—in particular, those of "order, oeconomy and attention."[25] Commerce introduces probity and punc-tuality. But it is important to note that Smith's argument makes these qualities emerge, not out of some vague national character, but as a direct response to the pursuit of self-interest in a commercial society.

Whenever commerce is introduced into any country, probity and punctuality always accompany it. These virtues in a rude and bar-barous country are almost unknown. Of all the nations in Europe, the Dutch, the most commercial, are the most faithfull to their word. The English are more so than the Scotch, but much inferiour to the Dutch, and in the remote parts of this country they are far less so than in the commercial parts of it. This is not at all to be imputed to national character, as some pretend. There is no natural reason why an Englishman or Scotchman should not be as punctual in performing agreements as a Dutchman. It is far more reduceable to self interest, that general principle which regulates the actions of every man, and which leads men to act in a certain manner from views of advantage, and is as deeply implanted in an Englishman as a Dutchman. A dealer is afraid of losing his character, and is scrupulous in observing every engagement. When a person makes perhaps 20 contracts in a day, he cannot gain so much by endeav-ouring to impose on his neighbours, as the very appearance of a cheat would make him lose. Where people seldom deal with one another, we find that they are somewhat disposed to cheat, because they can gain more by a smart trick than they can lose by the injury which it does their character. . . . Wherever dealings are frequent, a man does not expect to gain so much by any one contract as by probity and punctuality in the whole, and a prudent dealer, who is sensible of his real interest, would rather chuse to lose what he has a right to than give any ground for suspicion. Every thing of this kind is as odious as it is rare. When the greater part of the people are merchants they always bring probity and punctuality into fash-ion, and these therefore are the principal virtues of a commercial nation.[26]

---

proportion to it. The difference depends not on the quantity of money, but on the habits and manners which prevail." *Writings on Economics,* ed. Eugene Rotwein (Madison: University of Wisconsin Press, 1955), 50.

25. *Wealth of nations,* 412.

26. *Lectures,* 538–39; see also 528. Smith also had some harsh strictures, in this same passage, for politicians and, more particularly, ambassadors. "They whom we call politi-cians are not the most remarkable men in the world for probity and punctuality. Ambas-sadors from different nations are still less so; they are praised for any little advantage they

12   *History of Political Economy 22:1 (1990)*

Note also how clearly this passage foreshadows issues that have become of central concern to modern game theory: the evolution of cooperative modes of behavior and the importance of reputation in repeated market relationships.

V

Thus Smith is centrally concerned with the patterns of behavior that different social structures impose upon self-interested man. In this respect commercial societies emerge as a powerful force for the accumulation of moral capital because they reduce the extreme hierarchy of societies dominated by great wealth, where the pursuit of self-interest is inherently corrupting, and expand the vocational spheres where self-interest leads to just and honest behavior. This I take to be a reasonable reading of the central chapter of *The theory of moral sentiments,* "Of the Corruption of our Moral Sentiments, which is occasioned by this Disposition to admire the Rich and the Great, and to despise or neglect Persons of poor and mean Condition" (Part I, Section III, Chapter III). Smith argues there that "in the courts of princes, in the drawing-rooms of the great, where success and preferment depend, not upon the esteem of intelligent and well-informed equals, but upon the fanciful and foolish favour of ignorant, presumptuous and proud superiors; flattery and falsehood too often prevail over merit and abilities. In such societies the abilities to please, are more regarded than the abilities to serve. . . . The external graces, the frivolous accomplishments of that impertinent and foolish thing called a man of fashion, are commonly more admired than the solid and masculine virtues of a warrior, a statesman, a philosopher, or a legislator."[27]

If we grant that a commercial society reduces the social role of these largely landed-property-based rich and enlarges that of the other classes, especially the middle classes, some very important conclusions follow. This is so because the pursuit of self-interest by such classes is broadly congruent with behavior that Smith regards as moral, just, and honest.

> In the middling and inferior stations of life, the road to virtue and that to fortune, to such fortune, at least, as men in such stations can reasonably expect to acquire, are, happily in most cases, very

---

can take, and pique themselves a good deal on this degree of refinement. The reason of this is that nations treat with one another not above twice or thrice in a century, and they may gain more by one piece of fraud, than [lose] by having a bad character." Ibid., 539. Smith was referring to an earlier period in European history when ambassadors were not ordinarily exchanged during times of peace. See *Wealth of nations,* 731–32.

27. *Moral sentiments,* 63.

nearly the same. In all the middling and inferior professions, real and solid professional abilities, joined to prudent, just, firm, and temperate conduct, can very seldom fail of success. Abilities will even sometimes prevail where the conduct is by no means correct. Either habitual imprudence, however, or injustice, or weakness, or profligacy, will always cloud, and sometimes depress altogether, the most splendid professional abilities. Men in the inferior and middling stations of life, besides, can never be great enough to be above the law, which must generally overawe them into some sort of respect for, at least, the more important rules of justice. The success of such people, too, almost always depends upon the favour and good opinion of their neighbours and equals; and without a tolerably regular conduct these can very seldom be obtained. The good old proverb, therefore, That honesty is the best policy, holds, in such situations, almost always perfectly true. In such situations, therefore, we may generally expect a considerable degree of virtue; and, fortunately for the good morals of society, these are the situations of by far the greater part of mankind.[28]

Thus I interpret Smith as arguing, here and elsewhere, that the decline of the feudal order (or of a society dominated by large-scale landed-property owners) and the rise of a commercial society, will also strengthen the individual's personal incentives to behave in a manner consistent with his own definition of moral behavior. The pursuit of self-interest is far less likely to lead to a corruption of the moral sentiments in a commercial society than in one with an established, hereditary upper class.

Most important for our present concerns, Smith regards the growth of commerce as the solvent that itself dissolves the corrupting bonds of feudal ties and obligations. In doing this, it makes good government and, along with it, liberty and security, possible for the first time. Lest we should be in any doubt about the nature of these vital interconnections, Smith makes the assertion as explicitly as one might wish: "commerce and manufactures gradually introduced order and good government, and with them, the liberty and security of individuals, among the inhabitants of the country, who had before lived almost in a continual state of war with their neighbours, and of servile dependency upon their supe-

---

28. Ibid., 63. For an extended discussion of prudence, see Part VI. Section 1: "Of the Character of the Individual, so far as it affects his own Happiness; or of Prudence." Elsewhere Smith succinctly defines the virtues of prudence, justice, and beneficence as follows: "Concern for our own happiness recommends to us the virtue of prudence: concern for that of other people, the virtues of justice and beneficence: of which, the one restrains us from hurting, the other prompts us to promote that happiness." Ibid., 262.

riors. This, though it has been the least observed, is by far the most important of all their effects."[29]

The corrupting moral effects of "servile dependency" is a central theme of Smith's. It appeared prominently in his 1763 lectures, just four years after the publication of *The theory of moral sentiments,* in his discussion of the prevention of crime. Again, his conclusion was that it was the growth of commerce that, by reducing dependency, also prevented crime.

> We observe . . . that in cities where there is most police and the greatest number of regulations concerning it, there is not always the greatest security. In Paris the regulations concerning police are so numerous as not to be comprehended in several volumes. In London there are only two or three simple regulations. Yet in Paris scarce a night passes without somebody being killed, while in London, which is a larger city, there are scarce three or four in a year. On this account one would be apt to think that the more police there is the less security, but this is not the cause. In England as well as in France, during the time of the feudal government and as late as Queen Elizabeth's reign, great numbers of retainers were kept about the noblemen's houses, to keep the tenants in awe. These retainers, when turned out, had no other way of getting their subsistence but by committing robberies, and living on plunder, which occasioned the greatest disorder. A remain of the feudal manners, still preserved in France, gives occasion to the difference. The nobility at Paris keep far more menial servants than ours, who are often turned out on their own account or thro' the caprice of their masters, and, being in the most indigent circumstances, are forced to committ the most dreadfull crimes. In Glasgow, where almost nobody has more than one servant, there are fewer capital crimes than in Edinburgh. In Glasgow there is not one in several years; but not a year passes in Edinburgh without some such disorders. Upon this principle, therefore, it is not so much the police that prevents the commission of crimes as the having as few persons as possible to live upon others. Nothing tends so much to corrupt mankind as dependencey, while independencey still encreases the honesty of the people. The establishment of commerce and manufactures, which brings about this independency, is the best police for preventing crimes.[30]

29. *Wealth of nations,* 412.
30. *Lectures,* 486–87.

VI

I have argued that Smith views commercial societies as generating both additions to, as well as subtractions from, the stock of moral capital. How does he "net out" these two conflicting sets of forces? Obviously he never does so explicitly, although it is clear that his own preferences weigh strongly in favor of the commercial society as opposed to its historical predecessors. Two qualifications, however, are in order in closing.

First of all, Smith does appear, from a twentieth-century perspective, to be strangely complacent about the deleterious effects of the division of labor upon the working class. He offers the reader a devastating characterization of those effects.[31] Clearly, working-class parents underinvest in their children's education: "The education which low people's children receive is not indeed at any rate considerable; however, it does them an immense deal of service, and the want of it is certainly one of their greatest misfortunes."[32] Marx observed sarcastically that Smith believed that educational opportunities for working-class children should be enlarged, but only in "homoeopathic doses."[33] This is perhaps somewhat unfair to Smith, who recommended the establishment of parish schools, where the basic skills of reading, writing, and arithmetic could be taught to all, at a charge so modest "that even a common labourer may afford it."[34] Nevertheless it is fair to say that Smith's recommendations do seem limited in comparison to the enormity of the problem that he has identified.

Finally, a commercial society can be an effective builder of moral capital, but only under competitive conditions. Although Smith's argu-

31. At least Smith seems to have regarded them as devastating. It is not clear that we would all share his sense of loss at the decline of the "martial spirit" that flowed from the increasing division of labor. In the *Lectures* he stated: "Another bad effect of commerce is that it sinks the courage of mankind, and tends to extinguish martial spirit. . . . A man has . . . time to study only one branch of business, and it would be a great disadvantage to oblige every one to learn the military art and to keep himself in the practice of it. The defence of the country is therefore committed to a certain sett of men who have nothing else ado; and among the bulk of the people military courage diminishes. By having their minds constantly employed on the arts of luxury, they grow effeminate and dastardly." *Lectures*, 540.

32. Ibid.

33. Karl Marx, *Capital*, Modern Library Giant edition (New York: Random House), 362.

34. *Wealth of nations*, 785. The best single source of entry into Smith's treatment of the economic role of education is Mark Blaug, "The economics of education in classical political economy: a re-examination," in *Essays on Adam Smith*, ed. Andrew Skinner and Thomas Wilson (Oxford: Oxford University Press, 1975), ch. 16. See also Samuels, *Classical theory*, esp. 66–72, and E. G. West, *Education and the state* (Worcester and London: The Trinity Press, 1970).

ments about the importance of competitive conditions in achieving efficient resource allocation are familiar enough, it is not commonly realized that such competition was also essential to assure that, in the terminology of this paper, the moral capital of a commercial society does not quickly dissipate itself. This is a real possibility, because easily attained wealth is inherently corrupting. Although Smith's criticisms of the wealthy were usually directed at landowners, that is because great fortunes, in his day, were usually landed fortunes. Other classes would behave with similar self-indulgence and ostentation if they had the opportunity. This is because "a man of a large revenue, *whatever may be his profession*, thinks he ought to live like other men of large revenues; and to spend a great part of his time in festivity, in vanity, and in dissipation."[35] The great virtue of competitive capitalism, from this point of view, is that the intense pressures of the marketplace render such behavior extremely difficult or impossible on the part of the capitalist class. So long as profits are difficult to earn, and so long as competitive pressures keep the rate of profit low, the system may be relied upon to force the capitalist to display the traditional virtues associated with his class. However, the possibility of easily earned profits deprives society of the prudent and parsimonious capitalist. Nor does it end with the capitalist:

> besides all the bad effects to the country in general, which have already been mentioned as necessarily resulting from a high rate of profit; there is one more fatal, perhaps, than all these put together, but which, if we may judge from experience, is inseparably connected with it. The high rate of profit seems everywhere to destroy that parsimony which in other circumstances is natural to the character of the merchant. When profits are high, that sober virtue seems to be superfluous, and expensive luxury to suit better the affluence of his situation. But the owners of the great mercantile capitals are necessarily the leaders and conductors of the whole industry of every nation, and their example has a much greater influence upon the manners of the whole industrious part of it than that of any other order of men. If his employer is attentive and parsimonious, the workman is very likely to be so too; but if the master is dissolute and disorderly, the servant who shapes his work according to the pattern which his master prescribes to him, will shape his life too according to the example which he sets him. Accumulation is thus prevented in the hands of all those who are naturally the most disposed to accumulate; and the funds destined for the maintenance of productive labour receive no augmentation

35. *Wealth of nations*, 813–14 (emphasis added).

from the revenue of those who ought naturally to augment them the most. The capital of the country, instead of increasing, gradually dwindles away, and the quantity of productive labor maintained in it grows every day less and less. Have the exorbitant profits of the merchants of Cadiz and Lisbon augmented the capital of Spain and Portugal? Have they alleviated the poverty, have they promoted the industry of those two beggarly countries? Such has been the tone of mercantile expence in those two trading cities, that those exorbitant profits, far from augmenting the general capital of the country, seem scarce to have been sufficient to keep up the capitals upon which they were made. . . . Compare the mercantile manners of Cadiz and Lisbon with those of Amsterdam, and you will be sensible how differently the conduct and character of merchants are affected by the high and by the low profits of stock. . . . Light come light go, says the proverb; and the ordinary tone of expence seems everywhere to be regulated, not so much according to the real ability of spending as to the supposed facility of getting money to spend.[36]

One is almost tempted to say that the trouble with high profits is that it allows the capitalist to behave like a large landowner![37]

Thus Smith views a commercial society as one that, at the very least, can be relied upon to maintain stability in its stock of moral as well as physical capital. Under quite plausible circumstances, it can be relied upon to augment both stocks. But it should come as no great surprise to be told that competitive conditions are required in *both* cases.

The author is grateful to Stanley Engerman, Karl Habermeier, Russell Roberts, and George Stigler for helpful comments, and to David Levy for the initial encouragement that led to the writing of this paper.

36. Ibid., 612–13.
37. "It seldom happens . . . that a great proprietor is a great improver. . . . To improve land with profit, like all other commercial projects, requires an exact attention to small savings and small gains, of which a man born to a great fortune, even though naturally frugal, is very seldom capable. The situation of such a person naturally disposes him to attend rather to ornament which pleases his fancy, than to profit for which he has so little occasion." Ibid., 385. Thus the notorious indolence of landlords is not attributable to a view that land, in some sense, "cares for itself." Rather, their economic situation does not place them under any great pressure to be otherwise. Landlords "are the only one of the three orders whose revenue costs them neither labour nor care, but comes to them, as it were, of its own accord, and independent of any plan or project of their own. That indolence, which is the natural effect of the ease and security of their situation, renders them too often, not only ignorant, but incapable of that application of mind which is necessary in order to foresee and understand the consequences of any public regulation." Ibid., 265.

8

2   Charles Babbage: pioneer economist

> ... the arrangements which ought to regulate the interior economy of a
> manufactory, are founded on principles of deeper root than may have
> been supposed, and are capable of being usefully employed in preparing
> the road to some of the sublimest investigations of the human mind.[1]

Charles Babbage has recently been rediscovered as the "pioneer of the
computer."[2] He needs to be rediscovered a second time for his contribution
to the understanding of economics, especially for his penetrating and
original insights into the economic role played by technological change in
the course of industrial development. Indeed, it is fair to say that it was
Babbage's book which first introduced the factory into the realm of
economic analysis.

Babbage has lived a furtive, almost fugitive existence in the literature of
economics. Joseph Schumpeter, in his magisterial *History of Economic
Analysis*, refers to Babbage's book, *On the Economy of Machinery and
Manufactures*, as "a remarkable performance of a remarkable man."[3]
Nevertheless, although Schumpeter's well-known book is more than 1,200

This chapter first appeared in Herbert Hax, Nathan Rosenberg, and Karl Steinbuch, *Charles Babbage, Ein Pionier der Industriellen Organisation*, Verlag Wirtschaft und Finanzen GmbH, Dusseldorf, 1992. The author wishes to acknowledge the able assistance of Scott Stern in the preparation of this paper, and to thank Stanley Engerman for his customarily astute comments and suggestions. The Technology and Economic Growth Program of the Center for Economic Policy Research at Stanford University provided financial support for the research upon which the paper is based.

[1] Charles Babbage, *On the Economy of Machinery and Manufactures*, fourth edition, 1835; reprinted by Frank Cass & Co., London, 1963, p. 191. All further references to *On the Economy of Machinery and Manufactures* will mention only the page number of the 1963 edition.

[2] See the valuable biography by Anthony Hyman, *Charles Babbage: Pioneer of the Computer*, Princeton University Press, Princeton (NJ), 1982.

[3] Joseph Schumpeter, *History of Economic Analysis*, Oxford University Press, New York, 1954, p. 541.

24

dense pages long, the treatment of Babbage is confined to a single footnote. Mark Blaug, in his *Economic Theory in Retrospect*, uses the same adjective as Schumpeter. He cites Babbage's book only to point out its influence on John Stuart Mill's discussion of increasing returns to scale in chapter 9 of book I of Mill's *Principles of Political Economy*. Mill's treatment of that subject, Blaug states, "is heavily indebted to a remarkable book, *On the Economy of Machinery and Manufactures* (1833) by Charles Babbage."[4]

Babbage the economist deserves far better treatment than this. His book contains important contributions to economics which have received unduly short shrift. A book that, at the time of its publication, provided a considerable improvement upon a topic as seminal as Adam Smith's treatment of the division of labor and, at the same time, offered the first systematic analysis of the economies associated with increasing returns to scale, surely deserves to be rescued from the comparative obscurity of footnotes and parenthetic references.

I

Babbage's purpose in writing *On the Economy of Machinery and Manufactures* was to examine "the mechanical principles which regulate the application of machinery to arts and manufactures" (p. iii). The book is, in fact, invaluable for its detailed, nontechnical descriptions of the manufacturing technologies that were employed in English workshops at the beginning of the 1830s. Babbage had, himself, travelled extensively through the industrial districts of England as well as continental Europe. And he was, as we know from his other remarkable accomplishments, no casual observer. On the contrary, he saw everything through the inquiring eyes of someone searching for more general underlying principles, categories, or commonalities. He sought, continuously, for some basis for classification and meaningful comparison. In brief, he wanted to illuminate his subject matter by rendering it subject to quantification and calculation.

In fact, the relationship of Babbage the economist to Babbage the inventor is a close one. That is to say, the book is, in an important sense, a by-product of Babbage's lifelong preoccupation with the development of a calculating machine. Indeed, the opening sentence of the preface to the first edition of the book states that: "The present volume may be considered as one of the consequences that have resulted from the Calculating-Engine, the construction of which I have been so long superintending." Thus, the book shares a common provenance with the calculating engine. The power of systematic reasoning that Babbage invested in his attempt to develop

---

[4] Mark Blaug, *Economic Theory in Retrospect*, Cambridge University Press, Cambridge, third edition, 1978, p. 198.

26   **Dealing with an uncertain future**

such a machine is abundantly evident in the ways in which he organizes and classifies his data on the English industrial establishment in this book.[5]

This is particularly evident in chapter 11, "Of Copying," by far the longest chapter in the book. Babbage brings together in this chapter a wide array of industrial processes involving specific applications of printing, casting, moulding, engraving, stamping, punching, etc. The cheapness of machine operations in such processes turns upon the skill devoted to some original instrument or tool that subsequently may become the basis for many thousands of copies. The situation – involving the common denominator of a large fixed cost that lays the basis for cheap per-unit costs – is typical of the mass production technologies that were just beginning to emerge in Babbage's time.[6]

Babbage's travels through the manufacturing workshops of England were largely a consequence of the difficulties that he encountered in his own construction problems and his determination to become better informed concerning his technological options. Babbage's observations and descriptions are so informative that his book is well worth reading today just for its contribution to the history of technology, even if it were totally devoid of any other merit. Babbage even provides the reader with a guide for extracting useful and reliable information concerning productivity from factory visits.[7] The guide includes a suggested set of structured questions as well as some discreet methods of verifying the accuracy of responses by checking for the internal consistency of answers. He also offers suggestions when reliable information on factory output is not available:

When this cannot be ascertained, the number of operations performed in a given time may frequently be counted when the workman is quite unconscious that any person is observing him. Thus the sound made by the motion of a loom may enable the observer to count the number of strokes per minute, even though he is outside the building in which it is contained. (p. 117)

Babbage would certainly have made a good industrial spy!

If Babbage at times seems to be writing with an excessively didactic hand, it is partly because he believes that greater attention to the empirical world, and especially the activities inside a factory, would significantly elevate the quality of economic analysis and reasoning generally.

---

[5] For further discussion of the context in which Babbage came to write this book, see Hyman, *Charles Babbage*, chapter 8.

[6] See Babbage's discussion of the Navy Board's contract to make iron tanks for ships. Maudslay at first was reluctant to take the contract because it was "out of his line of business" but also because the holes for the large number of rivets ordinarily involved an expensive hand-punching process. The Navy Board subsequently offered a larger contract which Maudslay accepted because it then became worthwhile to introduce specialized tools. "The magnitude of the order made it worth his while to commence *manufacturer*, and to make tools for the express business" (p. 121). Babbage's italics.

[7] See chapter 12, "On the Method of Observing Manufactories."

Political economists have been reproached with too small a use of facts, and too large an employment of theory. If facts are wanting, let it be remembered that the closet-philosopher is unfortunately too little acquainted with the admirable arrangements of the factory; and that no class of persons can supply so readily, and with so little sacrifice of time, the data on which all the reasonings of political economists are founded, as the merchants and manufacturer; and, unquestionably, to no class are the deductions to which they give rise so important. Nor let it be feared that erroneous deductions may be made from such recorded facts: the errors which arise from the absence of facts are far more numerous and more durable than those which result from unsound reasoning respecting true data. (p. 156)

A person who could pen these words – especially the last sentence – obviously has something of importance to say to the present generation of economists![8]

II

Babbage's distinctly economic contribution is taken up in section II, the largest portion of the book, where he considers the "economic principles which regulate the application of machinery," after the purely "mechanical principles" that were the focus of section I. The central point is that, as soon as one undertakes to produce a product in large volume, to become a "manufacturer" rather than a "maker," it becomes necessary to devote careful and explicit attention to the organization of production, to "the whole system" (p. 121) of the factory. Moreover, a manufacturer must be prepared to utilize, and perhaps to design, tools made expressly for a specialized purpose. One needs to consider, in other words, the division of labor.

Babbage begins his critical chapter 19, "On the Division of Labour," by asserting that "Perhaps the most important principle on which the economy of a manufacture depends, is the *division of labour* [Babbage's *italics*] amongst the persons who perform the work" (p. 169).Babbage's most distinctive contributions to the discipline of economics are generally regarded as his contributions to this subject. That view will not be challenged. However, I will suggest that his analysis of the division of labor constitutes an advance upon the classic treatment of the subject of much greater dimensions than has yet been recognized. Indeed, Babbage himself, a man who did not suffer from excessive modesty, also understated the extent of his own improvement upon Adam Smith.

[8] At the same time, Babbage urged the undertaking of statistical estimation in order to improve decision-making within the business community: "The importance of collecting data, for the purpose of enabling the manufacturer to ascertain how many additional customers he will acquire by a given reduction in the price of the article he makes, cannot be too strongly pressed upon the attention of those who employ themselves in statistical inquiries" (p. 120). Babbage was the founder of the London Statistical Society.

As Babbage reminds his readers, Smith attributed the increased productivity flowing from the division of labor to "three different circumstances: first, to the increase of dexterity in every particular workman; secondly, to the saving of time, which is commonly lost in passing from one species of work to another; and, lastly, to the invention of a great number of machines which facilitate and abridge labour, and enable one man to do the work of many" (p. 175). Babbage goes on to assert that Smith has overlooked a key advantage that flows from the analysis of the *Wealth of Nations*, and that the analysis is therefore seriously incomplete.

When there is only a limited division of labor, each worker is required to perform a number of tasks, involving a variety of skills and physical capabilities. The supply of such skills and capabilities varies considerably, for reasons having to do with length of training, previous experience, and natural differences in physical endowment. Accordingly, the remuneration received by workers who supply different skills will also vary considerably.

However, when there is a limited division of labor the employer is required, in effect, to purchase "bundles" of labor. Consequently, a workman who is capable of performing highly skilled work will need to receive a wage appropriate to these high skill levels, even though he will spend much, perhaps most, of his time performing work of lower skill, and pay, levels.

Seen from this perspective, the great virtue of the division of labor is that it permits an "unbundling" of labor skills, and allows the employer to pay for each separate labor process no more than the market value of the lower capabilities commensurate with such work. Under an extensive division of labor, the employer is no longer confronted with the necessity of purchasing labor corresponding to higher skill levels than those required for the specific project at hand.

In Babbage's own words,

the master manufacturer, by dividing the work to be executed into different processes, each requiring different degrees of skill or of force, can purchase exactly that precise quantity of both which is necessary for each process; whereas, if the whole work were executed by one workman, that person must possess sufficient skill to perform the most difficult, and sufficient strength to execute the most laborious, of the operations into which the art is divided. (pp. 175–176; emphasis Babbage's)

In elaborating his analysis of this point, and examining its implications, Babbage reverts to Adam Smith's time-honored example of the division of labor in a pin factory. He presents a detailed enumeration of the sequence of steps involved in the English manufacture of pins – wire-drawing, wire-straightening, pointing, twisting, and cutting the heads, heading, tinning, and papering. For each separate step in the sequence, he identifies those who supply the labor – man, woman, boy, girl – and their rate of remuneration for each step. The wage rates of these separate labor inputs vary all the way from 4.5 pence per day up to 6 shillings per day (see table, p. 184). Taking into account the amount of time required for each step, and assuming that the highest-paid worker, the pin whitener (who earned 6 shillings a day at his specialty), could carry out each of the steps in pinmaking in the same amount of time as the individuals who perform each step under the prevailing division of labor, Babbage concludes that pins would cost 3.75 times as much as they actually did (p. 186). He then draws the generalization: "The higher the skill required of the workman in any one process of a manufacture, and the smaller the time during which it is employed, so much the greater will be the advantage of separating that process from the rest, and devoting one person's attention entirely to it" (pp. 168–187).

Years later, Babbage cogently restated his central point as follows:

The most effective cause of the cheapness produced by the division of labour is this:

By dividing the work to be executed into different processes, each requiring different degrees of skill, or of force, the master manufacturer can purchase exactly that precise quantity of both which is necessary for each process. Whereas if the whole work were executed by one workman, that person must possess sufficient skill to perform the most difficult, and sufficient strength to execute the most laborious, of those operations into which the art is divided.

Needle-making is perhaps the best illustration of the overpowering effect of this cause. The operatives in this manufacture consist of children, women, and men, earning wages varying from three or four shillings up to five pounds per week. Those who point the needles gain about two pounds. The man who hardens and tempers the needles earns from five to six pounds per week. It ought also to be observed that one man is sufficient to temper the needles for a large factory; consequently the time spent on each needle by the most expensive operative is excessively small.

But if a manufacturer insist on employing one man to make the whole needle, he must pay at the rate of five pounds a week for every portion of the labour bestowed upon it.[9]

This analysis of the benefits of an extensive division of labor was highly original. It did indeed constitute a major addition to Adam Smith's formulation, and it was precisely this point that exercised a heavy influence upon later economists, most especially, as we will see later, Marx. Nevertheless, Babbage also improved upon the formulation of Smith and others in several additional important respects that have not been widely recognized. This involved not only points of clarification but also points of analytical rigor.

Babbage observes that a more extensive division of labor leads to a

---

[9] Charles Babbage, *Passages from the Life of a Philosopher*, volume XI in *The Works of Charles Babbage* William Pickering, London, 1989, p. 328.

reduction in the time required for learning, and therefore to a shortening of the time period during which a new labor force entrant is employed in a relatively unproductive and unremunerative way (p. 170). Then he makes the important observation, not to be found in Adam Smith, that the conventional apprenticeship of five to seven years' duration was necessary in the past, not merely to allow the young man to acquire the requisite skills, but also "to enable him to repay by his labour, during the latter portion of his time, the expense incurred by his master at its commencement" (p. 170). If a new labor force entrant is required to learn only a single operation instead of many, he will much more quickly arrive at the stage where his employment generates a profit to his employer. If a competitive situation prevails among the masters, "the apprentice will be able to make better terms, and diminish the period of his servitude" (p. 170). Thus, the length of apprenticeship needs to be understood as determined not just by the time necessary to acquire a skill, but also by the time necessary for the master to reap a normal rate of return upon his investment in the human capital of his apprentice (p. 170). One does not need to interpret Babbage's analysis here with excessive generosity in order to see it as a tantalizing precursor of the contemporary work of Gary Becker and Jacob Mincer on learning-by-doing.[10]

Babbage also makes an extremely significant qualification to Adam Smith's central point that specialization leads to increased dexterity and therefore greater speed on the part of the workman who is no longer required to perform a number of separate operations. Babbage refers to Smith's example of nail-making. Smith had claimed that a smith, who was accustomed to make nails, but who was not solely occupied as a nailer, could only make 800 to 1,000 per day, "whilst a lad who had never exercised any other trade, can make upwards of two thousand three hundred a day" (p. 173). In the case of the boys in his example, Smith had added the (perhaps not insignificant) qualification, "when they exerted themselves."[11] Moreover, Smith, as reported in his lectures, had used the lower figure of two thousand, although he also added "and those incomparably better."[12]

Babbage believed that the case of nail-making is "rather an extreme one" (p. 173). Moreover, factories with an extensive division of labor tend also to pay on the basis of piecework, which renders comparisons of labor productivity more difficult, since this mode of payment provides stronger

[10] Babbage also adds, as a separate point, that greater division of labor will lead to reduced waste of materials in the learning process, and a consequent reduction in the cost and the price of the product (p. 171).

[11] Adam Smith, *Wealth of Nations*, 1776; Modern Library Reprint, New York, 1937, p. 8.

[12] Adam Smith, *Lectures on Justice, Police, Revenue and Arms*, reprinted by Kelley & Millman, New York, 1963, p. 166.

incentives to increase output. But he had a much more fundamental qualification to append to Smith's emphasis upon the greater dexterity acquired by the workman who continuously performs the same process. These advantages to repetition, he states, are merely ephemeral. Under stable conditions, less specialized workers will move more slowly down the relevant learning curves, but they will eventually approach, even if they never entirely attain, some lower labor cost asymptote. Thus, the gain from the constant repetition of a process "is not a permanent source of advantage; for, though it acts at the commencement of an establishment, yet every month adds to the skill of the workmen; and at the end of three or four years they will not be very far behind those who have never practiced any other branch of their art" (p. 173). Here, as elsewhere, Babbage makes skillful use of a primitive sort of time-period analysis, which enables him to distinguish between immediate and longer-term consequences.[13] Thus, even though Babbage makes these points in a context where he is ostensibly recounting what was, when he wrote, merely conventional wisdom, he in fact ended up providing a fresh and quite powerful new insight.

III

Adam Smith's third advantage of the division of labor was that it gave rise to inventions. Smith's treatment of the determinants of inventive activity is extremely sparse; the textual treatment of the subject in chapter 1 of the *Wealth of Nations* occupied not much more than a single page. In Smith's view, in the earlier stages of industrial development, most inventions were the work of the users, that is, workmen whose attention was increasingly fixed upon a single object. Eventually, however, when the division of labor gives rise to specialized makers of machinery, the ingenuity of these machine makers comes to play an increasingly important role; and finally, a more prominent role comes to be played by those to whom Smith refers as "philosophers or men of speculation, whose trade it is not to do any thing, but to observe every thing; and who, upon that account, are often capable of combining together the powers of the most distant and dissimilar objects."[14]

Babbage's discussion of the determinants of invention is far richer than that of Smith, and there is of course a perfectly straightforward reason. Smith, writing in the late 1760s and 1770s, was writing about, and

[13] See, in particular, Babbage's analysis of the impact of the introduction of machinery upon employment in chapter 32, "On the Effect of Machinery in Reducing the Demand for Labour."

[14] Smith, *Wealth of Nations*, p. 10. For a more extensive treatment of Smith's views on this subject, see Nathan Rosenberg, "Adam Smith and the Division of Labor: Two Views or One?" *Economica*, 57, no. 3 (May 1965).

commenting upon, a society that was still essentially pre-industrial. Babbage, on the other hand, wrote his book some sixty years later. The interval between the writing of the two books constituted the heyday of the British industrial revolution. Babbage is therefore analyzing a society where the division of labor had been carried to far greater lengths than the society that was known to Adam Smith. Indeed, very little of the descriptive accounts in Babbage's book, aside from the examples that Babbage deliberately chose from Smith's own book, dealt with machinery that would have been recognizable to the author of the *Wealth of Nations*.

A central point for Babbage is that an extensive division of labor is itself an essential prerequisite to technical change. This is so for two related reasons. First of all, technical improvements are not generally dependent upon a few rarely gifted individuals, although the more "beautiful combinations" are indeed the work of the occasional genius (p. 260). Rather, and secondly, inventive activity needs to be seen as a consequence as well as a cause of the division of labor. This is so because "The arts of contriving, of drawing, and of executing, do not usually reside in their greatest perfection in one individual; and in this, as in other arts, the *division of labor* must be applied" (p. 266; emphasis Babbage's).

It is also worth noting that Babbage shows an acute awareness of the economic forces that drive inventive capability in specific directions and that influence the timing of inventive effort. In fact, his observations deserve to be regarded as possibly the earliest treatment of the economic determinants of inventive activity. Technological change is not, for him, some totally exogenous phenomenon. On the contrary, he clearly sees the direction of technological improvements as responding to the relative prices of factor inputs, and the commitment of resources to the improvements of machinery as directly connected to the state of demand for the final product that the machines produce. In urging the importance of careful cost accounting, Babbage points out that one of its main advantages "is the indication which it would furnish of the course in which improvement should be directed" (pp. 203–204); a firm would invest in those technological improvement activities that offered the highest payoff in terms of cost reduction, but only if it had a close understanding of those costs. On the demand side, he observes that: "The inducement to contrive machines for any process of manufacture increases with the demand for the article" (p. 213). And he also observes that "overmanufacturing" is likely to lead to efforts to reduce costs through machinery improvement or the reorganization of the factory (p. 233). Babbage also suggests a highly valuable research project on the relationship between gluts and technological improvements. "It would be highly interesting, if we could trace, even approximately, through the history of any great manufacture, the effects of gluts in producing improvements in machinery, or in methods of working; and if we could shew what addition to the annual quantity of goods previously manufactured, was produced by each alteration." He then adds the conjecture: "It would probably be found, that *the increased quantity manufactured by the same capital, when worked with the new improvement, would produce nearly the same rate of profit as other modes of investment.*"[15]

It seems to be a reasonable claim that Babbage is the first observer of the events of the industrial revolution to call attention in an explicit way to the causal links between economic forces and inventive activity.

IV

Chapter 27 of Babbage's book, "On Contriving Machinery," provides valuable insights into the difficulties associated with the innovation process in the period when Britain was attaining to the status of "Workshop of the World."

Babbage expresses great concern over the difficulties of executing a new machine design and putting it into operating form in close accordance with the specifications of the inventor. This chapter clearly bears the painful imprint of the author's numerous frustrating experiences in designing highly complex machines in an age when machine making was still a relatively primitive art. This was a period when precision in the design and execution of new machinery was only just coming of age, but when the establishment of a new production facility was still attended by innumerable uncertainties with respect to the cost and performance of machinery of novel design. To be sure, the master machine-tool designer and builder, Henry Maudslay, inventor of the slide rest, makes an appearance in the pages of Babbage's book, but his contributions represented only the beginning of a long process of learning to work metals with higher degrees of precision. Indeed, Babbage thought it appropriate to include a separate chapter enumerating precisely these difficulties, in which he placed particular emphasis upon the problems involved in calculating the cost of new machines.[16]

Babbage stresses in several places the importance of accuracy in the actual paper design of a new machine. "It can never," he states, "be too strongly impressed upon the minds of those who are devising new machines, that to make the most perfect drawings of every part tends

---

[15] Pp. 233–234. Babbage's italics. See also pp. 158–159.
[16] Chapter 35, "Inquiries Previous to Commencing Any Manufactory."

essentially both to the success of the trial, and to economy in arriving at the result" (p. 262). It is clear from his admonitions on this matter that high-quality draughtsmanship could by no means be taken for granted. Never-theless, "if the exertion of moderate power is the end of the mechanism to be contrived, it is possible to construct the whole machine upon paper" (p. 261).

However, for more complex machinery where performance will depend heavily upon "physical or chemical properties" (p. 261), optimum design cannot be determined on paper alone, and testing and experimentation ("direct trial") will be unavoidable. One can piece together, from various chapters of the book, a vivid account of the difficulties confronting would-be innovators during a period characterized by rapid technical change, particularly in the realm of machine making itself.

Chapter 29, "On the Duration of Machinery," deals with what a later generation would call "technological obsolescence," especially as the problem applies to capital goods with long useful lives, "such as wind-mills, water-mills, and steam-engines" (p. 283). Babbage introduces a table (p. 284) of the average annual duty performed by steam engines in Cornwall over the period 1813–1833, as well as the "average duty of the best engines." These engines, which were employed in Cornwall's extensive mining operations, provide impressive evidence of improvements in the construc-tion and management of such engines. One wishes one had more infor-mation concerning their operation; nevertheless, on the face of it, they show a strong upward trend in performance. For the 21-year period as a whole the average duty of the *best* engines more than triples, from 26,400,000 in 1813 to 83,306,092 in 1833. Over the same period the average duty of all the engines rose from 19,456,000 to 46,000,000.

In such an environment, technological obsolescence is a dominating commercial consideration, and the physical life of a capital good becomes of secondary importance. Babbage here offers a powerful insight that, it seems fair to say, is still not fully absorbed today.

Machinery for producing any commodity in great demand, seldom actually wears out; new improvements, by which the same operations can be executed either more quickly or better, generally superseding it long before that period arrives: indeed, to make such an improved machine profitable, it is usually reckoned that in five years it ought to have paid itself, and in ten to be superseded by a better." (p. 285)

The effect of such obsolescence was a rapid downward revaluation of the market price for older machinery, which indeed is soon rendered commer-cially worthless. Babbage cites technological improvements in frames for making patent-net "not long ago." As a result, a machine that had cost £1200 and was still "in good repair" a few years later, sold for a mere £60.

But even more extreme evidence of the impact of rapid ongoing technological improvements in that trade was the decision to abandon the construction of unfinished machines "because new improvements had superseded their utility."[17]

Babbage ends this chapter by pointing out that the effect of competition with respect to durable goods had been to render them even less durable. When manufactured articles are transported a considerable distance, it is not uncommon for broken articles to be deemed unworthy of the cost of repair if the price of labor is higher than in its original place of manufacture. It is cheaper to purchase a new article (p. 292). This appears to be a practice of recent vintage when Babbage wrote.

V

In examining the innovation process specifically from the point of view of the developer of a potential new machine, rather than its possible user, Babbage warns his readers of the peculiar uncertainties of the technical problems involved. In situations that require testing what we would today call a prototype, the outcome of the tests may be especially sensitive to the quality of workmanship that was employed in producing the contrivance. Otherwise "an imperfect trial may cause an idea to be given up, which better workmanship might have proved to be practicable" (p. 264).

But there is another reason why the outcome of such a test may be inconclusive. The "art of making machinery" was undergoing such improvement "that many inventions which have been tried, and given up in one state of art, have at another period been eminently successful" (p. 264). This statement might serve as a remarkably appropriate epitaph to the author's own celebrated technical accomplishments. Indeed, one may read his conclusion as both an astute observation on the uncertainties associated with the innovative process during his own lifetime, and also as a personal and correct premonition concerning his own ambitious technical enterprise. "These considerations prove the propriety of repeating, at the termination of intervals during which the art of making machinery has received any great improvement, the trials of methods which, although founded upon just principles, had previously failed" (p. 265).

For the subset of inventions that survives the rigors and uncertainties of this experimental period, the commercial risks may prove to be as hazardous as the purely technical risks that had been overcome. The reason is

---

[17] P. 286. For a discussion of the complexity of the decision-making process when technological change is not only rapid, but is anticipated to continue to be rapid in the future, see Nathan Rosenberg, "On Technological Expectations," *Economic Journal* (September 1976); reprinted as chapter 5 in Rosenberg, *Inside the Black Box*.

36   **Dealing with an uncertain future**

simplicity itself. The machine may work perfectly well but produce its output "at a greater expense than that at which it can be made by other methods" (p. 265). Babbage at several points in the book had urged his readers to pay the most careful attention to *all* the costs that would be incurred in some prospective new machine, while at the same time admitting the difficulties of arriving at accurate estimates.

But there is still a further and final irony concerning the plight of the would-be innovator. Assuming that all previous hurdles and initial "tee-thing troubles" had been overcome, subsequent units of the product could be produced far more cheaply than the first. Babbage clearly identifies what later generations would refer to as a "learning curve." His words deserve to be quoted in full:

It has been estimated roughly, that the first individual of any newly-invented machine, will cost about five times as much as the construction of the second, an estimate which is, perhaps, sufficiently near the truth. If the second machine is to be precisely like the first, the same drawings, and the same patterns will answer for it; but if, as usually happens, some improvements have been suggested by the experience of the first, these must be more or less altered. When, however, two or three machines have been completed, and many more are wanted, they can usually be produced at much less than one-fifth of the expense of the original invention. (p. 266)

But the subsequent financial fortunes of such an innovator are by no means assured. Much would depend not only upon the subsequent demand for the innovation but upon the ability of the innovator to control and capture the flow of profits generated by the innovation. In a highly competitive environment of the sort described by Babbage, the profits might well be captured by others unless the innovator had some specific means that allowed him to appropriate the benefits – patents, secrecy, tacit knowledge, access to scarce skills, etc.

Babbage's analysis here takes on additional importance because it powerfully influenced Marx, who quoted Babbage's estimate approvingly.[18] In this particular context Marx was anxious to emphasize how the technological improvements in a machine shortened its life expectancy and thereby intensified the forces making for the prolongation of the working day on the part of the capitalists anxious to recoup their large investments as quickly as possible.[19] On the other hand, in volume III of *Capital* Marx, again drawing upon Babbage's treatment, called attention to "the far greater cost of operating an establishment based on a new invention as compared to later establishments, arising *ex suis ossibus*. This is so very true

[18] Karl Marx, *Capital*, vol. I, Foreign Languages Publishing House, Moscow, 1961, p. 405, footnote 1.   [19] *Ibid.*, especially footnote 2.

that the trail-blazers generally go bankrupt, and only those who later buy the buildings, machinery, etc., at a cheaper price make money out of it."[20] This is an intriguing statement on Marx's part, insofar as it portrays the capitalist, or at least the innovating capitalist, in a distinctly sympathetic way. But, more importantly, it would be essential to know how "generally" such bankruptcy occurs. Moreover, if this *were* generally the case, and if technological change were as central to long-term capitalist growth as Marx consistently asserted, it would constitute a powerful argument for the social necessity of high profits in order to compensate the occasional successful innovator for undertaking such great risks. Not surprisingly, Marx does not draw this implication.

VI

Babbage's concern with the division of labor as it relates to technological improvements leads him to a significant extension of his analysis into the field of international trade. His main concern was with a special issue: the restrictions that had recently been imposed by parliament upon the export of certain classes of machinery. Such restrictions, in his view, represented a needless and, indeed, counterproductive pandering to the interests of the users of machinery, who feared the prospect of commercial competition from foreigners equipped with the latest machinery. But Babbage perceives[21] that Britain was already well on the way to developing a dynamic comparative advantage in the making of machinery. In his view, if the country could maintain its superiority in the manufacture of machinery, it would have little to fear from the acquisition of high-quality machinery by overseas competitors.

Babbage distinguishes sharply between the ability to contrive new machines and the ability to manufacture them. Even if the ability to contrive were equally distributed among countries, "the means of execution" are nevertheless different (p. 365). These means of execution obviously include the highly skilled makers of machinery, a class of workers who are "as a body, far more intelligent that those who only use it" (p. 364). In a regime of rapid technological change, the country with a higher skill capability will continue to have much speedier access to the best machinery. By allowing domestic manufacturers the opportunity to sell their products abroad, the country will in fact solidify its superiority in machine making (pp. 370–373). It will enrich itself by enlarging the class of machine makers. Such workmen

---

[20] *Ibid.*, vol. III, Foreign Languages Publishing House, Moscow, 1959, p. 103. See also chapter 5 below, pp. 95–97.   [21] Chapter 34, "On the Exportation of Machinery."

38   **Dealing with an uncertain future**

possess much more skill, and are paid much more highly than that class who merely *use* it; and, if a free exportation were allowed, the more valuable class would, undoubtedly, be greatly increased; for, notwithstanding the high rate of wages, there is no country in which it can at this moment be made, either so well or so cheaply as in England. We might, therefore, supply the whole world with machinery, at an evident advantage, both to ourselves and our customers. (p.372; emphasis Babbage's)

The separate strands of Babbage's argument in this chapter are not entirely distinct. On the one hand, he asserts that, in the absence of trade restrictions, English machine users will always have the advantage of prior access to the best machines. On the other hand, he also asserts that such access is not a sufficient condition for commercial success. Even if foreign competitors have equal access to the best technology, they will not compete successfully so long as they fail to achieve the admirable organizational adaptations of the industrial economy that have already been achieved in England. Here Babbage seems to have come full circle, to the overarching theme of the book: the advantages accruing to a society that manages to organize its economic life in close accordance with the dictates of the division of labor.

This seems to be the spirit of his response to the charge that the elimination of restrictions on machinery exports will provide foreigners with machinery that will threaten England's competitive advantage.

It is contended that by admitting the exportation of machinery, foreign manufacturers will be supplied with machines equal to our own. The first answer which presents itself to this argument is supplied by almost the whole of the present volume; *That in order to succeed in a manufacture, it is necessary not merely to possess good machinery, but that the domestic economy of the factory should be most carefully regulated.*[22]

Of course, for the larger economy outside the "domestic economy of the factory," appropriate regulation should be understood to include the force of competition: "it is only in countries which have attained a high degree of civilization, and in articles in which there is a great competition amongst the producers, that the most perfect system of the division of labour is to be observed" (p. 169). And countries that can maintain a more advanced division of labor, in this enlarged sense, than their foreign competitors, need not be excessively concerned over their prospective competitiveness.

---

[22] P. 376. Babbage's italics. Substantially the same point is made several pages later. "The fact that England can, notwithstanding her taxation and her high rate of wages, actually undersell other nations, seems to be well established: and it appears to depend on the superior goodness and cheapness of those raw materials of machinery the metals, – on the excellence of the tools, – and on the admirable arrangements of the domestic economy of our factories" (p. 374).

VII

Chapter 20, "On the Division of Mental Labours," is a fascinating chapter for several reasons. It involves, to begin with, a direct application of Babbage's reasoning on the division of labour in the previous chapter, to the specific realm of the activities of the human mind. Second, it contains an extensive discussion of Babbage's own work on a "calculating engine," placed in the larger context of his analysis of the application of machine methods to industrial production. And, third, it provides an absorbing historical account of the project that culminated in Babbage's own efforts to develop a calculating-engine.

Starting with this third point, these efforts had their origin, remarkably enough, in the accidental perusal of Smith's *Wealth of Nations* by a French government official who happened upon the volume in a bookstore. A Monsieur Prony had been charged by the French government with the Herculean task of superintending the production of a series of logarithmic and trigonometric tables that would facilitate the transition to the recently adopted decimal system.[23]

The tables that M. Prony was to calculate were to occupy no less than seventeen large folio volumes.

Il fut aisé à M. de Prony de s'assurer que même en s'associant trois ou quatre habiles co-operateurs, la plus grande durée presumable de sa vie, ne lui suffirai pas pour remplir ses engagements. Il était occupé de cette fâcheuse pensée lorsque, se trouvant devant la boutique d'un marchand de livres, il apperçut la belle edition Anglaise de Smith, donnée a Londres en 1776; il ouvrit le livre au hazard, et tomba sur le premier chapitre, qui traite de *la division du travail*, et où la fabrication des épingles est citée pour exemple. A peine avait-il parcouru les premières pages, que, par une espèce d'inspiration, il conçut l'expédient de mettre ses logarithmes en *manufacture* comme les épingles. (p. 193; emphasis Babbage's)

M. Prony then proceeded with a threefold division of labor including (1) "five or six of the most eminent mathematicians in France," (2) seven or eight persons, not eminent mathematicians, but persons possessed of a "considerable acquaintance with mathematics," and (3) a group whose number varied between sixty and eighty, who generated the final tables "using nothing more than simple addition and subtraction" (p. 194)

[23] The decimal system was, of course, adopted in France but not in England. Babbage points out the advantages of the decimal system in facilitating monetary calculations, and observes that "it becomes an interesting question to consider whether our own currency might not be converted into one decimally divided. The great step, that of abolishing the guinea, has already been taken without any inconvenience, and but little is now required to render the change complete" (p. 124). Babbage's countrymen were, of course, to wait for more than a century before acquiring the conveniences of this conversion. For other purposes, such as measurement of length and weight, they are still waiting.

40   **Dealing with an uncertain future**

M. Prony's procedure, Babbage astutely observes, "much resembles that of a skillful person about to construct a cotton or silk-mill, or any similar establishment" (p. 195). None of the well-educated groups involved in the project played any role in the "dog-work" of actual calculation. It was, of course, Babbage's intention that his calculating engine would provide a machine substitute for all of the work performed by the third group.

Babbage completes the specification of the neat parallelism of the division of labor between the mechanical and mental domains:

> We have seen, then, that the effect of the *division of labour*, both in mechanical and in mental operations, is, that it enables us to purchase and apply to each process precisely that quantity of skill and knowledge which is required for it: we avoid employing any part of the time of a man who can get eight or ten shillings a day by his skill in tempering needles, in turning a wheel, which can be done for sixpence a day; and we equally avoid the loss arising from the employment of an accomplished mathematician in performing the lowest processes of arithmetic. (p 201)

But the improvements in the cost of calculation which are now on the horizon, and which are the offspring of the division of labor, are by no means exhausted by purely financial considerations. For, in Babbage's view, as a country progresses in its arts and manufactures, continued progress comes to depend increasingly upon a growing intimacy between science and industry. In the final chapter of the book (chapter 35), "On the Future Prospects of Manufactures as Connected with Science," Babbage argues that science itself is becoming subject to the same law of the division of labor that is the central theme of the book. Science needs to be cultivated as a full-time, specialized activity by those with the "natural capacity and acquired habits" (p. 379). Such specialization is unavoidable because "the discovery of the great principles of nature demands a mind almost exclusively devoted to such investigations; and these, in the present state of science, frequently require costly apparatus, and exact an expense of time quite incompatible with professional avocations" (p. 380). Babbage's reference to "costly apparatus" is especially apposite. One of the most costly of all research instruments today is a large Cray computer!

Babbage closes a long apotheosis to science by pointing out that the progress of science itself will be increasingly governed by progress in the ability to calculate: "It is the science of *calculation*, – which becomes continually more necessary at each step of our progress, and which must ultimately govern the whole of the applications of science to the arts of life."[24]

---

[24] Pp. 387–388. Babbage's italics. It is interesting to note that, in the very next paragraph, Babbage anticipates precisely the question that so troubled Jevons several decades later in his book, *The Coal Question*, Macmillan and Co., London, 1865. Babbage recognizes the threat posed to a society increasingly dependent upon the power of steam, that "the coal-

In short, it is Babbage's view that mankind's future prospects will be dominated by the fact that "machinery has been taught arithmetic" (p. 390). Babbage was of course remarkably prescient, but the possibility of teaching machinery arithmetic would have to await the age of electronics.

VIII

Thus, Babbage's analysis involves a long chain of reasoning that has its origin in the division of labor; from there, Babbage spells out what he perceives as its far-reaching implications through the realms of technology and then even science. But one further feature, of great significance, has so far been neglected. The extension of the division of labor can and was necessarily leading to the establishment of large factories.[25] Indeed, Babbage provides the first extended discussion in the literature of economics of an issue of immense future significance: the economies associated with large-scale production. The chapter devoted to this topic, chapter 22, "On the Causes and Consequences of Large Factories," in turn powerfully influenced the treatment of this topic by two of the most influential, perhaps *the* two most influential economists of the nineteenth century, John Stuart Mill and Karl Marx.

Babbage had shown in chapter 19, "On the Division of Labour," that a critical advantage of that division was that it enabled the employer to purchase only the precise amount of each higher skill category, and no more, that was required by the different processes under his roof. Ideally, although the ideal was hardly ever fully achieved, no worker was ever paid at a rate that was higher than that appropriate to his assigned activity. But in chapter 22 he specifies an important implication of such an arrangement. In order to produce at minimum cost, it will be necessary to expand the factory by some multiple whose size will depend upon the specific labor requirements imposed by the division of labor. It follows from the principle of the division of labor that *"When the number of processes into which it is most advantageous to divide it, and the number of individuals to be employed by it are ascertained, then all factories which do not employ a direct multiple of this latter number, will produce the article at a greater cost"* (p. 212; emphasis Babbage's).

mines of the world may ultimately be exhausted." Nevertheless, with the growth of knowledge he appears to be confident that substitute sources of power will be found. He identifies one possibility upon which research is presently being conducted in the United Kingdom: tidal power. "(T)he sea itself offers a perennial source of power hitherto almost unapplied. The tides, twice in each day, raise a vast mass of water, which might be made available for driving machinery" (p. 388).

25 The importance of this insight cannot be overstated, for the rise of the large manufacturing enterprise is central to the arguments of both Marx and Schumpeter. For a further discussion, see chapters 3 and 5 below.

42   **Dealing with an uncertain future**

Babbage adds a variety of other circumstances that, he believes, will offer advantages to manufacturing establishments of great size. The most common denominator involves the indivisibility of certain valuable inputs which fail to be fully utilized in smaller establishments. These would include the availability of higher-wage workmen who are skilled in adjusting or repairing machines;[26] a small factory with few machines could not fully utilize such a highly skilled worker. Similarly, the introduction of lighting for night work, or an accounting department, involve sizable fixed costs that are also under-utilized at low levels of output. The possibilities for effectively utilizing waste materials are greater in a larger plant, and this is sometimes further facilitated by "the union of the trades in one factory, which otherwise might have been separated" (p. 217) Agents who are employed by large factories frequently provide services that cost little more than those provided to smaller establishments, even though the benefits of the service to the large factory are far more valuable.

Finally, Babbage quotes approvingly a Report of the Committee of the House of Commons on the Wool Trade (1806) which asserts that large factories can afford the risks and experiments to generate technological change that are not feasible for the "little master manufacturers."

it is obvious, that the little master manufacturers cannot afford, like the man who possesses considerable capital, to try the experiments which are requisite, and incur the risks, and even losses, which almost always occur, in inventing and perfecting new articles of manufacture, or in carrying to a state of greater perfection articles already established ... The owner of a factory ... being commonly possessed of a large capital, and having all his workmen employed under his own immediate superintendence, may make experiments, hazard speculation, invent shorter or better modes of performing old processes, may introduce new articles, and improve and perfect old ones, thus giving the range to his tastes and fancy, and, thereby alone enabling our manufacturers to stand the competition with their commercial rivals in other countries. (p. 223)

IX

Babbage's treatment, although obviously of limited scope, was nevertheless a pioneering first effort to identify the economic advantages of bigness on which first John Stuart Mill and later Karl Marx drew extensively.[27] It has

---

[26] Although Babbage does not make it clear why such a worker needs to be in constant attendance so long as the machines are above some minimal threshold of reliability.

[27] Mill's treatment of the specific issue of the division of labor, although coming almost three-quarters of a century after Adam Smith, constituted no substantial improvement over Smith's treatment. As Blaug observes of Mill's *Principles of Political Economy*: "Book 1, chapter 8, on the division of labor, adds little to Adam Smith's treatment and may be passed over without loss." Blaug, *Economic Theory in Retrospect*, p. 198.

often been asserted that Marx was the first economist to identify the sources making for a tendency for firms to expand in size. But that priority, if denied to Babbage, certainly belongs to Mill, whose analysis well preceded that of Marx. Chapter 9, book I, of Mill's hugely successful *Principles of Political Economy* (1848), titled "Of Production on a Large, and Production on a Small Scale," is the first systematic treatment of increasing returns to large-scale production. Mill acknowledges his debt to Babbage in the opening paragraph of this chapter. He points out that there are advantages to large-scale enterprise

when the nature of the employment allows, and the extent of the possible market encourages, a considerable division of labour. The larger the enterprise, the farther the division of labour may be carried. This is one of the principle causes of large manufactories. Even when no additional subdivision of the work would follow an enlargement of the operations, there will be good economy in enlarging them to the point at which every person to whom it is convenient to assign a special occupation, will have full employment in that occupation.[28]

Mill illustrates this statement by an extensive quotation from Babbage's chapter "On the Causes and Consequences of Large Factories." The extract covered most of the points that we have just discussed and it amounted to two full pages of Babbage's original text. Mill included an even more extensive extract from Babbage on the optimal payment arrangements for workers in the first (1848) and second (1849) editions of his *Principles*.

Marx's intellectual indebtedness to Babbage on the matter of increasing returns to large-scale production appears to be at least as extensive as Mill's and is amply acknowledged, especially by the use of numerous citations and quotations. But Babbage's influence on Marx is even more pervasive, as would be revealed by a close textual comparison of Babbage's treatment of the causes and consequences of the division of labor with that of Marx in the two central chapters of volume I of *Capital*: chapter 14 on "Division of Labour and Manufacture," and chapter 15 on "Machinery and Modern Industry." It would take us much too far afield to explore this relationship in detail. The essential point is that Marx's most fundamental criticisms of capitalism as a social and economic system turn upon its peculiar division of labor. The degradation of the worker under advanced capitalism, especially the dehumanizing effects of specialization, and the systematic tendency to deprive the worker of skills and to incorporate those skills into the machine, are all consequences of the division of labor as treated by Babbage.

Marx even takes his definition of a machine from Babbage. According to

[28] Mill, *Principles*, p. 132.

44   Dealing with an uncertain future

Marx, "The machine, which is the starting-point of the industrial revolution, supersedes the workman, who handles a single tool, by a mechanism operating with a number of similar tools, and set in motion by a single motive power, whatever the form of that power may be."[29] Marx here cites as his authority Babbage's statement from his chapter (19) on the division of labor: "The union of all these simple instruments, set in motion by a single motor, constitutes a machine."[30]

Much of Marx's critique of capitalism flows from examining exactly those characteristics of the division of labor that Babbage had identified as sources of improved efficiency in the factory. However, Marx considers them from a very different perspective: specifically, from the point of view of the welfare of the worker. From Babbage's perspective, "One great advantage which we may derive from machinery is from the check which it affords against the inattention, the idleness, or the dishonesty of human agents" (p. 54). Putting aside the matter of dishonesty, Marx sees the introduction of machinery as introducing an entirely new form of oppression and loss of the worker's essential humanity.

In handicrafts and manufacture, the workman makes use of a tool, in the factory, the machine makes use of him. There the movements of the instrument of labour proceed from him, here it is the movements of the machine that he must follow. In manufacture the workmen are parts of a living mechanism. In the factory we have a lifeless mechanism independent of the workman, who becomes its mere living appendage. (Marx, *Capital*, p. 422)

Additionally, of the system of manufacture, Marx states: "It converts the labourer into a crippled monstrosity, by forcing his detail dexterity at the expense of a world of productive capabilities and instincts; just as in the States of La Plata they butcher a whole beast for the sake of his hide or his tallow" (*ibid.*, p. 360). The freedom of the capitalist, under the division of labor, to purchase labor of lower skills, translates into "deskilling" from the laborer's point of view. Babbage's continuous citation of the "advantages" of the division of labor in making it possible to insert women, boys, and girls at very low pay into jobs formerly performed by men readily translates into Marx's searing indictment of capitalism precisely *because* of its intensive exploitation of the division of labor.

Within the capitalist system all methods for raising the social productiveness of labour are brought about at the cost of the individual labourer; all means for the development of production transform themselves into means of domination over, and exploitation of, the producers; they mutilate the labourer into a fragment of a

[29] Marx, *Capital*, p. 376.
[30] See also Babbage, *Economy of Machinery*, p. 12, and Karl Marx, *The Poverty of Philosophy*, Foreign Languages Publishing House, Moscow, pp. 132–133.

man, degrade him to the level of an appendage of a machine, destroy every remnant of charm in his work and turn it into a hated toil; they estrange from him the intellectual potentialities of the labour-process in the same proportion as science is incorporated in it as an independent power; they distort the conditions under which he works, subject him during the labour-process to a despotism the more hateful for its meanness; they transform his life-time into working-time, and drag his wife and child beneath the wheels of the Juggernaut of capital. (Marx, *Capital*, p. 645)

It is tempting to conclude that Marx's analysis of the division of labor and its consequences is the same as that of Babbage, only considered dialectically!

I have attempted to show why Babbage continues to be deserving of our attention, not only as the pioneer of the computer, but as an original contributor to the development of economic ideas. Moreover, these two roles were, as we have seen, closely connected by Babbage's own personal experiences. His prolonged frustrations over the attempt to construct a working computer led him to many of the profound and precocious insights that are developed in his book. The book has much to offer to any reader today who wishes to understand the difficulties confronting the innovative impulse in the early days of industrialization. Babbage's difficulties were, of course, far greater than those of most innovators because the goal he had set for himself was so breathtakingly ambitious. In confronting his own difficulties as a computer pioneer more than a century ahead of its time, Babbage in fact became, however reluctantly, a pioneer economist.

If the world has eventually beaten a path back to Babbage's door as a result of the computer revolution, a strong case can now be made that a second path to that door remains to be beaten. For Babbage, as we have seen, also pioneered in the analysis of technological change. The subject suffered a long neglect when the main thrust of economic analysis came to be dominated by the neoclassical analysis of comparative statics in the late nineteenth century. With only a few notable exceptions, including the seminal work of Schumpeter and Kuznets, economists devoted little attention to either the causes or consequences of technological change until the 1950s.

The revival doubtless owed a great deal to the reawakening of interest in problems of long-term economic growth in less-developed countries as well as in the industrialized west. The renewed interest was reinforced, within the economics profession, by the researches of Jacob Schmookler, Moses Abramovitz, Robert Solow, and others, which pointed forcefully to two things: (1) the existence of economic forces that powerfully shape both the rate and the direction of inventive activity; and (2) the prominent role played by technological change in generating long-term economic growth.

46   **Dealing with an uncertain future**

Babbage's book, *On the Economy of Machinery and Manufactures*, continues to have much to say to readers who are concerned with the causes as well as the consequences of technological change. But it can, of course, equally well be read for the sheer intellectual excitement it provides in following a first-class mind as it attempts to comprehend, and to impose order upon, newly emerging forms of economic activity and organization.

9

Karl Marx on the Economic Role of Science

Nathan Rosenberg

University of Wisconsin

> It is not the articles made, but how they are made, and by what instruments, that enables us to distinguish different economical epochs. [MARX 1906, p. 200]

This paper examines Marx's treatment of rising resource productivity and technological change under capitalism. Little attention has been given to Marx's view of the role which science plays in these processes. It is obvious that Marx (and Engels) attach the greatest importance to the development of modern science, but the way in which scientific progress meshes with the rest of the Marxian system has not been fully understood. The paper analyzes Marx's treatment of the factors which account for the growth of scientific knowledge as well as capitalist society's changing capacity to incorporate this knowledge into the productive process.

The purpose of this paper is to examine certain aspects of Marx's treatment of rising resource productivity and technological change under capitalism. Many of the most interesting aspects of Marx's treatment of technological change have been ignored, perhaps because of the strong polemical orientation which readers from all shades of the political spectrum seem to bring to their reading of Marx. As a result, much has been written about the impact of the machine upon the worker and his family, the phenomenon of alienation, the relationship between technological change, real wages, employment, etc. At the same time, a great deal of what Marx had to say concerning some 300 years of European capitalist development has received relatively little attention. This applies to his views dealing with the complex interrelations between science, technology, and economic development.

It is a well-known feature of the Marxian analysis of capitalism that Marx views the system as bringing about unprecedented increases in

The author is grateful to Professors Stanley Engerman and Eugene Smolensky for critical comments on an earlier draft.

713

human productivity and in man's mastery over nature. Marx and Engels told their readers, in *The Communist Manifesto*, that "the bourgeoisie, during its rule of scarce one hundred years, has created more massive and more colossal productive forces than have all preceding generations together. Subjection of Nature's forces to man, machinery, application of chemistry to industry and agriculture, steam-navigation, railways, electric telegraphs, clearing of whole continents for cultivation, canalisation of rivers, whole populations conjured out of the ground—what earlier century had even a presentiment that such productive forces slumbered in the lap of social labour?" (Marx and Engels 1951, 1: 37). No single question, therefore, would seem to be more important to the whole Marxian analysis of capitalist development than the question: Why is capitalism such an immensely productive system by comparison with all earlier forms of economic organization? The question, obviously, has been put before, and certain portions of Marx's answer are in fact abundantly plain. In particular, the social and economic structure of capitalism is one which creates enormous incentives for the generation of technological change. Marx and Engels insist that the bourgeoisie is unique as a ruling class because, unlike all earlier ruling classes whose economic interests were indissolubly linked to the maintenance of the status quo, the very essence of bourgeois rule is technological dynamism.[1] Capitalism generates unique incentives for the introduction of new, cost-reducing technologies.

The question which I am particularly interested in examining is the role which is played, within the Marxian framework, by science and scientific progress in the dynamic growth of capitalism. For surely the growth in resource productivity can never have been *solely* a function of the development of capitalist institutions. It is easy to see the existence of such institutions as a necessary condition but hardly as a sufficient condition for such growth. Surely the technological vitality of an emergent capitalism was closely linked up with the state of scientific knowledge and with industry's capacity to exploit such knowledge.

Marx's (and Engels's) position, briefly stated, is to affirm that science is, indeed, a fundamental factor accounting for the growth in resource productivity and man's enlarged capacity to manipulate his natural environment for the attainment of human purposes. However, the statement requires two immediate and highly significant qualifications, which will constitute our major concern in this paper: (1) science does not, according to Marx, function in history as an independent variable; and (2) science has come to play a critical role as a systematic contributor to increasing productivity only at a very recent (from Marx's perspective)

---

[1] "The bourgeoisie cannot exist without constantly revolutionising the instruments of production, and thereby the relations of production, and with them the whole relations of society. Conservation of the old modes of production in unaltered form, was, on the contrary, the first condition of existence for all earlier industrial classes" (Marx and Engels 1951, 1:36).

point in history. The ability of science to perform this role had necessarily to await the fulfillment of certain objective conditions. What these conditions were has not been understood adequately.

I

Marx's treatment of scientific progress is consistent with his broader historical materialism. Just as the economic sphere and the requirements of the productive process shape man's political and social institutions, so do they also shape his scientific activity at all stages of history. Science does not grow or develop in response to forces internal to science or the scientific community. It is not an autonomous sphere of human activity. Rather, science needs to be understood as a social activity which is responsive to economic forces. It is man's changing needs as they become articulated in the sphere of production which determine the direction of scientific progress. Indeed, this is generally true of all human problem-solving activity, of which science is a part. As Marx states in the introduction to his *Critique of Political Economy*: "Mankind always takes up only such problems as it can solve; since, looking at the matter more closely, we will always find the problem itself arises only when the material conditions necessary for its solution already exist or are at least in the process of formulation" (Marx 1904, pp. 12–13).

Marx views specific scientific disciplines as developing in response to problems arising in the sphere of production. The materialistic conception of history and society involves the rejection of the notion that man's intellectual pursuits can be accorded a status independent of material concerns. It emphasizes the necessity of systematically relating the realm of thinking and ideas to man's material concerns. Thus, the scientific enterprise itself needs to be examined in that perspective. "Feuerbach speaks in particular of the perception of natural science; he mentions secrets which are disclosed only to the eye of the physicist and chemist: but where would natural science be without industry and commerce? Even this 'pure' natural science is provided with an aim, as with its material, only through trade and industry, through the sensuous activity of men" (Marx and Engels 1947, p. 36). Egyptian astronomy had developed out of the compelling need to predict the rise and fall of the Nile, upon which Egyptian agriculture was so vitally dependent (Marx 1906, p. 564, n. 1). The increasing (if still "sporadic") resort to machinery in the seventeenth century was, says Marx, "of the greatest importance, because it supplied the great mathematicians of that time with a practical basis and stimulant to the creation of the science of mechanics."[2] The difficulties encountered with

---

[2] Marx 1906, pp. 382–83. Engels states: "Like all other sciences, mathematics arose out of the *needs* of men; from the measurement of land and of the content of vessels; from the computation of time and mechanics" (Engels 1939, p. 46; emphasis Engels's. Cf. Marx 1906, p. 564).

gearing as waterpower was being harnessed to larger millstones was "one of the circumstances that led to a more accurate investigation of the laws of friction."[3]

These themes are repeated by Engels, who asserts that "from the very beginning the origin and development of the sciences has been determined by production."[4] In accounting for the rise of science during the Renaissance, his first explanation again drew upon the requirements of industry.

> If, after the dark night of the Middle Ages was over, the sciences suddenly arose anew with undreamt-of force, developing at a miraculous rate, once again we owe this miracle to production. In the first place, following the crusades, industry developed enormously and brought to light a quantity of new mechanical (weaving, clock-making, milling), chemical (dyeing, metallurgy, alcohol), and physical (spectacles) facts, and this not only gave enormous material for observation, but also itself provided quite other means for experimenting than previously existed, and allowed the construction of *new* instruments; it can be said that really systematic experimental science now became possible for the first time.[5]

Moreover, in a letter written in 1895, Engels stated: "If, as you say, technique largely depends on the state of science, science depends far more still on the *state* and the *requirements* of technique. If society has a technical need, that helps science forward more than ten universities. The whole of hydrostatics (Torricelli, etc.) was called forth by the necessity for regulating the mountain streams of Italy in the sixteenth and seventeenth centuries. We have only known about electricity since its technical applicability was discovered" (Marx and Engels 1951, 2: 457, Letter from Engels to H. Starkenburg, January 25, 1895; emphasis Engels's).

---

[3] Marx 1906, p. 411. He adds: "In the same way the irregularity caused by the motive power in mills that were put in motion by pushing and pulling a lever, led to the theory, and the application, of the flywheel, which afterwards plays so important a part in Modern Industry. In this way, during the manufacturing period, were developed the first scientific and technical elements of Modern Mechanical Industry."

[4] Engels 1954, p. 247. Earlier in the paragraph, he had stated: "The successive development of the separate branches of natural science should be studied. First of all, astronomy, which, if only on account of the seasons, was absolutely indispensable for pastoral and agricultural peoples. Astronomy can only develop with the aid of mathematics. Hence this also had to be tackled. Further, at a certain stage of agriculture and in certain regions (raising of water for irrigation in Egypt), and especially with the origin of towns, big building structures and the development of handicrafts, mechanics also arose. This was soon needed also for navigation and war. Moreover, it requires the aid of mathematics and so promoted the latter's development."

[5] Ibid., p. 248. The editor of Engels's unfinished manuscript points out that Engels had written in the margin of the manuscript opposite this paragraph: "Hitherto, what has been boasted of is what production owes to science, but science owes infinitely more to production."

This statement is probably the most explicit and direct assertion in the writings of Marx and Engels that factors affecting the demand for science are overwhelmingly more important than factors affecting its supply. Scientific knowledge is acquired when a social need for that knowledge has been established. Science is, however, not an initiating force in the dynamics of social change. Developments in this sphere are a response to forces originating elsewhere. Thus, Marx and Engels appear to be presenting a purely demand-determined explanation of the social role of science. Scientific enterprise supplies that which industry demands, and therefore the changing direction of the thrust of science needs to be understood in terms of the changing requirements of industry.

II

In this section I will argue that, while the demand-oriented component of the argument just presented is indeed a major part of the Marxian view, there are also vital but less conspicuous elements in Marx's argument which have been ignored. Without these additional and more neglected elements one cannot explain a central thesis which emerges out of Marx's view: namely, that it is only at a particular time in human history that science is enlisted in a crucial way in the productive process. It is only at a very recent point in history, Marx argues, that the marriage of science and industry occurs. Moreover, this marriage does *not* coincide with the historical emergence of capitalism. In fact, Marx is quite explicit that the union of science and industry comes only centuries after the arrival of modern capitalism and the emergence of sophisticated bodies of theoretical science. If arguments based upon the existence of capitalist incentives and demand forces generally were a sufficient explanation, the full-scale industrial exploitation of science would have come at a much earlier stage in Western history. But it did not. Why?

Stripped to its essentials, Marx's answer is that the handicraft and manufacturing stages of production lacked the technological basis which would *permit* the application of scientific knowledge to the solution of problems of industrial production.[6] This essential technological basis

[6] Since the subsequent discussion turns directly upon the Marxian periodization scheme, it is important to remind the reader of the meaning which Marx attaches to the terms "handicraft," "manufacture," and "modern industry." Engels expressed Marx's meanings succinctly as follows: "We divide the history of industrial production since the Middle Ages into three periods: (1) handicraft, small master craftsmen with a few journeymen and apprentices, where each laborer produces the complete article; (2) manufacture, where greater numbers of workmen, grouped in one large establishment, produce the complete article on the principle of division of labor, each workman performing only one partial operation, so that the product is complete only after having passed successively through the hands of all; (3) modern industry, where the product is produced by machinery driven by power, and where the work of the laborer is limited to superintending and correcting the performances of the mechanical agent" (Engels 1910, pp. 12–13).

emerged only with modern industry. The immense and growing productivity of nineteenth century British industry was really, in Marx's view, the resultant of three converging sets of forces: (1) the unique incentive system and capacity for accumulation provided by capitalist institutions, (2) the availability of bodies of scientific knowledge[7] which were directly relevant for problem-solving activities in industry, and (3) a technology possessing certain special characteristics. It is this last category which is least understood and to which we therefore now turn.

Historically, capitalist relationships were introduced in an unobtrusive way, by the mere quantitative expansion in the number of wage-laborers employed by an individual owner of capital (Marx 1906, p. 367). The independent handicraftsman, operating with a few journeymen and apprentices, gradually shifted into the role of a capitalist as his relationship with these men assumed the form of a permanent system of wage payments and as the number of such laborers increased.[8] The system of manufacture, therefore, while introducing social relationships drastically different from the handicraft system of the medieval guilds which preceded it,[9] initially employed the same technology.[10]

From Marx's mid-nineteenth-century vantage point, the system of manufacture had actually been the dominant one throughout most of the history of capitalism—from "roughly speaking . . . the middle of the 16th to the last third of the 18th century" (Marx 1906, p. 369; see also p. 787).

---

[7] Actually, Marx's use of the term "science" was sufficiently broad that it included bodies of systematized knowledge far beyond what we ordinarily mean when we speak today of pure or even applied science—e.g., engineering and machine building. It was not a term which he attempted to use with precision. In *Theories of Surplus Value*, for instance, he refers to science simply as "the product of mental labour" (Marx 1963, pt. 1, p. 353).

[8] "With regard to the mode of production itself, manufacture, in its strict meaning, is hardly to be distinguished, in its earliest stages, from the handicraft trades of the guilds, otherwise than by the greater number of workmen simultaneously employed by one and the same individual capital. The workshop of the medieval master handicraftsman is simply enlarged" (Marx 1906, p. 353. Cf. Marx and Engels 1947, pp. 12–13).

[9] "With manufacture was given simultaneously a changed relationship between worker and employer. In the guilds the patriarchal relationship between journeyman and master maintained itself; in manufacture its place was taken by the monetary relation between worker and capitalist—a relationship which in the countryside and in small towns retained a patriarchal tinge, but in the larger, the real manufacturing towns, quite early lost almost all patriarchal complexion" (Marx and Engels 1947, p. 52).

[10] Machinery had sometimes been employed in earlier periods, but Marx clearly regarded these instances as exceptional. "Early in the manufacturing period the principle of lessening the necessary labour-time in the production of commodities, was accepted and formulated: and the use of machines, especially for certain simple first processes that have to be conducted on a very large scale, and with the application of great force, sprang up here and there. Thus, at an early period in paper manufacture, the tearing up of the rags was done by paper mills; and in metal works, the pounding of the ores was effected by stamping mills. The Roman Empire had handed down the elementary form of all machinery in the water-wheel" (Marx 1906, p. 382). In a footnote Marx makes the extremely interesting observation that "the whole history of the development of machinery can be traced in the history of the corn mill" (ibid., p. 382, n. 3).

Manufacture involved a significant regrouping of workers and a redefini-
tion of the responsibilities of each. Whereas a medieval handicraftsman
would himself perform a succession of operations upon a product, the
manufacturing system divided up the operation into a succession of steps,
each one of which was allocated to a separate workman.[11]

The essence of the manufacturing system, therefore, is a growing specialization on the part of the individual worker. While this in turn has psychological and social consequences of the greatest importance for the worker
with which Marx was very much concerned,[12] it continued to share with
the earlier handicraft system an essential feature. That is to say, although
the product now passed through a succession of hands, and although this
reorganization raised the productivity of labor, it nevertheless perpetuated
the industrial system's reliance upon human skills and capacities.[13]
Whereas the critical skill was formerly that of the guild craftsman, it is
now the unremitting repetition of a narrowly defined activity on the part
of the detail laborer. More precisely, the productive process now pressed
against the constraints imposed by the limited strength, speed, precision,
and, indeed, the limited number of limbs, of the human animal.

So long as the worker continues to occupy strategic places in the productive process, that process is limited by all of his human frailties. And, of
course, the individual capitalist is, in many ways, continually pressing the
worker against those limits. But the point which Marx is making here is of
much broader significance: The application of science to the productive

[11] "The needlemaker of the Nuremberg Guild was the cornerstone on which the
English needle manufacture was raised. But while in Nuremberg that single artificer
performed a series of perhaps 20 operations one after another, in England it was not
long before there were 20 needlemakers side by side, each performing one alone of those
20 operations; and in consequence of further experience, each of those 20 operations was
again split up, isolated, and made the exclusive function of a separate workman" (ibid.,
pp. 370–71).
[12] "While simple co-operation leaves the mode of working by the individual for the
most part unchanged, manufacture thoroughly revolutionises it, and seizes labour-power
by its very roots. It converts the labourer into a crippled monstrosity, by forcing his
detail dexterity at the expense of a world of productive capabilities and instincts; just
as in the States of La Plata they butcher a whole beast for the sake of his hide or his
tallow" (ibid., p. 396).
[13] "For a proper understanding of the division of labour in manufacture, it is essential
that the following points be firmly grasped. First, the decomposition of a process of
production into its various successive steps coincides, here, strictly with the resolution
of a handicraft into its successive manual operations. Whether complex or simple, each
operation has to be done by hand, retains the character of a handicraft, and is therefore
dependent on the strength, skill, quickness, and sureness, of the individual workman in
handling his tools. The handicraft continues to be the basis. This narrow technical basis
excludes a really scientific analysis of any definite process of industrial production, since
it is still a condition that each detail process gone through by the product must be capable
of being done by hand and of forming, in its way, a separate handicraft. It is just because
handicraft skill continues, in this way, to be the foundation of the process of production
that each workman becomes exclusively assigned to a partial function, and that for the
rest of his life, his labour-power is turned into the organ of this detail function" (ibid.,
pp. 371–72).

process involves dealing with impersonal laws of nature and freeing itself from all dependence upon the organic. It involves calculations concerning the behavior of natural phenomena. It involves the exploitation of reliable physical relationships which have been established by scientific disciplines. It involves a degree of predictability of a purely objective sort, from which the uncertainties and subjectivities of human behavior have been systematically excluded. Science, in short, can only incorporate its findings in impersonal machinery. It cannot be incorporated in human beings with their individual volitions, idiosyncracies, and refractory temperaments. The manufacturing period shared with the earlier handicraft system the essential feature that it was a tool-using economy where the tools were subject to human manipulation and guidance. It is this element of human control, the continued reliance upon the limited range of activities of the human hand, and not the nature of the power source, Marx insists, which is decisive in distinguishing a machine from a tool.

> The machine proper is . . . a mechanism that, after being set in motion, performs with its tools the same operations that were formerly sone by the workman with similar tools. Whether the motive power is derived from man, or from some other machine, makes no difference in this respect. From the moment that the tool proper is taken from man, and fitted into a mechanism, a machine takes the place of a mere implement. The difference strikes one at once, even in those cases where man himself continues to be the prime mover. The number of implements that he himself can use simultaneously, is limited by the number of his own natural instruments of production, by the number of his bodily organs. . . . The number of tools that a machine can bring into play simultaneously, is from the very first emancipated from the organic limits that hedge in the tools of a handicraftsman.[14]

III

What, then, is the distinctive technological feature of modern industry? It is that, for the first time, the design of the productive process is carried out on a basis where the characteristics of the worker and his physical

[14] Ibid., p. 408; see also p. 410. In his early work, *The Poverty of Philosophy*, Marx had stated: "The machine is a unification of the instruments of labour, and by no means a combination of different operations for the worker himself. 'When, by the division of labour, each particular operation has been simplified to the use of a single instrument, the linking-up of all these instruments, set in motion by a single engine, constitutes— a machine.' (Babbage, *Traité sur l'Economie des Machines*, etc., Paris 1833). Simple tools; accumulation of tools; composite tools; setting in motion of a composite tool by a single hand engine, by men; setting in motion of these instruments by natural forces, machines; system of machines having one motor; system of machines having one automatic motor— this is the progress of machinery" (Marx, n.d., pp. 132–33. This book was first published in 1847).

endowment are no longer central to the organization and arrangement of capital. Rather, capital is being designed in accordance with a completely different logic, a logic which explicitly incorporates principles of science and engineering.[15] The subjectivity of a technology adapted, out of necessity, to the capacities (or, better, the debilities) of the worker is rejected in favor of the objectivity of machinery which has been designed in accordance with its own laws and the laws of science.

> In Manufacture it is the workmen who, with their manual implements, must, either singly or in groups, carry on each particular detail process. If, on the one hand, the workman becomes adapted to the process, on the other, the process was previously made suitable to the workman. This subjective principle of the division of labour no longer exists in production by machinery. Here, the process as a whole is examined objectively, in itself, that is to say, without regard to the question of its execution by human hands, it is analysed into its constituent phases; and the problem, how to execute each detail process, and bind them all into a whole, is solved by the aid of machines, chemistry, etc.[16]

The shift from the hand-operated to the machine-operated process is a momentous one, for the simple reason that machine processes are susceptible to continuous and indefinite improvement, whereas hand processes are not.[17] The factory system makes possible the virtual routinization of productivity improvement.[18] By breaking down the productive process

[15] There is an important learning experience at the technological level before this can be done well. "It is only after considerable development of the science of mechanics, and accumulated practical experience, that the form of a machine becomes settled entirely in accordance with mechanical principles, and emancipated from the traditional form of the tool that gave rise to it" (Marx 1906, p. 418, n. 1). A typical aspect of the innovation process, therefore, is that machines go through a substantial process of modification after their first introduction (see ibid., p. 442).

[16] Ibid., pp. 414–15. Later, Marx adds: "The implements of labour, in the form of machinery, necessitate the substitution of natural forces for human force, and the conscious application of science, instead of rule of thumb. In Manufacture, the organization of the social labour-process is purely subjective; it is a combination of detail labourers; in its machinery system, Modern Industry has a productive organism that is purely objective, in which the labourer becomes a mere appendage to an already existing material condition of production" (p. 421).

[17] "As soon as a machine executes, without man's help, all the movements requisite to elaborate the raw material, needing only attendance from him, we have an automatic system of machinery, and one that is susceptible of constant improvement in its details" (ibid., p. 416).

[18] In a valuable article, "Karl Marx and the Industrial Revolution," Paul Sweezy argues that many of the important differences between Marx and his classical predecessors reduced to the fact that the classical economists "took as their model an economy based on manufacture, which is an essentially conservative and change-resistant economic order; while Marx, recognizing and making full allowance for the profound transformation effected by the industrial revolution, took as his model an economy based on modern machine industry" (Sweezy 1968, p. 115).

into objectively identifiable component parts, it creates a structure of activities which is readily amenable to rigorous analysis. "The principle, carried out in the factory system, of analysing the process of production into its constituent phases, and of solving the problems thus proposed by the application of mechanics, of chemistry, and of the whole range of the natural sciences, becomes the determining principle everywhere."[19] Thus, historical development has brought technology to a point where it has become, for the first time, an object of scientific analysis and improvement.

> A characteristic feature is, that, even down into the eighteenth century, the different trades were called "mysteries" (mystères); into their secrets none but those duly initiated could penetrate. Modern Industry rent the veil that concealed from men their own social process of production, and that turned the various spontaneously divided branches of production into so many riddles, not only to outsiders, but even to the initiated. The principle which it pursued, of resolving each process into its constituent movements, without regard to their possible execution by the hand of man, created the new modern science of technology. The varied, apparently unconnected, and petrified forms of the industrial processes now resolved themselves into so many conscious and systematic applications of natural science to the attainment of given useful effects. Technology also discovered the few main fundamental forms of motion, which, despite the diversity of the instruments used, are necessarily taken by every productive action of the human body; just as the science of mechanics sees in the most complicated machinery nothing but the continual repetition of the simple mechanical powers.
>
> Modern Industry never looks upon and treats the existing form of a process as final. The technical basis of that industry is therefore revolutionary, while all earlier modes of production were essentially conservative.[20]

In its most advanced form, therefore, "modern industry . . . makes science a productive force distinct from labour and presses it into the service of capital" (Marx 1906, p. 397).

Before capitalism could reach this stage of self-sustaining technological

---

[19] Marx 1906, p. 504. The manufacturing stage needs to be seen as an essential step in the introduction of science into the productive process. The application of science required that productive activity be broken down into a series of separately analyzable steps. The manufacturing system, even though it continued to rely upon human skills, accomplished precisely this when it replaced the handicraftsman with a number of detail laborers. In this important sense it "set the stage" for the advent of modern industry.

[20] Ibid., p. 532. Marx (1959) examines the vast possibilities for capital-saving innovations and improvements in an advanced capitalist economy in *Capital*, vol. 3, chaps. 4 and 5.

dynamism, however, another critical condition needed to be fulfilled. Machinery cannot fully liberate the economy from the output ceiling imposed by dependence upon human skills and capacities so long as these things continue to be essential in the production of the machines themselves. In the early stages of modern industry, machines were, inevitably, produced by direct reliance upon human skills and capacities. The manufacturing system responded to the demand for the new inventions by creating new worker specializations.[21] While this sufficed in the early stages of the development of modern industry, improvements in machine design and performance and increasing size eventually came up increasingly against the limitations of the human machine maker.

> Modern Industry was crippled in its complete development, so long as its characteristic instrument of production, the machine, owed its existence to personal strength and personal skill, and depended on the muscular development, the keenness of sight, and the cunning of hand, with which the detail workmen in manufactures and the manual labourers in handicrafts, wielded their dwarfish implements. Thus, apart from the dearness of the machines made in this way, a circumstance that is ever present to the mind of the capitalist, the expansion of industries carried on by means of machinery, and the invasion by machinery of fresh branches of production, were dependent on the growth of a class of workmen, who, owing to the almost artistic nature of their employment, could increase their numbers only gradually, and not by leaps and bounds. But besides this, at a certain stage of its development, Modern Industry became technologically incompatible with the basis furnished for it by handicraft and Manufacture. The increasing size of the prime movers, of the transmitting mechanism, and of the machines proper, the greater complication, multiformity and regularity of the details of these machines, as they more and more departed from the model of those originally made by manual labour, and acquired a form, untrammelled except by the conditions under which they worked, the perfecting of the automatic system, and the use, every day more unavoidable, of a more refractory material, such as iron instead of wood—the solution of all these problems, which sprang up by the force of circumstances, everywhere met

[21] "As inventions increased in number, and the demand for the newly discovered machines grew larger, the machine-making industry split up, more and more, into numerous independent branches, and division of labour in these manufactures was more and more developed. Here, then, we see in Manufacture the immediate technical foundation of Modern Industry. Manufacture produced the machinery, by means of which Modern Industry abolished the handicraft and manufacturing systems in those spheres of production that it first seized upon" (Marx 1906, p. 417).

with a stumbling-block in the personal restrictions which even
the collective labourer of Manufacture could not break through,
except to a limited extent. Such machines as the modern hydraulic press, the modern powerloom, and the modern carding
engine, could never have been furnished by Manufacture.[22]

The vital step, therefore, is the establishment of the technological conditions which would make it possible to use machinery in the construction
of machines, thus bypassing the central constraint of the old manufacturing system. "Modern Industry had therefore itself to take in hand the
machine, its characteristic instrument of production, and to construct
machines by machines. It was not till it did this, that it built up for itself
a fitting technical foundation, and stood on its own feet. Machinery,
simultaneously with the increasing use of it, in the first decades of this
century, appropriated, by degrees, the fabrication of machines proper."[23]
Marx singles out, not only the new power sources which offered gigantic
quantities of energy subject to careful human regulation, but also that
indispensable addition to the equipment at the disposal of the machine
maker, the slide rest. This simple but ingenious device of Henry Maudsley
replaces, as Marx perceptively notes, not any particular tool, "but the
hand itself" (Marx 1906, p. 408). In this sense it is a strategic technological
breakthrough, fully comparable in importance to the steam engine.

The improvements in the machinery-producing sector constitute a
quantum leap in the technological arsenal at man's disposal. They make
it possible to escape the physical limitations of a tool-using culture. They
do this, ironically as Marx points out, by providing machines which
reproduce the actions of a hand-operated tool, but do so on a "cyclopean
scale."[24]

---

[22] Ibid., pp. 417–18. Marx saw the improvements in the means of communication
and transportation as particularly significant in pushing the productive process beyond
the limitations inherent in the manufacturing system. "The means of communication
and transport became gradually adapted to the modes of production of mechanical
industry, by the creation of a system of river steamers, railways, ocean steamers, and
telegraphs. But the huge masses of iron that had now to be forged, to be welded, to be
cut, to be bored, and to be shaped, demanded, on their part, cyclopean machines, for
the construction of which the methods of the manufacturing period were utterly
inadequate" (pp. 419–20).

[23] Ibid., p. 420. Marx saw this process as culminating during his own time. "It is only
during the last 15 years (i.e., since about 1850), that a constantly increasing portion of
these machine tools have been made in England by machinery, and that not by the same
manufacturers who make the machines" (p. 408).

[24] "If we now fix our attention on that portion of the machinery employed in the
construction of machines, which constitutes the operating tool, we find the manual
implements reappearing, but on a cyclopean scale. The operating part of the boring
machine is an immense drill driven by a steam-engine; without this machine, on the
other hand, the cylinders of large steam-engines and of hydraulic presses could not be
made. The mechanical lathe is only a cyclopean reproduction of the ordinary footlathe;
the planing machine, an iron carpenter, that works on iron with the same tools that the
human carpenter employs on wood; the instrument that, on the London wharves, cuts

IV

Thus, I would interpret the Marxian position to be that it is the changing requirements of industry and the altering perception of economic needs which provide the stimulus to the *pursuit* of specific forms of scientific knowledge. But I would also conclude that the Marxian position cannot be adequately described as a demand-induced approach without doing a severe injustice to the subtlety of Marx's historical analysis.[25] For the ability to apply science to the productive sphere turns upon industry's changing *capacity* to utilize such knowledge, a capacity which Marx explicitly recognizes has been subjected to great changes over the course of recent history. Indeed, Marx himself, as I have tried to establish, devoted considerable effort to the elucidation of the factors which have shaped society's altering capacity to absorb the fruits of scientific knowledge.[26]

Nor did Marx argue that the historical sequence in which scientific disciplines actually developed was also directly determined by economic needs. For example, in discussing the relative pace of development in industry and agriculture, he states that productivity growth in agriculture had, historically, to await the development of certain scientific disciplines, and therefore came later, whereas industry progressed more rapidly than agriculture at least in large part because the scientific knowledge upon

---

the veneers, is a gigantic razor; the tool of the shearing machine, which shears iron as easily as a tailor's scissors cut cloth, is a monster pair of scissors; and the steam hammer works with an ordinary hammer head, but of such a weight that not Thor himself could wield it. These steam hammers are an invention of Nasmyth, and there is one that weighs over 6 tons and strikes with a vertical fall of 7 feet, on an anvil weighing 36 tons. It is mere child's play for it to crush a block of granite into powder, yet it is not less capable of driving, with a succession of light taps, a nail into a piece of soft wood" (ibid., p. 421; see also pp. 492–93).

[25] At one point Marx presents what one might be tempted to call a Toynbeean "challenge-response" mechanism to account for the emergence of high productivity societies. It is not true, he says, "that the most fruitful soil is the most fitted for the growth of the capitalist mode of production. This mode is based on the dominion of man over nature. Where nature is too lavish, she 'keeps him in hand, like a child in leading-strings.' She does not impose upon him any necessity to develop himself. It is not the tropics with their luxuriant vegetation, but the temperate zone, that is the mother country of capital. It is not the mere fertility of the soil, but the differentiation of the soil, the variety of its natural products, the changes of the seasons, which form the physical basis for the social division of labour, and which, by changes in the natural surroundings, spur man on to the multiplication of his wants, his capabilities, his means and modes of labor. It is the necessity of bringing a natural force under the control of society, of economising, of appropriating or subduing it on a large scale by the work of man's hand, that first plays the decisive part in the history of industry" (ibid., pp. 563–64).

[26] In this light, there is no necessary conflict between Marx's materialist conception of history and his treatment of science as a productive force under advanced capitalism. I therefore disagree with the following statement of Bober: "Marx intends to offer a materialistic conception of history. Yet he frequently stresses the power of science as a component of modern technique and production. The incorporation of science in the foundation of his theory is no more defensible than the inclusion of all other nonmaterial phenomena" (Bober 1965, p. 21).

which industry relied had developed earlier. "Mechanics, the really scientific basis of large-scale industry, had reached a certain degree of perfection during the eighteenth century. The development of chemistry, geology and physiology, the sciences that *directly* form the specific basis of agriculture rather than of industry, does not take place till the nineteenth century and especially the later decades."[27]

This strongly suggests at least some degree of independence and autonomy on the part of science in shaping the sequence of industrial change, in spite of the fact that, as we saw earlier, Marx and Engels usually emphasize the cause-effect relationships which run from industry to science. If the growth in agricultural productivity is dependent upon progress in specific subdisciplines of science, and if the existence of profitable commercial opportunities in agriculture cannot "induce" the production of the requisite knowledge, then factors internal to the realm of science must be conceded to play a role independent of economic needs.

Moreover, it is especially curious to find that Engels is content to state, as quoted earlier, that "from the very beginning the origin and development of the sciences has been determined by production" (Engels 1954, p. 247). For Engels himself, in the *Dialectics of Nature*, had also presented a classification scheme for the sciences which emphasized a hierarchy of increasing complexity based upon the forms of motion of the matter being analyzed. Increasing complexity is identified with the movement from the inorganic to the organic, from mechanics to physics to chemistry to biology.[28] Engels even goes so far as to speak of an

---

[27] Marx 1968, pt. 2, p. 110. In *The German Ideology* Marx and Engels stated that "the science of mechanics perfected by Newton was altogether the most popular science in France and England in the eighteenth century" (Marx and Engels 1947, p. 56).

[28] "Hegel's division (the original one) into mechanics, chemics, and organics, fully adequate for the time. Mechanics: the movement of masses. Chemics: molecular (for physics is also included in this and, indeed, both—physics as well as chemistry—belong to the same order) motion and atomic motion. Organics: the motion of bodies in which the two are inseparable. For the organism is certainly *the higher unity which within itself unites mechanics, physics, and chemistry into a whole* where the trinity can no longer be separated. In the organism, mechanical motion is effected directly by physical and chemical change, in the form of nutrition, respiration, secretion, etc., just as much as pure muscular movement" (Engels 1954, pp. 331–32; emphasis Engels's). For Engels's entire treatment of the subject, see ibid., pp. 322–408. In his book, *Herr Eugen Duhring's Revolution in Science*, Engels draws a sharp distinction between the sciences concerned with inanimate nature and those concerned with living organisms. The former group of sciences (mathematics, astronomy, mechanics, physics, chemistry) are susceptible to mathematical treatment "to a greater or less degree." No such precision is possible in the sciences concerned with living organisms. "In this field there is such a multitude of reciprocal relations and causalities that not only does the solution of each question give rise to a host of other questions, but each separate problem can usually only be solved piecemeal, through a series of investigations which often requires centuries to complete; and even then the need for a systematic presentation of the interrelations makes it necessary again and again to surround the final and ultimate truths with a luxuriant growth of hypotheses" (Engels 1939, pp. 97–99).

"inherent sequence,"[29] which he clearly believes has structured the *historical* sequence in which nature's secrets have been progressively uncovered. But, if one accepts this intuitively plausible view, then surely there is much more to "the origin and development of the sciences" than can be accounted for by the specific demands being generated in the productive sphere. Surely the historical fact that the biological sciences came to the assistance of agriculture long after the mechanical sciences were being utilized by industry is a sequence originating, not in economic needs, but in the differing degrees of complexity of these scientific disciplines. Engels's formulations particularly seem to overemphasize the importance of demand-induced incentives to the neglect of supply side considerations, even though he is obviously sensitive to these supply variables in other contexts.

In Engels's defense one must recall, of course, the unfinished, indeed often merely fragmentary condition of his *Dialectics of Nature*.[30] It is entirely possible that, had he the opportunity, he would have resolved these apparent inconsistencies. But it is expecting far too much to look to either Marx or Engels for the resolution of these deep and thorny problems. We are still, today, a long way from being able to incorporate the history of science in an orderly manner into our understanding of the economic development of the Western world.[31]

Conclusion

There are several possible meanings which can be attached to the statement that "the origin and development of the sciences has been determined by production."

1. Science depends upon industry for financial support.

2. The expectation of high financial returns is what motivates individuals (and society) to pursue a particular scientific problem.

3. The needs of industry serve as a powerful agent in calling attention to certain problems (Pasteur's studies of fermentation and silkworm epidemics).

[29] "Classification of the sciences, each of which analyzes a single form of motion, or a series of forms of motion that belong together and pass into one another, is therefore the classification, the arrangement, of these forms of motion themselves according to their inherent sequence, and herein lies its importance" (Engels 1954, p. 330; see also Zvorikine 1963, pp. 59–74).

[30] See Engels 1954, "Preface."

[31] The most ambitious attempt to fill this void is the fascinating but seriously flawed four-volume work by the late J. D. Bernal, *Science in History* (1971). His *Science and Industry in the Nineteenth Century* (London, 1953) is more restricted in scope and far more consistently persuasive. Nevertheless, *Science in History* displays an immense erudition, and all but the most remarkably well-informed readers will learn much from, and be greatly stimulated by, its contents.

4. The normal pursuit of productive activities throws up physical evidence of great importance to certain disciplines (metallurgy and chemistry, canal building and geology). As a result, industrial activities have, as a byproduct of their operation, provided the flow of raw observations upon which sciences have built and generalized.

5. The history of individual sciences, including an account of their varying rates of progress at different periods in history, can be adequately provided by an understanding of the changing economic needs of society.

I believe that Marx and Engels subscribed to propositions 1–4 without qualification. I believe they often *sounded* as if they subscribed to the fifth proposition. However, I think the preceding discussion has established that they subscribed to the fifth proposition only subject to certain qualifications—qualifications which strike me as being, collectively, more interesting than the original proposition.

References

Bernal, J. D. *Science and Industry in the Nineteenth Century*. London: Routledge & Kegan Paul, 1953.
———. *Science in History*. 4 vols. Cambridge, Mass.: M.I.T. Press, 1971.
Bober, M. M. *Karl Marx's Interpretation of History*. New York: Norton, 1965.
Engels, Frederick. *Socialism: Utopian and Scientific*. Chicago: Kerr, 1910.
———. *Herr Eugen Duhring's Revolution in Science*. New York: International, 1939.
———. *The Dialectics of Nature*. Moscow: Foreign Languages, 1954.
Marx, Karl. *A Contribution to the Critique of Political Economy*. Chicago: Kerr, 1904.
———. *Capital*. Vol. 1. Chicago: Kerr, 1906.
———. *Capital*. Vol. 3. Moscow: Foreign Languages, 1959.
———. *Theories of Surplus Value*. 3 pts. Moscow: Progress, 1963.
———. *The Poverty of Philosophy*. Moscow: Foreign Languages, n.d.
Marx, Karl, and Engels, Frederick. *The German Ideology*. New York: International, 1947.
———. *Selected Works*. 2 vols. Moscow: Foreign Languages, 1951.
Sweezy, Paul. "Karl Marx and the Industrial Revolution." *Events, Ideology and Economic Theory*, edited by Robert Eagly. Detroit: Wayne State Univ. Press, 1968.
Zvorikine, A. "Technology and the Laws of its Development." *The Technological Order*, edited by Carl F. Stover. Detroit: Wayne State Univ. Press, 1963.

[10]

Marx as a Student of Technology

by Nathan Rosenberg

I

    This paper will attempt to demonstrate that a major reason for the fruitfulness of Marx's framework for the analysis of social change was that Marx was, himself, a careful student of technology. By this I mean not only that he was fully aware of, and insisted upon, the historical importance and the social consequences of technology. That much is obvious. Marx additionally devoted much time and effort to explicating the distinctive characteristics of technologies, and to attempting to unravel and examine the inner logic of individual technologies. He insisted that technologies constitute an interesting subject, not only to technologists, but to students of society and social pathology as well, and he was very explicit in the introduction of technological variables into his arguments.

    I will argue that, quite independently of whether Marx was right or wrong in his characterization of the future course of technological change and its social and economic ramifications, his formulation of the problem still deserves to be a starting point for any serious investigation of technology and its ramifications. Indeed, the following statement by Marx, amazingly fresh over a century later, reads like a prolegomenon to a history of technology which still remains to be written:

> A critical history of technology would show how little any of the inventions of the eighteenth century are the work of a single individual. Hitherto there is no such book. Darwin has interested us in the history of Nature's Technology, i.e.,

In preparing this paper, I have had the considerable benefit of comments and suggestions from Jens Christiansen, Paul David, David Mowery, and Stanley Engerman. I am grateful also to the National Science Foundation for financial support.

56

in the formation of the organs of plants and animals, which organs serve as instruments of production for sustaining life. Does not the history of the productive organs of man, of organs that are the material basis of all social organization, deserve equal attention? And would not such a history be easier to compile since, as Vico says, human history differs from natural history in this, that we have made the former, but not the latter? Technology discloses man's mode of dealing with Nature, the process of production by which he sustains his life, and thereby also lays bare the mode of formation of his social relations, and of the mental conceptions that flow from them.[1]

In what follows, I will focus first upon Marx's alleged technological determinism, second on his views on the characteristics of Modern Industry which are responsible for its high degree of technological dynamism, and finally on the special importance which Marx attaches to the role of the capital-goods sector in the generation of technological change. An important question regarding Marx's treatment of technology is, quite simply, what it was about his method or approach which made him so much more perceptive on this subject than any of his contemporaries. I think a few tentative methodological observations, upon which I will elaborate later, may be useful at the outset.

The method of historical materialism which Marx utilized was one which emphasized the interactions and conflicts of social classes and institutions, not individuals. Thus for Marx invention and innovation, no less than other socioeconomic activities, were best analyzed as social processes rather than as inspired flashes of individual genius. The focus of Marx's discussion of technological change is thus not upon individuals, however heroic, but upon a collective, social process in which the institutional and economic environments play major roles.

Marx's historical approach was one which emphasized the discontinuous nature of social evolution, an evolutionary process which was, for him, moving forward under capitalism, just as it had under earlier forms of social organization. Rather than viewing capitalism as the final, logical outcome of a smooth, lengthy evolutionary process, Marx treated it as simply one stage in the process of historical evolution, while looking for the unique features of the capitalist forces of production and attempting to understand them in dynamic terms.

I would argue that the dialectical method is the most important factor in understanding the methodological basis for Marx's unique insights. Rather than positing some unidirectional chain of causation for technological change, Marx offers a far richer mode of analysis, one which emphasizes the mutual interactions and feedbacks between economy and technology. His analysis of the rise of the system of "machinofacture" and its implications for technological change, which I will examine in this paper, is an important example of the insights yielded by such a method.

II

First of all, it is necessary to advert briefly to the oft-repeated view that Marx was a technological determinist.[2] If by this we mean that technological forces are the decisive factor in generating socioeconomic changes—that technological factors are, so to speak, the independent variable in generating social change, which constitutes the dependent variable—it is easy to demonstrate that Marx subscribed to no such simplistic view. No doubt certain passages can be cited to support such an interpretation—most notably, of course, the statement from *The Poverty of Philosophy* that "The handmill gives you society with the feudal lord; the steam-mill, society with the industrial capitalist."[3] But such an interpretation, relying upon a few such aphoristic assertions, often tossed out in the heat of debate (as the quotation from *The Poverty of Philosophy* was thrown out in criticizing Proudhon) finds little support in Marx's own treatment of the major historical episodes with which he was concerned. Indeed, in a process no less central to Marx than the historical rise of capitalism itself, technological factors play no immediate role at all. For Marx, capitalism developed in Western Europe basically in response to growing markets and related opportunities for profit-making associated with the geographic explorations of the fifteenth

century. The *locus classicus* for this view is, of course, the opening pages of the *Communist Manifesto*:

> The discovery of America, the rounding of the Cape,
> opened up fresh ground for the rising bourgeoisie. The
> East-Indian and Chinese markets, the colonization of Ameri-
> ca, trade with the colonies, the increase in the means of
> exchange and in commodities generally, gave to commerce,
> to navigation, to industry, an impulse never before known,
> and thereby, to the revolutionary element in the tottering
> feudal society, a rapid development.
>
> The feudal system of industry, under which industrial
> production was monopolized by closed guilds, now no longer
> sufficed for the growing wants of the new markets. The
> manufacturing system took its place. The guild-masters were
> pushed on one side by the manufacturing middle class; divi-
> sion of labor between the different corporate guilds vanished
> in the face of division of labor in each single workshop.
>
> Meantime the markets kept ever growing, the demand
> ever rising. Even manufacture no longer sufficed. Thereupon,
> steam and machinery revolutionized industrial production.
> The place of manufacture was taken by the giant, Modern
> Industry, the place of the industrial middle class, by indus-
> trial millionaires, the leaders of whole industrial armies, the
> modern bourgeois.
>
> Modern industry has established the world-market, for
> which the discovery of America paved the way. This market
> has given an immense development to commerce, to naviga-
> tion, to communication by land. This development has, in its
> turn, reacted on the extension of industry; and in propor-
> tion as industry, commerce, navigation, railways extended, in
> the same proportion the bourgeoisie developed, increased its
> capital, and pushed into the background every class handed
> down from the Middle Ages.[4]

I have taken the liberty of quoting at length from a familiar source because this passage is, it seems to me, a definitive
refutation of the view that Marx was a technological determinist. The question is: What are the factors which *initiate*
change? What are the factors which cause other factors to
change? A resolute technological determinist would presumably
argue that the entire process of European expansion was initi-

ated by navigational improvements which in turn generated the growth of overseas markets. But this is clearly not Marx's own view here. In fact, Marx states *twice* that the improvements in navigation were caused by the prior growth in markets and commercial opportunities. The passage makes it unmistakably clear that the technological changes associated with the two stages of capitalist development—the manufacturing system and Modern Industry—were responses to an expanding universe of profit-making opportunities.

For Marx, then, capitalist relationships emerged when the growth of profit-making opportunities led to an expansion in the size of the productive unit beyond that which was characteristic of the medieval craft workshop. The mere quantitative expansion of such workshops led eventually to qualitative changes of a most basic sort in social relationships.[5] Although the system of manufacture totally dominated the first two and a half centuries of Western capitalism and led to major transformations in social relationships,[6] it was not associated with any major technological innovations. "With regard to the mode of production itself, manufacture, in its strict meaning, is hardly to be distinguished, in its earliest stages, from the handicraft trades of the guilds, otherwise than by the greater number of workmen simultaneously employed by one and the same individual capital. The workshop of the mediaeval master handicraftsman is simply enlarged."[7]

To regard Marx as a technological determinist, then, is tantamount to ignoring his dialectical analysis of the nature of historical change.[8] The essence of this view is that the class struggle, the basic moving force of history, is itself the product of fundamental contradictions between the forces of production and the relations of production. At any point in historical time, new productive forces emerge, not exogenously or as some mysterious *deus ex machina*, but rather as a dialectical outcome of a larger historical process in which *both* the earlier forces and relations of production play essential roles. As Marx forcefully put it: "It must be kept in mind that the new forces of production and relations of production do not develop out of *nothing*, nor drop from the sky, nor from the womb of the self-positing Idea; but from within and in antithesis to the existing development of production and the inherited, traditional relations of property."[9]

Thus, for Marx the basic rhythm of human history is the outcome of this dialectical interaction between the forces and the relations of production. To categorize Marx as a technological determinist one would have to demonstrate first that he does *not* intend his historical argument to proceed in a dialectical form. I think it is easy to demonstrate that he does.

III

If Marx was not a technological determinist he did, nonetheless, attach great importance to technological factors. The reasons for this are made clear in Chapter 7 of the first volume of *Capital*. Technology is what mediates between man and his relationship with the external, material world. But in acting upon that material world, man not only transforms it for his own useful purposes (that is to say, "Nature becomes one of the organs of his activity"[10]) but he also, unavoidably, engages in an act of self-transformation and self-realization. "By thus acting on the external world and changing it, he at the same time changes his own nature."[11] Technology, therefore, is at the center of those activities which are distinctively human. For technology comprises those instruments which determine the effectiveness of man's pursuit of goals which are shaped not only by his basic instinctive needs, but also those formulated and shaped in his own brain. "A spider conducts operations that resemble those of a weaver, and a bee puts to shame many an architect in the construction of her cells. But what distinguishes the worst architect from the best of bees is this, that the architect raises his structure in imagination before he erects it in reality. At the end of every labor process, we get a result that already existed in the imagination of the laborer at the commencement."[12]

The informed student of society, therefore, can infer much concerning the nature of a society, its intellectual attainments, its organization, and its dominant social relationships, by studying the instruments of human labor. But again it needs to be insisted that Marx's position here cannot be reduced to a crude technological determinism. In a highly perceptive passage which is sometimes cited as evidence of his technological determinism, Marx is, in fact, pointing to what can be *inferred* about the nature of earlier societies from their remaining artifacts. "Relics of by-gone instruments of labor possess the same importance for the investigation of extinct economical forms of society, as do fossil bones for the determination of extinct species of animals. It is not the articles made, but how they are made, and by what instruments, that enables us to distinguish different economical epochs. Instruments of labor not only supply a *standard* of the degree of development to which human labor has attained, but they are also *indicators* of the social conditions under which that labor is carried on."[13] I believe this passage is evidence of technological determinism in about the same sense that one is entitled to say that a thermometer *determines* body temperature or a barometer *determines* atmospheric pressure. All such statements are equally specious and misleading in mixing up measurement with causation.

The decisive technological changes with which Marx is concerned begin around the middle of the eighteenth century. It is at this point that Britain began her transition from an industrial system of manufacture to what Marx calls Modern Industry. The general outline of his analysis, as presented in Chapters 13-15 of *Capital*, is well known and need not be repeated here. Rather, I will focus on certain specific features which, I believe, are still insufficiently appreciated.

First of all, Marx posed and dealt with a basic question concerning the nature of technology which has never received the attention it deserves. It is widely accepted that modern capitalist societies have achieved high levels of productivity because of the systematic application of scientific knowledge to the productive sphere. As Kuznets has stated: "The epochal innovation that distinguishes the modern economic epoch is the extended application of science to problems of economic production."[14] Our awareness of the importance of modern science (an awareness which is not, of course, confined to its purely economic significance) has led to a mushrooming interest in the history of science, which is now a thoroughly respectable academic discipline. But although we study the history of science (in some cases with the financial support of the National Science Foundation), the study of the history of technology is still largely (although by no means entirely) neglected. And yet to the extent that we are interested in the economic importance of science, we need to study the history of technology, because not all technologies will permit, or will permit in equal degrees, the *application* of scientific knowledge to the productive sphere. The growth of science, *by itself,* is not a sufficient condition for the growth of productivity. To believe that it is, is to ignore the mediating role of technology between man and nature. It was one of Marx's most important accomplishments to have posed precisely this question: What are the characteristics of technologies which make it possible to apply scientific knowledge to the productive sphere? Moreover, I think Marx suggested an answer which was quite adequate for his own historical period, given the nature of the industrial technology of his day and the state of scientific development. Still, this immensely important question needs to be posed and studied anew for the far more complex technologies, as well as the far more sophisticated bodies of scientific knowledge, which have emerged in the century since Marx wrote *Capital.* From the vantage point of the mid-nineteenth century, Marx's answer ran along the following lines.

The manufacturing system, which was the dominant mode of production of early capitalism, developed a high degree of worker specialization. Whereas the medieval handicraftsmen performed a whole range of operations in the production of a single commodity, the manufacturing system broke down the productive process into a series of discrete steps, and assigned each step to a separate detail laborer. However, although this growing specialization of work had highly significant consequences with which Marx was intensely concerned, it nevertheless shared a basic feature in common with the medieval handicraft system: a continued reliance upon human skills and capacities.

> Whether complex or simple, each operation has to be done by hand, retains the character of a handicraft, and is therefore dependent upon the strength, skill, quickness, and sureness, of the individual workman in handling his tools.

The handicraft continues to be the basis. This narrow technical basis excludes a really scientific analysis of any definite process of industrial production, since it is still a condition that each detail process gone through by the product must be capable of being done by hand and of forming, in its way, a separate handicraft. It is just because handicraft skill continues, in this way, to be the foundation of the process of production, that each workman becomes exclusively assigned to a partial function, and that for the rest of his life, his labor power is turned into the organ of this detail function.[15]

Although, therefore, the manufacturing system achieved a growth in productivity through the exploitation of a new and more extensive division of labor, a rigid ceiling to the growth in productivity continued to be imposed by limitations of human strength, speed, and accuracy. Marx's point, indeed, is more general: science itself can never be extensively applied to the productive process so long as that process continues to be dependent upon forces the behavior of which cannot be predicted and controlled with the strictest accuracy. Science, in other words, must incorporate its principles in impersonal machinery. Such machinery may be relied upon to behave in accordance with scientifically established physical relationships. Science, however, cannot be incorporated into technologies dominated by large-scale human interventions, for human action involves too much that is subjective and capricious. More generally, human beings have wills of their own and are therefore too refractory to constitute reliable, i.e., controllable, inputs in complex and interdependent productive processes.

The decisive step, then, was the development of a machine technology which was not heavily dependent upon human skills or volitions, where the productive process was broken down into a series of separately analyzable steps. The historic importance of the manufacturing system was that it had provided just such a breakdown. The historic importance of Modern Industry was that it incorporated these separate steps into machine processes to which scientific knowledge and principles could now be routinely applied. "The principle, carried out in the factory system, of analyzing the process of production into its constituent phases, and of solving the problems thus proposed by the application of mechanics, of chemistry, and of the whole range of the natural sciences, becomes the determining principle everywhere."[16] When this stage has been reached, Marx argues, technology becomes, for the first time, capable of indefinite improvement:

> Modern industry rent the veil that concealed from men their own social process of production, and that turned the various, spontaneously divided branches of production into so many riddles, not only to outsiders, but even to the initiated. The principle which it pursued, of resolving each process into its constituent movements, without any regard to their possible execution by the hand of man, created the new modern science of technology. The varied, apparently unconnected, and petrified forms of the industrial processes now resolved themselves into so many conscious and systematic applications of natural science to the attainment of given useful effects. Technology also discovered the few main fundamental forms of motion, which despite the diversity of the instruments used, are necessarily taken by every productive action of the human body; just as the science of mechanics sees in the most complicated machinery nothing but the continual repetition of the simple mechanical powers.[17]

I suggest that Marx's insight into the historical interrelationships between science and technology was extraordinarily perceptive and that it ought to be treated as a starting point for the vastly more complex interrelationships which have characterized the last century of capitalist development.[18]

IV

In the remainder of this paper I propose to concentrate upon Marx's analysis of the unique role and importance of the capital-goods sector. Although Marx is generally recognized as the father of the two-sector model, this recognition has been confined primarily to the usefulness of such models in the explanation of the inherent instability of capitalist economies, after the fashion in which Marx employed such models in the second volume of *Capital*. His work, however, suggests much

more than this. The identification and isolation of a capital-
goods producing sector offers rich possibilities for the further
understanding of the form and the mechanism of diffusion of
technological change, as well as other critical aspects of the
behavior of capitalist societies.

In the early stages of the development of Modern Industry,
machinery was produced by handicraft and manufacturing
methods.[19] Although such methods were sufficient in the early
stages, the growth in machine size and complexity and requirements for improvement in machine design and performance
characteristics created demands which proved to be incompatible with the limited capacities of handicraft and manufacturing
technologies. Indeed, "Such machines as the modern hydraulic
press, modern powerloom, and the modern carding engine, could
never have been furnished by Manufacture."[20] The realization
of the full productive possibilities of Modern Industry therefore
required that machine techniques be employed in the construction of the machines themselves. This is the final stage in the
"bootstrap" operation, the stage by which Modern Industry
completes its liberation from the constraints of the old technology. "Modern Industry had therefore itself to take in hand
the machine, its characteristic instrument of production, and to
construct machines by machines. It was not till it did this, that
it built up for itself a fitting technical foundation, and stood on
its own feet. Machinery, simultaneously with the increasing use
of it, in the first decades of this century, appropriated, by
degrees, the fabrication of machines proper."[21]

Once this stage of technological maturity has been attained, modern capitalism may be regarded as being in full
possession of those extraordinary technological means which
sharply distinguish it from all earlier stages in the development
of man's productive capacities:

> So soon . . . as the factory system has gained a certain
> breadth of footing and a definite degree of maturity, and.
> especially, so soon as its technical basis, machinery, is itself
> produced by machinery; so soon as coal mining and iron
> mining, the metal industries, and the means of transport
> have been revolutionized; so soon, in short, as the general
> conditions requisite for production by the modern industrial

> system have been established, this mode of production ac-
> quires an elasticity, a capacity for sudden extension by leaps
> and bounds that finds no hindrance except in the supply of
> raw material and the disposition of the produce.[22]

It was one of Marx's enduring accomplishments that he
was among the first to perceive the inevitability of the trend
toward bigness. This perception was, again, firmly rooted in his
careful study of technological forces at work in mid-nineteenth
century British capitalism. Marx asserted in Chapter 25 of the
first volume of *Capital* ("The General Law of Capitalist Accumulation") the decisive economic advantages of capitalist
production on a large scale. The nature of these advantages is
carefully categorized and analyzed, and numerous specific examples are presented in Chapter 5 of the third volume ("Economy in the Employment of Constant Capital").

When, as a result of the process of capital accumulation,
the capitalist economy has acquired a sufficiently large comple-
ment of capital goods, and therefore also a well-defined sector
devoted to the production of capital goods, the system at this
stage acquires a new source of productive dynamism. First of all
there are the opportunities, when the scale of production is
sufficiently large, for the exploitation of what we have come to
call indivisibilities:

> In a large factory with one or two central motors the
> cost of these motors does not increase in the same ratio as
> their horse power and, hence, their possible sphere of activity.
> The cost of the transmission equipment does not grow in the
> same ratio as the total number of working machines which
> it sets in motion. The frame of a machine does not become
> dearer in the same ratio as the mounting number of tools
> which it employs as its organs, etc. Furthermore, the con-
> centration of means of production yields a saving on buildings
> of various kinds not only for the actual workshops, but also
> for storage, etc. The same applies to expenditures for fuel,
> lighting, etc. Other conditions of production remain the
> same, whether used by many or by few.[23]

Furthermore, when production takes place on a sufficiently
large scale, it eventually becomes worthwhile to take steps to
utilize waste, or by-product, materials. "The general require-

ments for the reemployment of these 'excretions' are: large quantities of such waste, such as are available only in large-scale production, improved machinery whereby materials, formerly useless in their prevailing form, are put into a state fit for new production; scientific progress, particularly chemistry, which reveals the useful properties of such waste."[24]

Most generally, the existence of a large stock of capital goods now provides powerful economic incentives for innovations of a capital-saving nature. That is to say, there now exist great opportunities for increasing the rate of profit "by reducing the value of the constant capital required for commodity production."[25] This involves not only the development of improved machinery—steam engines which deliver a greater amount of power with the same expenditure of capital and fuel—but also *technological change in the machinery-producing sector itself.* As a result of such improvements in the machine-building sector, "although the value of the fixed portion of constant capital increases continually with the development of labor on a large scale, it does not increase at the same rate."[26] At this most advanced stage of capitalist development, inter-industry relationships come to play a most important role, because the rate of profit in one industry now becomes a function of labor productivity in another industry. "What the capitalist thus utilizes are the advantages of the entire system of the social division of labor. It is the development of the productive power of labor in its exterior department, in that department which supplies it with means of production, whereby the value of the constant capital employed by the capitalist is relatively lowered and consequently the rate of profit is raised."[27]

From an even broader perspective, the rate of profit may be increased by any capital-saving innovations, in whatever form. A large class of such innovations will therefore include all measures which reduce the turnover period of capital. From an economy-wide point of view, this has been precisely the effect of the communications revolution, one of the effects of which was a drastic reduction in the requirements for circulating capital. Marx deals with this source of capital-saving in Chapter 4 of the third volume of *Capital* ("The Effect of the Turnover on the Rate of Profit"):

The chief means of reducing the time of circulation is improved communications. The last 50 years have brought about a revolution in this field, comparable only with the industrial revolution of the latter half of the eighteenth century. On land the macadamized road has been displaced by the railway, on sea the slow and irregular sailing vessel has been pushed into the background by the rapid and dependable steamboat line, and the entire globe is being girdled by telegraph wires. The Suez Canal has fully opened East Asia and Australia to steamer traffic. The time of circulation of a shipment of commodities to East Asia, at least twelve months in 1847 . . . , has now been reduced to almost as many weeks. The two large centers of the crises of 1825-1857, America and India, have been brought from 70 to 90 percent nearer to the European industrial countries by this revolution in transport. . . . The period of turnover of the total world commerce has been reduced to the same extent, and the efficacy of the capital involved in it has been more than doubled or trebled. It goes without saying that this has not been without effect on the rate of profit.[28]

All this from someone who is often described as treating the process of technological innovation as if it were purely a labor-saving phenomenon!

One further point which deserves to be made here is that Marx does not regard the reliance upon a new power source as the crucial element in the development of machines. Indeed, as he points out, in many of the early machines man was himself the prime mover. The distinctive element, as our earlier discussion has suggested, is the transfer of the control over the tool out of human hands.[29] This transfer of control involves a quantum leap forward, since "the number of tools that a machine can bring into play simultaneously is from the very first emancipated from the organic limits that hedge in the tools of a handicraftsman."[30] Furthermore, modern technology has even, *mirabile dictu*, invented a substitute for the human hand itself in the form of Henry Maudsley's slide rest.[31] This simple but ingenious device, as Marx perceptively notes, replaces not any particular tool, "but the hand itself." In this sense the slide rest is a technological breakthrough fully comparable in importance to the steam engine.

In his discussion of technological change within the capital goods sector, Marx has many acute observations which are tossed out without further development. New inventions often contain inefficient design features at the outset because the inventor has not shaken himself totally free of an earlier technology which is being displaced and whose operating principles have been rendered irrelevant. Marx observes:

> To what an extent the old forms of the instruments of production influenced their new forms at first starting, is shown by, amongst other things, the most superficial comparison of the present powerloom with the old one, of the modern blowing apparatus of a blast-furnace with the first inefficient mechanical reproduction of the ordinary bellows, and perhaps more strikingly than in any other way, by the attempts before the invention of the present locomotive, to construct a locomotive that actually had two feet, which after the fashion of a horse, it raised alternately from the ground. It is only after considerable development of the science of mechanics, and accumulated practical experience, that the form of a machine becomes settled entirely in accordance with mechanical principles, and emancipated from the traditional form of the tool that gave rise to it.[32]

It is a shame that posterity has been deprived of some sketch of the ill-fated, two-footed locomotive! But, more seriously, the last sentence can be read as a striking anticipation of some of the central ideas of Abbott Payson Usher, probably the most careful twentieth-century student of the history of technology.[33] For Marx is insistent that technology has to be understood as a social process. The history of invention is, most emphatically, not the history of inventors. Here, as in so many other realms, Marx's position cannot be understood without dealing with the basic methodological question: What is the most appropriate unit of analysis? His answer is that for questions pertaining to long-term changes in technology, the individual is *not* the appropriate unit. In this particular instance Marx is insisting that technological change cannot be adequately understood by examining the contributions of single individuals, even though he often acknowledges the noteworthy contributions of such individuals. Rather, one needs to examine the way in which larger social forces continually alter the focus of technological problems which require solutions. Within this framework one may then examine how the productive process has, in the past, shaped the development of scientific and technological knowledge and skills.[34] One is then in a position to explore the social process of problem formulation and eventual solution. In all of this, however, although individual human beings are, inevitably, the actors, the *dramatis personae* of the historical process, the actual unfolding of the plot turns upon the larger social forces which shape their actions. Within this larger framework it is possible to see the efforts and contributions of *numerous* individuals even though those twin bastions of individualism, the patent office and writers of history textbooks, require that the names of *single* individuals be written alongside the names of particular inventions. But what is really involved is a process of a cumulative accretion of useful knowledge, to which many people make essential contributions, even though the prizes and recognition are usually accorded to the one actor who happens to have been on the stage at a critical moment.

Usher would agree with Marx's stricture, quoted earlier, that "a critical history of technology would show how little any of the inventions of the eighteenth century are the work of a single individual." Usher's own analysis turns upon the study of problem formulation in dealing with technology, focusing especially upon the process which he describes as "the setting of the stage." It is the correct setting of the stage which makes possible the eventual act of insight leading to the solving of the problem (whether Watt's separate condenser or Bessemer's converter). As Usher points out: "Our analysis . . . redefines the question. It is not necessary to explain the final act of insight; the task now consists in explaining how the stage is set to suggest the solution of the perceived problem."[35] Moreover, this is not the end of the process, because the initial act of insight is likely to lead to crude and primitive solutions. "The setting of the stage leads directly to the act of insight by which the essential solution of the problem is found. But this does not bring the process to an end. Newly perceived relations must be thoroughly mastered, and effectively worked into the entire context of which they are a part. The solution must, therefore, be studied critically, understood in its fullness, and learned as a technique of thought or action. This final stage can be described as critical revision."[36]

I would regard the completion of Usher's stage of critical revision as bringing us to essentially the same point in the development of a technology that Marx had in mind in referring to the process by which "the form of a machine becomes settled entirely in accordance with mechanical principles, and emancipated from the traditional form of the tool that gave rise to it." Marx was aware of the regular need for something resembling Usher's final stage of critical revision and attached considerable importance to it. Indeed, there is implicit in Marx's analysis a kind of "life cycle" in the development of new techniques of production. New machines, when first introduced, are usually economically inefficient for two quite distinct reasons. First of all, the initial model has not yet had the opportunity to be subjected to a rigorous examination of its operations from which methods for performance improvement can be expected to flow. Marx pointed to continual improvements

> which lower the use-value, and therefore the value, of existing machines, factory buildings, etc. This process has a particularly dire effect during the first period of newly introduced machinery, before it attains a certain stage of maturity, when it continually becomes antiquated before it has time to reproduce its own value. This is one of the reasons for the flagrant prolongation of the working time usual in such periods, for alternating day and night shifts, so that the value of the machine may be reproduced in a shorter time without having to place the figures for wear and tear too high. If, on the other hand, the short period in which the machinery is effective (its short life vis-à-vis the anticipated improvements) is not compensated in this manner, it gives up so much of its value to the product through moral depreciation that it cannot even compete with hand-labor.[37]

The early model, therefore, is recognized to have a short life expectancy—a high rate of "moral depreciation"—and this expectation that it will shortly be swept away by the competition of improved models is an ever present consideration in the mind of the capitalist.

Eventually the new machine, having been subjected to a series of design improvements, assumes a relatively stabilized form, and at this point it becomes possible for the capital-goods sector to develop techniques for producing the machine more cheaply. This is where the capital-goods sector plays its critical role in the ongoing competitive process:

> After machinery, equipment of buildings, and fixed capi-
> tal in general, attain a certain maturity, so that they remain
> unaltered for some length of time at least in their basic con-
> struction, there arises a similar depreciation due to improve-
> ments in the methods of reproducing this fixed capital. The
> value of the machinery, etc., falls in this case not so much
> because the machinery is rapidly crowded out and depre-
> ciated to a certain degree by new and more productive ma-
> chinery, etc., but because it can be reproduced more cheaply.
> This is one of the reasons why large enterprises frequently
> do not flourish until they pass into other hands, i.e., after
> their first proprietors have been bankrupted, and their suc-
> cessors, who buy them cheaply, therefore begin from the
> outset with a smaller outlay of capital.[38]

Marx emphasized in several other places the high cost of the early machine models by comparison with the later ones.[39] His argument suggests a great deal, not only about the process through which a capitalist economy generates new techniques, but also about the speed with which new techniques will be spread throughout the economy.[40]

I do not propose to discuss the question whether Usher's work was influenced by Marx. That is not, in my view, terribly important. But I do want to insist upon the fruitfulness of certain ways of conceptualizing the technological process under capitalism which Marx suggested but never developed beyond some precocious and suggestive hints. I want also to render my judgment that American students of Marx, in creating a mode of analysis which they call "the Marxist tradition," have not been faithful, in at least one important respect, to the mode of analysis initiated by Marx himself. For Marx, as I have argued,

74

was a close student both of the history of technology and its newly emerging forms.

These strictures are only somewhat less applicable to the British Marxian tradition. For although it is true that the two leading British figures in the history of technology, J.D. Bernal and Joseph Needham, have frequently adverted to the strong Marxian component of their thinking, they have not, any more than others, followed Marx's hints or elaborated upon his insights concerning the development of modern industrial technology. This is a task which still remains to be undertaken.

Notes

1. Karl Marx, *Capital*, Vol. 1, Modern Library edition, p. 406, n. 2. All citations to the first volume of *Capital* are to this edition. The pagination is the same as in the Kerr edition.
2. This view goes back more than 50 years in the professional economics literature. See Alvin Hansen, "The Technological Interpretation of History," *Quarterly Journal of Economics,* November 1921, pp. 72-83.
3. Karl Marx, *The Poverty of Philosophy* (Moscow, n.d.), p. 105. The sentences which precede the one quoted above make Marx's meaning perfectly clear and reasonable. "Social relations are closely bound up with productive forces. In acquiring new productive forces men change their mode of production; and in changing their mode of production, in changing the way of earning their living, they change all their social relations." Moreover, as Marx points out later, "The hand-mill presupposes a different division of labor from the steam-mill" (ibid., p. 127). Surely one need not be a technological determinist to subscribe to these observations
4. Karl Marx and Friedrich Engels, *The Manifesto of the Communist Party*, in Karl Marx and Friedrich Engels, *Selected Works*, Vol. 1 (Moscow, 1951), p. 34. See also *Capital*, p. 823; *The Poverty of Philosophy*, pp. 129-33; and Karl Marx, *Grundrisse* (New York, 1973), pp. 505-11.
5. Marx, *Capital*, pp. 337-38, 367.
6. "While simple co-operation leaves the mode of working by the individual for the most part unchanged, manufacture

thoroughly revolutionizes it, and seizes labor power by its very roots. It converts the laborer into a crippled monstrosity, by forcing his detail dexterity at the expense of a world of productive capabilities and instincts; just as in the States of La Plata they butcher a whole beast for the sake of his hide or his tallow" (ibid., p. 396).

7. Ibid., p. 353. Note also that Marx's panegyrics on the technological dynamism of capitalism apply, *not* to capitalism throughout its history, but only to capitalism as it existed in the century or so before the writing of the *Communist Manifesto*. "The bourgeoisie, *during its rule of scarce one hundred years,* has created more massive and more colossal productive forces than have all preceding generations together" (Marx and Engels, *Manifesto*, p. 37, emphasis added).

8. For a forthright statement of technological determinism, see the work of the anthropologist Leslie A. White. According to White, a social system is "a function of a technological system." Furthermore, "Technology is the independent variable, the social system the dependent variable. Social systems are therefore determined by systems of technology; as the latter change, so do the former" (*The Science of Culture* [New York, 1971], p. 365).

9. Marx, *Grundrisse*, p. 278. Emphasis Marx's. Elsewhere he states: "Whenever a certain stage of maturity has been reached, the specific historical form is discarded and makes way for a higher one. The moment of arrival of such a crisis is disclosed by the depth and breadth attained by the contradictions and antagonisms between the distribution relations, and thus the specific historical form of their corresponding production relations, on the one hand, and the productive forces, the production powers and the development of their agencies, on the other hand. A conflict then ensues between the material development of production and its social form" (Karl Marx, *Capital*, Vol. 3 [Moscow, 1959], p. 861).

10. Marx, *Capital*, Vol. 1, p. 199.

11. Ibid., p. 198.

12. Ibid.

13. Ibid., p. 200, emphasis added. The paleontological mode of reasoning is continued after the passage quoted. Marx adds in a footnote on the same page: "However little our written histories up to this time notice the development of material production, which is the basis of all social life, and therefore

of all real history, yet prehistoric times have been classified in accordance with the results, not of so-called historical, but of materialistic investigations. These periods have been divided, to correspond with the materials from which their implements and weapons are made, viz., into the stone, the bronze, and the iron ages."

14. Simon Kuznets, *Modern Economic Growth* (New Haven, 1966), p. 9.

15. *Capital,* Vol. 1, pp. 371-72.

16. Ibid., p. 504.

17. Ibid., p. 532. For further discussion of these and related issues, see Nathan Rosenberg, "Karl Marx on the Economic Role of Science," *Journal of Political Economy,* July-August 1974, pp. 713-28.

18. For some tentative exploration of these relationships, see Nathan Rosenberg, "Science, Invention and Economic Growth," *Economic Journal,* March 1974, pp. 90-108.

19. "As inventions increased in number, and the demand for the newly discovered machines grew larger, the machine-making industry split up, more and more, into numerous independent branches, and division of labor in these manufactures more and more developed. Here, then, we see in Manufacturing the immediate technical foundation of Modern Industry. Manufacturing produced the machinery, by means of which Modern Industry abolished the handicraft and manufacturing systems in those spheres of production that it first seized upon" (*Capital,* Vol. 1, p. 417).

20. Ibid., p. 418.

21. Ibid., p. 420. See also pp. 417-18 and 421.

22. Ibid., p. 492.

23. Karl Marx, *Capital,* Vol. 3, p. 79.

24. Ibid., p. 100. Later Marx adds: "The most striking example of utilizing waste is furnished by the chemical industry. It utilizes not only its own waste, for which it finds new uses, but also that of many other industries. For instance, it converts the formerly almost useless gas-tar into aniline dyes, alizarin, and, more recently, even into drugs" (ibid., p. 102).

25. Ibid., p. 80.

26. Ibid., p. 81. See also p. 84.

27. Ibid., pp. 81-82.

28. Ibid., p. 71.

29. "From the moment that the tool is taken from man, and

fitted into a mechanism, a machine takes the place of a mere implement" (*Capital*, Vol. 1, p. 408).

30. Ibid.
31. Ibid., p. 420.
32. Ibid., p. 418.
33. See Abbott Payson Usher, *A History of Mechanical Inventions*, rev. ed. (Cambridge, Mass., 1954), especially Chapter 4, "The Emergence of Novelty in Thought and Action."
34. In all of this, the natural environment plays a critical role. "It is not the tropics with their luxuriant vegetation, but the temperate zone that is the mother country of capital. It is not the mere fertility of the soil, but the differentiation of the soil, the variety of its natural products, the changes of the seasons, which form the physical basis for the social division of labor, and which, by changes in the natural surroundings, spur man on to the multiplication of his wants, his capabilities, his means and modes of labor. It is the necessity of bringing a natural force under the control of society, of economizing, of appropriating or subduing it on a large scale by the work of man's hand, that first plays the decisive part in the history of industry" (*Capital*, pp. 563-64).
35. *A History of Mechanical Inventions*, p. 78.
36. Ibid., p. 65.
37. *Capital*, Vol. 3, p. 112.
38. Ibid.
39. Ibid., p. 103, and *Capital*, Vol. 1, p. 442. Marx cites Babbage for supporting evidence in both places and Ure in the former. Both arguments—with respect to improvements in machine design and improvements in techniques for producing the machines—are combined in *Capital*, Vol. 1, p. 442: "When machinery is first introduced into an industry, new methods of reproducing it more cheaply follow blow upon blow, and so do improvements, that not only affect individual parts and details of the machine, but its entire build. It is, therefore, in the early days of the life of machinery that this special incentive to the prolongation of the working day makes itself felt most acutely."
40. See Nathan Rosenberg, "Factors Affecting the Diffusion of Technology," *Explorations in Economic History*, Fall 1972, pp. 3-33.

3   Joseph Schumpeter: radical economist

I

This chapter will deal with Schumpeter's book, *Capitalism, Socialism and Democracy*, as the mature statement of the most radical scholar in the discipline of economics in the twentieth century.

Of course, I do not mean to suggest that Joseph Schumpeter held views on the organization of the economy, or society generally, that make it appropriate to label him as a radical in the political sense. In his social and political views Schumpeter was anything but radical. In fact, one could make a case – although I do not propose to do so – that Schumpeter was not merely conservative in his social views, but reactionary. In his most private thoughts, as suggested by a recent biography, he seemed to possess an insatiable longing for the glorious later days of the Hapsburg monarchy. Moreover, the most charitable characterization of his attitude toward Nazi Germany in the darkest days of the 1930s and the Second World War is that he was ambivalent.

The reason I propose to call Schumpeter a radical is that he urged the rejection of the most central and precious tenets of neo-classical theory. Indeed, I want to insist that very little of the complex edifice of neo-classical economics, as it existed in the late 1930s and 1940s, survives the sweep of Schumpeter's devastating assaults. But in examining Schumpeter's criticisms, it is not my primary intention to enlist his authority in an attack upon neo-classical economics. Rather, I propose to show that the quintessential, later Schumpeter, the author of *Capitalism, Socialism and Democracy*, held views that were not only genuinely radical, but that are deserving of far more serious attention than they receive today, even, or perhaps especially,

This chapter was first presented at the meetings of the Schumpeter Society in Kyoto, in August, 1992. That meeting marked the fiftieth anniversary of the publication of *Capitalism, Socialism, and Democracy*.

47

48   **Dealing with an uncertain future**

from scholars who think of themselves as working within the Schumpeterian tradition. While this chapter focuses on *Capitalism, Socialism, and Democracy*, I draw upon Schumpeter's other writings to round out the argument and interpretation that I am proposing.

II

I begin by quoting from Schumpeter's preface to the Japanese edition of *The Theory of Economic Development*, for in that preface Schumpeter sketches out what is probably the most precise and succinct statement of his own intellectual agenda that he ever committed to print. That agenda focuses not only upon the understanding of how the economic system generates economic change, but also upon how that change occurs as a result of the working out of purely endogenous forces:

If my Japanese readers asked me before opening the book what it is that I was aiming at when I wrote it, more than a quarter of a century ago, I would answer that I was trying to construct a theoretic model of the process of economic change in time, or perhaps more clearly, to answer the question how the economic system generates the force which incessantly transforms it ... I felt very strongly that ... there was a source of energy within the economic system which would of itself disrupt any equilibrium that might be attained. If this is so, then there must be a purely economic theory of economic change which does not merely rely on external factors propelling the economic system from one equilibrium to another. It is such a theory that I have tried to build.[1]

It should be noted that these words were published in 1937, when Schumpeter was, as we know, already at work on *Capitalism, Socialism and Democracy*. In fact, I regard *Capitalism, Socialism and Democracy* as the fulfillment of precisely the intellectual agenda that Schumpeter articulated in the passage to his Japanese readers that I have just quoted.

Of course, an account of how and why economic change took place was precisely something that could not be provided within the "rigorously static" framework of neo-classical equilibrium analysis, as Schumpeter referred to it. Schumpeter also observed that it was Walras' view that economic theory was only capable of examining a "stationary process," that is, "a process which actually does not change of its own initiative, but merely produces constant rates of real income as it flows along in time." As Schumpeter interprets Walras:

[1] Joseph Schumpeter, Preface to Japanese edition of *Theorie Der Wirtschaftlichen Entwicklung*, as translated by I. Nakayama and S. Tobata, Tokyo, Iwanami Shoten, 1937. As reprinted in *Essays of J.A. Schumpeter*, ed. Richard V. Clemence, Addison-Wesley, Cambridge (MA), 1951, p. 158.

He would have said (and, as a matter of fact, he did say it to me the only time that I had the opportunity to converse with him) that of course economic life is essentially passive and merely adapts itself to the natural and social influences which may be acting on it, so that the theory of a stationary process constitutes really the whole of theoretical economics and that as economic theorists we cannot say much about the factors that account for historical change, but must simply register them.[2]

The critical point here is that Schumpeter directly rejects the view of Walras that economic theory must be confined to the study of the stationary process, and that it cannot go farther than demonstrating how departures from equilibrium, such as might be generated by a growth in population or in savings, merely set into motion forces that restore the system to an equilibrium path. In proposing to develop a theory showing how a stationary process can be disturbed by internal as well as external forces, Schumpeter is suggesting that the essence of capitalism lies not in equilibrating forces but in the inevitable tendency of that system to *depart* from equilibrium – in a word, to disequilibrate. Equilibrium analysis fails to capture the essence of capitalist reality. Lest there should be any doubt about Schumpeter's position on this critical matter, we cite his own forceful formulation: "Whereas a stationary feudal economy would still be a feudal economy, and a stationary socialist economy would still be a socialist economy, stationary capitalism is a contradiction in terms."[3]

Although Schumpeter did in fact make important use of Walrasian general equilibrium in his analysis of the circular flow in a stationary state, he used the concept precisely as a means of demonstrating how capitalist economies would behave *if they were deprived of their essential feature*: that is, innovative activities that are the primary generator of economic change.

It is important to understand this methodological use that Schumpeter makes of the neo-classical analysis of a stationary economic process. As Schumpeter stated: "In appraising the performance of competitive enterprise, the question whether it would or would not tend to maximize production in a perfectly equilibrated stationary condition of the economic process is ... almost, though not quite, irrelevant."[4]

The reason it is not completely irrelevant is that the model of a stationary competitive process helps us to understand the behavior of an economy that possesses no internal forces generating economic change. Thus, the model of a Walrasian circular flow constitutes Schumpeter's starting point in understanding the essential elements of capitalist reality because it shows

[2] *Ibid.*, pp. 2–3.
[3] Joseph Schumpeter, "Capitalism in the Postwar World," in *Essays of J.A. Schumpeter*, ed. Clemence, p. 174.
[4] Joseph Schumpeter, *Capitalism, Socialism and Democracy*, second edition, George Allen & Unwin, Ltd., London, 1943, p. 77.

how that system would behave in the absence of its most distinctive feature – innovation. It is an invaluable abstraction precisely because it makes it possible to trace out with greater precision the impact of innovative activity. This is the role served by the Walrasian conception of the circular flow in Schumpeter's analysis of business cycles as well as growth.

Of course, one can always adopt the position that Schumpeter and neo-classical economics address very different questions, and that the theoretical analysis of each is valid in its particular intellectual context. Newton's law of gravity, after all, was not invalidated by Mendeleev's periodic table of the elements. Each theory was devised to account for different classes of phenomena. They do not contradict each other and they may, therefore, be simultaneously valid – or invalid.

I believe that there is something to be said in support of such a position. But I am not at all confident that the Schumpeter of part II of *Capitalism, Socialism and Democracy* would have been satisfied with it. Schumpeter's position seems to be that, if you want to understand what capitalism is all about as an economic system, the fundamental question is how it generates economic change rather than how it restores stability. Not all theoretical frameworks are equally useful in analyzing the essential feature of modern capitalism. And again, the essential feature, in Schumpeter's view, is economic change. This is because the capitalist form of economic organization has a built-in logic that dominates the behavior of that economic system. Thus, economists who purport to have something to say that is pertinent to the contemporary operation of capitalism have the obligation to deal with certain distinctive patterns of capitalist behavior and to explain their consequences. The behavior of capitalism is totally dominated by the continual working out of its inner logic, the essence of which is economic change resulting from the impact of the innovation process.

Equilibrium analysis, on the other hand, focuses upon adjustment mechanisms that are only peripheral, and not central, to the logic of capitalist organization and incentives. Therefore a theoretical approach that neglects persistent disequilibrium, instability and growth is an approach that deals with processes that are, at best, phenomena of secondary importance, or only mere epiphenomena.[5]

III

I do not propose to examine in any detail Schumpeter's views on innovation, or the breadth of his definition of innovation, since these are

---

[5] For a perceptive examination of the limits of equilibrium analysis in the context of innovation studies, see Richard R. Nelson, "Schumpeter and Contemporary Research on the Economics of Innovation," unpublished manuscript, Columbia University, February 1992.

familiar to all readers of his major works. I do, however, propose to underline the rather radical implications that Schumpeter himself drew from the primacy that he attached to innovation – implications that have received little attention. The dynamic forces that are inherent in the capitalist structure lead Schumpeter to treat capitalism as a system whose essential feature is an evolutionary process and not the mechanisms that force the system to revert to an equilibrium after some external force has produced a small departure from that equilibrium. For those who find the term "disequilibrium analysis" too paradoxical to be useful as a description of Schumpeter's mode of economic analysis, I suggest the propriety of the term "evolutionary." My justification is a simple one: it is Schumpeter's own frequently used term in *Capitalism, Socialism and Democracy*:

The essential point to grasp is that in dealing with capitalism we are dealing with an evolutionary process ... Capitalism ... is by nature a form or method of economic change and not only never is but never can be stationary. And this evolutionary character of the capitalist process is not merely due to the fact that economic life goes on in a social and natural environment which changes and by its changes alters the data of economic action; this fact is important and these changes (wars, revolutions and so on) often condition industrial change, but they are not its prime movers. Nor is this evolutionary character due to a quasi-automatic increase in population and capital or to the vagaries of monetary systems of which exactly the same thing holds true.[6]

I ask readers of *Capitalism, Socialism and Democracy* to ponder the far-reaching implications of this statement. For it involves not only the recognition of the inherently dynamic nature of capitalism. It involves also nothing less than the rejection of the competitive ideal itself, as that ideal is enshrined not only in economists' models but also in decades of government regulation and, in the United States, in a full century of anti-trust legislation. In this view, textbook competition is not an ideal state to be pursued. The welfare implications of the competitive ideal reflect a mistaken preoccupation with the distinctly secondary issue of how the economy allocates an existing stock of resources; whereas the far more significant concern for Schumpeter is how successful an economic system is at generating growth – growth in a qualitative as well as a quantitative sense. In my own reading, this deserves to be regarded as the central message of *Capitalism, Socialism and Democracy*. Capitalists survive, if they survive at all, by learning to live in, and to participate in, a "perennial gale of creative destruction ... the problem that is usually being visualized is how capitalism administers existing structures, whereas the relevant problem is how it creates and destroys them."[7] I call attention to the

---

[6] Schumpeter, *Capitalism, Socialism and Democracy*, p. 82. See also *ibid.*, p. 58.
[7] *Ibid.*, p. 84.

significant fact that Schumpeter attached so much importance to this last observation that he repeated it, almost verbatim, in the preface to the second edition of *Capitalism, Socialism and Democracy*.[8]

In my view, if one is looking for a distinctively "Schumpeterian hypothesis," it lies in this definition of the essential nature of the competitive process. Perhaps this should not be regarded as a hypothesis, since it is difficult to reduce it to a testable, potentially refutable form. It is more in the nature of a conception or, better, to use a favorite Schumpeterian term, a "vision" of the essential nature of capitalism. It is a vision in which it is a mistake to reduce monopoly to the purely restrictive and anti-social consequences that are normally ascribed to it, since monopoly power is often a temporary adjunct of the process of creative destruction. The Schumpeter of *Capitalism, Socialism and Democracy* does indeed attach considerable significance to the growth in the absolute size of the firm in the course of the twentieth century. At the same time, I would like to insist that a "Schumpeterian hypothesis," which postulates a strong association between market power and innovation, is an extreme oversimplification of a much more sophisticated – and much more radical – view of the meaning of competition.[9]

Thus, Schumpeter is involved in an explicit rejection of the central neoclassical notion that atomistic competition offers unique welfare advantages. In *Capitalism, Socialism and Democracy* he posits a novel conception of competition based upon innovation as a central element in a disequilibrium process that leads the economy to higher levels of income, output, and, presumably, well-being. In the course of the twentieth century the large-scale firm, with its internal research capabilities, has become the dominant engine of technical progress. This is a main theme of *Capitalism, Socialism and Democracy*, as opposed to his earlier book, *The Theory of Economic Development*. Schumpeter's argument is certainly closely tied to bigness and to the dismissal of the virtues of perfect competition. It recognizes some degree of monopoly power as a passing phase of the innovation process. But rejecting the virtues of perfect competition is not the same thing as saying that monopoly power is inherently favorable to innovation.

Thus it is not sufficient to argue that because perfect competition is impossible under modern industrial conditions – or because it always has been impossible – the large-scale establishment or unit of control must be accepted as a necessary evil inseparable from the economic progress which it is prevented from sabotaging by the forces inherent in its productive apparatus. What we have got to accept is that it

---

[8] *Ibid.*, p. x.
[9] See Nelson, "Schumpeter and Contemporary Research on the Economics of Innovation," for an illuminating discussion of this issue.

has come to be the most powerful engine of that progress and in particular of the long-run expansion of total output not only in spite of, but to a considerable extend through, this strategy which looks so restrictive when viewed in the individual case and from the individual point of time. In this respect, perfect competition is not only impossible but inferior, and has no title to being set up as a model of ideal efficiency.[10]

Indeed, the perennial gale of creative destruction is continually sweeping away entrenched monopoly power that appeared so secure until a new innovation consigned it to the scrapheap of history. That is precisely why the perennial gale is such a critically important economic force.

IV

But there is much more to Schumpeter the radical anti-neo-classicist than has been suggested so far. This becomes apparent as soon as it is recognized that innovation, the central feature of capitalist reality, is not a product of a decision-making process that can be described or analyzed as "rational":

the assumption that business behaviour is ideally rational and prompt, and also that in principle it is the same with all firms, works tolerably well only within the precincts of tried experience and familiar motive. It breaks down as soon as we leave those precincts and allow the business community under study to be faced by – not simply new situations, which also occur as soon as external factors unexpectedly intrude but by – new possibilities of business action which are as yet untried and about which the most complete command of routine teaches nothing. Those differences in the behaviour of different people which within those precincts account for secondary phenomena only, become essential in the sense that they now account for the outstanding features of reality and that a picture drawn on the Walras-Marshallian lines ceases to be true – even in the qualified sense in which it is true of stationary and growing processes: it misses those features, and becomes wrong in the endeavour to account by means of its own analysis for phenomena which the assumptions of that analysis exclude.[11]

It is, of course, difficult to imagine a more profound rejection of neo-classical economics than is embodied in Schumpeter's forceful assertion that the most important feature of capitalist reality – innovation – is one to which rational decision-making has no direct application. The nature of the innovation process, the drastic departure from existing routines, is inherently one that cannot be reduced to mere calculation, although subsequent imitation of the innovation, once accomplished, can be so reduced. Innovation is the creation of knowledge that cannot, and therefore should

[10] Schumpeter, *Capitalism, Socialism and Democracy*, p. 106.
[11] Joseph Schumpeter, *Business Cycles*, 2 vols., McGraw-Hill Book Company, New York, 1939, vol. I, pp. 98–99.

54   **Dealing with an uncertain future**

not, be "anticipated" by the theorist in a purely formal manner, as is done in the theory of decision-making under uncertainty. In Schumpeter's view, it would be entirely meaningless to speak of "the future state of the world," as that state is not merely unknown, but also indefinable in empirical and historical terms. Serious doubt is thus cast on what meaning, if any, can be possessed by intertemporal models of equilibrium under uncertainty, in which the essential nature of innovation is systematically neglected.

Thus, if rationality is reduced in the neo-classical world more and more to the tautology that people do the best they can, given the whole gamut of constraints they face – among the most important of which is the informational constraint – then accepting Schumpeter's concept of innovation means that human actions are always second best in a way that ultimately cannot be subjected to further analysis. For rational behavior, in Schumpeter's view, is most significant in a world of routine and repetition of similar events. (Needless to say, the modern literature on rational expectations does not overcome Schumpeter's strictures here. The "rationality" of rational expectations is limited by currently available information, and thus the inherent uncertainty concerning the future is not eliminated).

But this is not the end of Schumpeter's rather complex treatment of the role of rationality. If one considers rationality in the long historical context, Schumpeter mounts an argument in *Capitalism, Socialism and Democracy* the essential element of which is that capitalism, considered as a civilization, has continuously enlarged the social space within which rationalistic attitudes and habits of thought come to prevail.[12] In chapter 11, "The Civilization of Capitalism," Schumpeter argues that capitalism has expanded the sphere within which "rational cost-profit calculations" could be carried out. Moreover,

primarily a product of the evolution of economic rationality, the cost-profit calculus in turn reacts upon that rationality; by crystallizing and defining numerically, it powerfully propels the logic of enterprise. And thus defined and quantified for the economic sector, this type of logic or attitude or method then starts upon its conqueror's career, subjugating – rationalizing – man's tools and philosophies, his medical practice, his picture of the cosmos, his outlook on life, everything in fact including his concepts of beauty and justice and his spiritual ambitions.[13]

This aspect of Schumpeter's argument – what he himself might have described as his own "economic sociology" – is, in my opinion, analytically brilliant, breathtaking in its sweep and, historically, substantially correct. I regret that it is impossible here to examine his argument in detail. I remind

---

[12] Contrast this view with Babbage's treatment of rationality and the "Mental Division of Labour" in the previous chapter.
[13] Schumpeter, *Capitalism, Socialism and Democracy*, pp. 123–124.

you of it now because it is the linch pin of Schumpeter's argument that capitalism will eventually "self-destruct." The self-destruction is inevitable because, in his view, the historical expansion of rationality brings in its wake two crucial consequences.

The first is that rationality challenges and unfrocks beliefs and institutions that cannot survive the searching and corrosive glare of a (presumably narrow) rationality: "When the habit of rational analysis of, and rational behavior in, the daily tasks of life has gone far enough, it turns back upon the mass of collective ideas and criticizes and to some extent 'rationalizes' them by way of such questions as why there should be kings and popes or subordination or tithes or property."[14]

The second consequence is that, as capitalism expands the sphere to which rationality applies, it learns eventually how to supplant the entrepreneur, the human "carrier" of innovation, with institutions that do away with the social leadership of the entrepreneur himself. The entrepreneurial function itself becomes rationalized – or bureaucratized – with the growth of the large firm. "For . . . it is now much easier than it has been in the past to do things that lie outside familiar routine – innovation itself has been reduced to routine. Technological progress is increasingly becoming the business of teams of trained specialists who turn out what is required and make it work in predictable ways."[15]

Of course, the growth of large-scale enterprise and the "obsolescence of the entrepreneurial function" led Schumpeter, through the rich argument of his economic and political sociology, to his conclusion that capitalism cannot survive. The ideology and social myths that once sustained it cannot survive its tendency to "automatize progress"[16] and thus to reveal its new-found ability to do without the leadership and vitality once provided by the entrepreneur and the bourgeoisie.

My own view – with the easy wisdom of fifty years of retrospection – is that Schumpeter much overstated the extent to which technological progress would become automatized. I believe that this, in turn, is partly due to his intensive focus upon the earliest stages in the innovation process, and to his failure to consider the degree to which commercial success is dependent upon subsequent stages in the carrying out of an innovation. But, regrettably, these issues cannot be explored here. What is essential to my examination of Schumpeter the radical is the observation that, both in the past and in the future, it is Schumpeter's view that a rational approach to the innovation process is incompatible with capitalist institutions. So long as the function was carried out by the individual entrepreneur, it was an act based upon intuition and charismatic leadership; when capitalist

---

[14] *Ibid.*, p. 122.   [15] *Ibid.*, p. 132.   [16] *Ibid.*, p. 134.

56   **Dealing with an uncertain future**

institutions eventually, at some future date, succeed in subjecting innovation to a rationalized routine, those institutions will, *ipso facto*, lose their lustre and social justification, and be replaced by a socialized state.

Thus, in a world where capitalist institutions continue to prevail, innovation calls upon a decision-making process that goes beyond rational calculation. When capitalist development eventually leads to the institutionalization of innovation, the organizational basis of the economy will, Schumpeter believes, be transformed into some form of socialism. In neither case, ironically, does Schumpeter concede a significant role for the neo-classical analysis of rational behavior.

V

Schumpeter's radical anti-neo-classical stance extends even to the issue of what it is that constitutes the *explicanda* of economic analysis. It is normal practice for neo-classical economists to take tastes and technology as exogenously given, and to seek to examine issues of resource allocation by explicit reference to changes in incomes and relative prices.[17]

Thus, Schumpeter's assault upon neo-classical economics includes even his deliberate violation of the *sanctum sanctorum* of the neo-classical citadel: the commitments to the exogeneity of consumer preferences and the associated virtues of consumer sovereignty. His belief that the central problem of the economist is to account for economic change over time undoubtedly played an important role in sharpening his perception of the forces influencing consumer preferences:

Innovations in the economic system do not as a rule take place in such a way that first new wants arise spontaneously in consumers and then the productive apparatus swings round through their pressure. We do not deny the presence of this nexus. It is, however, the producer who as a rule initiates economic change, and consumers are educated by him if necessary; they are, as it were, taught to want new things, or things which differ in some respect or other from those which they have been in the habit of using. Therefore, while it is permissible and even necessary to consider consumers' wants as an independent and indeed the fundamental force in a theory of the circular flow, we must take a different attitude as soon as we analyse *change*.[18]

Schumpeter made the same essential point later on in *Business Cycles*:

We will, throughout, act on the assumption that consumers' initiative in changing their tastes – i.e., in changing that set of our data which general theory comprises in

---

[17] See George Stigler and Gary Becker, "De Gustibus non est Disputandum," *American Economic Review*, 67 (1977), pp. 76–90.

[18] Joseph Schumpeter, *The Theory of Economic Development*, Harvard University Press, Cambridge (MA), 1949, p. 65 Schumpeter's italics. (first published in German in 1911).

the concepts of "utility functions" or "indifference varieties" – is negligible and that all change in consumers' tastes is incident to, and brought about by, producers' actions. This requires both justification and qualification.

The fact on which we stand is, of course, common knowledge. Railroads have not emerged because any consumers took the initiative in displaying an effective demand for their service in preference to the services of mail coaches. Nor did the consumers display any such initiative wish to have electric lamps or rayon stockings, or to travel by motorcar or airplane, or to listen to radios, or to chew gum. There is obviously no lack of realism in the proposition that the great majority of changes in commodities consumed has been forced by producers on consumers who, more often than not, have resisted the change and have had to be educated up by elaborate psychotechnics of advertising.[19]

Although modern economists have, of course, investigated the consequences of endogenous preferences for welfare judgments, most have considered it better, for reasons of division of labor with other disciplines, in particular psychology, to neglect the investigation of why and how tastes change.[20] But Schumpeter asserted that innovation, the fundamental driving force of the historical evolution of capitalism, would mould tastes as well as technology in unexpected ways. The implications, both for the development of the economic and social systems, as well as for microeconomic welfare judgments were, as Schumpeter recognized, potentially radical. Just before his death in 1950 he severely criticized economists for the uncritical belief that so many seem to harbor in the virtues of consumers' choice:

First of all, whether we like it or not, we are witnessing a momentous experiment in malleability of tastes – is not this worth analyzing? Second, ever since the physiocrats (and before), economists have professed unbounded respect for the consumers' choice – is it not time to investigate what the bases for this respect are and how far the traditional and, in part, advertisement-shaped tastes of people are subject to the qualification that they might prefer other things than those which they want at present as soon as they have acquired familiarity with these other things? In matters of education, health, and housing there is already practical unanimity about this – but might the principle not be carried much further? Third, economic theory accepts existing tastes as data, no matter whether it postulates utility functions or indifference varieties or simply preference directions, and these data are made the starting point of price theory. Hence, they must be considered as independent of prices. But considerable and persistent changes in prices obviously do react upon tastes. *What, then, is to become of our theory and the whole of microeconomics?* It is investigations of this kind, that might break new ground, which I miss.[21]

[19] Schumpeter, *Business Cycles*, vol. I, p. 73.
[20] See, for example, Milton Friedman, *Price Theory*, Aldine Publishing Company, New York, 1976, p. 13.
[21] Joseph Schumpeter, "English Economists and the State-Managed Economy," *Journal of Political Economy* (1949), pp. 380–381. Schumpeter's italics.

The earlier discussion of Schumpeter's analysis of innovation has already anticipated his unwillingness to treat technological change, as well as consumers' tastes, as an exogenous phenomenon. But it is necessary to distinguish between the earlier Schumpeter of *The Theory of Economic Development* (1911) and the later Schumpeter of *Capitalism, Socialism and Democracy* (1942). In his earlier book, Schumpeter looked upon invention as an exogenous activity and upon innovation as endogenous. Whereas inventors conducted their activities off the economic stage and contributed their artifacts to a pool of invention, the timing of the entrepreneurial decision to draw from this pool was decisively shaped by economic forces. But the later Schumpeter saw both invention and innovation as generated by economic forces inside the large firm with its own internal research capabilities. The reason for the change in Schumpeter's views during this period is not far to seek: the economic world, the object of Schumpeter's studies, had changed substantially during the period between the publication of the two books. Schumpeter's altered views were an acknowledgment of empirical changes that had occurred during his own professional lifetime.

Schumpeter's insistence upon the role of endogenous forces applies, not only to technology, but also to science itself. The rationalizing influence of the capitalistic mentality and institutions created "the growth of rational science" as well as its "long list of applications."[22] Significantly, Schumpeter cites as examples not only "Airplanes, refrigerators, television and that sort of thing . . ." but also the "modern hospital." Although one might be surprised at the appearance here of an institution that is not commonly operated on a profitmaking basis, Schumpeter's explanation is illuminating. It is

fundamentally because capitalist rationality supplied the habits of mind that evolved the methods used in these hospitals. And the victories, not yet completely won but in the offing, over cancer, syphilis and tuberculosis will be as much capitalist achievements as motorcars or pipe lines or Bessemer steel have been. In the case of medicine, there is a capitalist profession behind the methods, capitalist both because to a large extent it works in a business spirit and because it is an emulsion of the industrial and commercial bourgeoisie. But even if that were not so, modern medicine and hygiene would still be by-products of the capitalist process just as is modern education.[23]

Thus, Schumpeter insisted that both science and technology, normally so far from the world of phenomena examined by neo-classical economics, are in reality highly endogenous to the economic world, subject to the gravitational pull of economic forces. In one of the last articles published during his own lifetime, Schumpeter identified his views with those of Marx

---

[22] Schumpeter, *Capitalism, Socialism and Democracy*, p. 125.   [23] *Ibid.*, pp. 125–126.

on the role played by western capitalism in accounting for progress in both science and technology. Schumpeter observed that Marx had, in the *Communist Manifesto*, "launched out on a panegyric upon bourgeois achievement that has no equal in economic literature." After quoting a relevant portion of the text, he says:

No reputable "bourgeois" economist of that or any other time – certainly not A. Smith or J.S. Mill – ever said as much as this. Observe, in particular, the emphasis upon the creative role of the business class that the majority of the most "bourgeois" economists so persistently overlooked and of the business class as such, whereas most of us would, on the one hand, also insert into the picture non-bourgeois contributions to the bourgeois success – the contributions of non-bourgeois bureaucracies, for instance – and, on the other hand, commit the mistake (for such I believe it is) to list as independent factors science and technology, whereas Marx's sociology enabled him to see that these as well as "progress" in such fields as education and hygiene were just as much the products of the bourgeois culture – hence, ultimately, of the business class – as was the business performance itself.[24]

Did Schumpeter then believe, along with Marx, in the economic interpretation of history? I suggest that he did, with certain qualifications. However, the qualifications that Schumpeter imposed upon the economic interpretation of history were of a sort that, if anything, actually strengthened its usefulness as a device for explaining economic change. It is important here to recall that the first four chapters of *Capitalism, Socialism and Democracy* are devoted entirely to an examination of Marx's views on a range of subjects. Schumpeter offered a sympathetic and approving treatment of the economic interpretation of history; moreover, almost all of his own writing fits conveniently into that interpretation. But Schumpeter also compresses the economic interpretation into just two propositions:

1. The forms or conditions of production are the fundamental determinants of social structures which in turn breed attitudes, actions and civilizations.
2. The forms of production themselves have a logic of their own; that is to say, they change according to necessities inherent in them so as to produce their successors merely by their own working.[25]

Schumpeter asserts that "Both propositions undoubtedly contain a large amount of truth and are, as we shall find at several turns of our way, invaluable working hypotheses."[26] His main qualification, if that is what it really is, is his insistence upon the importance of lags, that is, social forms that persist after they have lost their economic rationale. It is far from clear that Marx would have disagreed with such a qualification, since Marx was much too sophisticated a historian to believe that economic changes

[24] Joseph Schumpeter, "The Communist Manifesto in Sociology and Economics," *Journal of Political Economy* (1949), p. 293. See also *Capitalism, Socialism and Democracy*, chapter 1.
[25] Schumpeter, *Capitalism, Socialism and Democracy*, pp. 11–12.   [26] *Ibid.*, p. 12.

60   **Dealing with an uncertain future**

generated the "appropriate" social changes instantaneously. Schumpeter, in making the qualification about lags, adds that Marx, although perhaps not fully appreciating their implications, would not have taken the simplistic position involved in denying them a role:

> Social structures, types and attitudes are coins that do not readily melt. Once they are formed they persist, possibly for centuries, and since different structures and types display different degrees of this ability to survive, we almost always find that actual group and national behaviour more or less departs from what we should expect it to be if we tried to infer it from the dominant forms of the productive process. Though this applies quite generally, it is most clearly seen when a highly durable structure transfers itself bodily from one country to another. The social situation created in Sicily by the Norman conquest will illustrate my meaning. Such facts Marx did not overlook but he hardly realized all their implications.[27]

VI

Whether or not one concludes, as I do, that Schumpeter believed in a form of the economic interpretation of history, he clearly was strongly committed to the view that economic phenomena, in order to be meaningfully examined, must be studied in an historical context. Since I have spent a significant portion of my own professional life studying economic behavior in historical contexts, I am naturally pleased to be able to invoke the authority of Schumpeter in support of such an approach. At the same time, I believe that this interpretation of Schumpeter is more than a merely self-serving exercise on my part.

The fact is that most of what Schumpeter wrote qualifies as history, both economic and intellectual. Not only *Capitalism, Socialism and Democracy* but, in addition, *Business Cycles* and his posthumous *History of Economic Analysis* are historical works. His commitment to the historical approach was deeply rooted in his thought. Schumpeter had a profound appreciation of the path-dependent nature of economic phenomena and therefore of economic analysis itself.[28] More than this. The very subject matter of economics, in Schumpeter's view, *is* history. Economics is about economic change as it has occurred over historical time. That is why he insists upon the importance of studying capitalism as an evolutionary process. It is also why he assigns such a limited importance to the study of stationary economic processes. And these things have a great deal to do with Schumpeter's highest regard for some of Marx's contributions to economic analysis:

---

[27] *Ibid.*, pp. 12–13.
[28] For a more precise definition of path dependence and further analysis of the relationship between modern economic theory and historical analysis, see chapter 1 in this book.

Joseph Schumpeter: radical economist

There is . . . one thing of fundamental importance for the methodology of economics which he actually achieved. Economists always have either themselves done work in economic history or else used the historical work of others. But the facts of economic history were assigned to a separate compartment. They entered theory, if at all, merely in the role of illustrations, or possibly of verifications of results. They mixed with it only mechanically. Now Marx's mixture is a chemical one; that is to say, he introduced them into the very argument that produces the results. He was the first economist of top rank to see and to teach systematically how economic theory may be turned into historical analysis and how the historical narrative may be turned into *histoire raisonnée*.[29]

This passage, it seems to me, is also the best explanation for Schumpeter's frequent expression of admiration for, and intellectual indebtedness to Marx.

I can think of no better way of closing this chapter than by reminding you of certain views that Schumpeter expressed in chapter 2 of his *History of Economic Analysis*. After stating that a "scientific" economist is to be identified by the demonstrated command over three techniques – history, statistics, and theory – he goes on to say:

Of these fundamental fields, economic history – which issues into and includes present-day facts – is by far the most important. I wish to state right now that if, starting my work in economics afresh, I were told that I could study only one of the three but could have my choice, it would be economic history that I should choose. And this on three grounds. First, the subject matter of economics is essentially a unique process in historic time. Nobody can hope to understand the economic phenomena of any, including the present, epoch who has not an adequate command of historical facts and an adequate amount of historical sense or of what may be described as *historical experience*. Second, the historical report cannot be purely economic but must inevitably reflect also "institutional" facts that are not purely economic; therefore it affords the best method for understanding how economic and non-economic facts *are* related to one another and how the various social sciences *should* be related to one another. Third, it is, I believe, the fact that most of the fundamental errors currently committed in economic analysis are due to a lack of historical experience more often than to any other shortcoming of the economist's equipment.[30]

It is sad to have to conclude with the observation that some knowledge of history is still not regarded as essential to competent economic analysis. Indeed, judging by the curricula of the graduate programs in American universities today, the very idea would appear to be distinctly perverse and alien. In this, as in so many other respects, Schumpeter the radical economist still has a great deal to teach us.

[29] *Ibid.*, p. 44.

[30] Joseph Schumpeter, *History of Economic Analysis*, Oxford University Press, New York, 1954, pp. 12–13. Schumpeter's italics.

[12]

George Stigler: Adam Smith's Best Friend

Nathan Rosenberg

Stanford University

Let me begin by admitting that I had to overcome a certain amount of diffidence in preparing this paper. George Stigler was, of course, one of the great economists of his generation, and his writings are well known to most economists. Or, to put it somewhat differently, no economist of our day can possibly be regarded as well informed who is not at least reasonably familiar with Stigler's main contributions to the discipline. Saying something new about his writings would therefore not be easy. Moreover, I realized that I would be presenting the paper to an audience that would include people who knew Stigler well, certainly much better than I did, although I believe I knew him fairly well. Finally, adding to my diffidence was the awareness that, if there is such a thing as a Chicago School—and of course there is—I am the only person on this program who is not a member of it.

But then I took reassurance on two grounds: (1) Stigler's contributions to the history of economic thought have no doubt received far less attention than most of his other writings. There is a straightforward economic explanation, of course. As Stigler himself once pointed out, this subject "is perhaps the last unsubsidized research area in economics" (Stigler 1965, p. v). (2) More important, it was one of Stigler's own cardinal principles that the biographical facts of a scholar's life ought to be quite irrelevant to an examination and evaluation of his professional contributions. In his own words: "science consists of the arguments and the evidence that lead *other* men to accept or reject scientific views. Science is a social enterprise, and

I thank Stanley Engerman and Milton Friedman for incisive comments on an earlier draft.

[*Journal of Political Economy*, 1993, vol. 101, no. 5]
© 1993 by The University of Chicago. All rights reserved. 0022-3808/93/0105-0009$01.50

those parts of a man's life which do not affect the relationships between that man and his fellow scientists are simply extra-scientific. When we are told that we must study a man's life to understand what he really meant, we are being invited to abandon science" ([1976] 1982, p. 91). Armed with this reassurance, let me proceed.

The first thing that needs to be said about Stigler's work in the history of economic thought is that it was not the product of a casual interest. It was, in fact, his first and lasting love. He was, I think it fair to say, never far away from the subject. To begin with, Stigler spent a year at Northwestern before going on for his Ph.D. at the University of Chicago. His master's thesis at Northwestern, I am informed, dealt with issues in the history of economic thought. His doctoral dissertation was a careful, rigorous examination of the emergence of "modern" production and distribution theories between 1870 and 1895. The dissertation, written under the supervision of Frank Knight, was submitted to the University of Chicago in 1938. It was subsequently revised with an additional chapter on John Bates Clark and published under the title *Production and Distribution Theories* in 1941. Stigler's special interest in this period, 1870–95, persisted through his entire professional life, as we shall see.

Stigler's book was quickly accepted as the most authoritative treatment of the emergence of the "marginal revolution" that began in the early 1870s and culminated in the marginal productivity theory of the 1890s. Joseph Schumpeter, who did not dispense praise casually, said of the book: "This excellent work by a competent theorist is perhaps the best survey in existence of the theoretical work of that period's leaders and is strongly recommended" (Schumpeter 1954, p. 849). Characteristically, Schumpeter added that "this recommendation does not imply agreement in every point of fact or evaluation."

Stigler's research and writing in the history of economic thought did not end with his dissertation and book. His first published article was "The Economics of Carl Menger" (1937); the last article published during his own lifetime was an article on Charles Babbage's contribution to mathematical economics: "Charles Babbage (1791 + 200 = 1991)" (1991). In between 1937 and 1991, he published a steady flow of papers on the history of the discipline. He touched certain bases that one might expect, coming back most often to Adam Smith, but also to David Ricardo and to John Stuart Mill, in addition to all the major contributors to the creation and adoption of the marginal utility approach. But he also found time for lesser-known figures such as Stuart Wood and, perhaps more surprisingly, even Bernard Shaw and Sidney Webb. It is impossible to deal with all of this in a very short space. Rather, I shall call attention, in an admittedly somewhat subjective way, to the high points of this large body of material and, especially, to what I regard as some very original thought that has received relatively little attention from professional economists.

Stigler's approach to the history of economics has a consistent central feature, one that is better conveyed in fact by describing it as an interest in the emergence of economic *analysis,* or even economic *science,* rather than economic thought. Stigler's interest lay in extracting a core theoretical system, cleansed of an author's irrelevant digressions or precommitments to particular policy recommendations. Indeed, this interest doubtless helps to account for his decision to focus, in his doctoral dissertation, on the separate contributions to the emergence of the marginal productivity theory between 1870 and 1895. For "it was in this quarter-century that economic theory was transformed from an art, in many respects literary, to a science of growing rigor" (1941, p. 1).

In approaching the writings of earlier economists, therefore, the goal should be to discover and to explicate "the essential structure of the author's analytical system. Our understanding is better the larger the share of the man's work we can deduce from the analytical system. Indeed, we may use prediction to test our understanding. One who understands the first five chapters of Ricardo should be able to write his chapters on taxation" ([1969] 1982, p. 110). I commend this test to all of you—or at least to your students.

Stigler employs this perspective most fruitfully throughout his historical papers. It forms the basis for his central criticism of the *Wealth of Nations,* that "stupendous palace erected upon the granite of self-interest" (1982, p. 136). For, if we assume that self-interest is indeed the dominant force controlling the actions of people when they are commercially engaged, why is it so strangely absent from the political arena? On what basis is Smith entitled to reject the invocation of self-interest as a guide to legislative behavior (see Stigler 1971*a*)?

The connections that these questions bear to the literature of public choice (James Buchanan and Gordon Tullock) are obvious, as are the connections with Stigler's important contributions to the literature of economic regulation. Perhaps not surprisingly, Stigler's "Theory of Economic Regulation" (1971*b*) was published in the same year as "Smith's Travels on the Ship of State." As Stigler expressed it elsewhere, "The discipline that assumes man to be a reasonably efficient utility maximizer is singularly ill-suited to assuming that the political activity of men bears little relationship to their desires. . . . We live in a world that is full of mistaken policies, but they are not mistaken for their supporters" (1982, pp. 9–10).

But there is a second element, in addition to the search for a central analytical core, that defines Stigler's research in intellectual history.

It is so fundamental, indeed so elemental, that I almost hesitate to introduce it. Stigler believed that the progress of economics as a discipline had to be measured in terms of its ability to develop propositions that could be subjected to empirical testing and refutation. Economics for Stigler was always an empirical as well as an analytical discipline. Successful theories are more general than those that they displace, but the ability to encompass a wider range of phenomena needs to march forward hand in hand with the search for refutable implications.

Surprising as it may sound, no previous scholar had ever examined the development of the discipline with anything like the same insistence that intellectual progress had to be measured in terms of its ability to generate empirically refutable implications. Indeed, it was precisely the failure to do so that accounted for the painfully slow progress of utility theory after the additive utility function was introduced in the 1870s.

> Had specific tests been made of the implications of theories, the unfruitfulness of the ruling utility theory as a source of hypotheses in demand would soon have become apparent. Had these economists sought to establish true economic theories of economic behavior—that is, to isolate uniformities of economic events that permitted prediction of the effects of given conditions—they would not long have been content with the knowledge that demand curves have negative slopes. They would have desired knowledge on the relative elasticities of demand of rich and poor, the effects of occupation and urbanization on demand, the role of income changes, the difference between short- and long-run reactions to price changes, and a whole host of problems which we are just beginning to study. They would have given us an economic theory which was richer and more precise. [(1950) 1965, p. 155]

It is clear that Stigler became increasingly empirical in the course of his professional life. This is reflected in his strong insistence on refutability and therefore on the extracting of testable implications from theories and actually subjecting them to empirical tests. One obvious contribution to this growing concern was his extended stay at the National Bureau, but it would be well worth exploring—as I have not done—the influence of Karl Popper, whom Stigler met at the first meeting of the Mont Pelerin Society in 1947. Another obvious source of influence or, perhaps better, mutual influence throughout Stigler's professional life was Milton Friedman, who also attended that meeting.

An important milestone in Stigler's already growing interest in empirical testing was his critique of the kinky oligopoly demand curve (Stigler 1947a). As he observed of that article many years later, "My appraisal of the theory in 1947 was stimulated more by a growing interest in the empirical testing of theories than by the intrinsic interest in the kinked demand curve" ([1978] 1982, p. 227).[1] Using Bureau of Labor Statistics wholesale prices from 1929 to 1937, Stigler tested and rejected several implications of the kinked demand curve theory. The response to his tests, on the part of the defenders of the theory, took a variety of forms. Stigler noted "one characteristic these defenders of the theory of kinked demand curves all share: the belief that they need not provide evidence to support the theory. If my criticisms could be rejected, apparently there has been a presumption that the theory is acceptable: theories, like other citizens, are presumed innocent until shown to be guilty" (p. 228).

Stigler's strong empirical bent did much to clarify, as well as to enrich, the study of the history of the discipline. On the matter of clarification, consider the interminable discussions of whether Ricardo adhered to a labor theory of value, in the sense that the relative values of commodities are exclusively determined by the relative quantities of labor required in their production. In his splendid article "Ricardo and the 93 Per Cent Labor Theory of Value," Stigler points out that "the failure to distinguish between analytical and empirical propositions has been a source of much misunderstanding in economics. An analytical statement concerns functional relationships; an empirical statement takes account of the quantitative significance of the relationships" ([1958] 1965, p. 341). As soon as one distinguishes between functional relationships (analytical) and the quantitative significance of the relationships (empirical), it is easy to establish that, while Ricardo never argued that quantities of labor are the *sole* determinants of relative values, he did believe in an empirical labor theory of value.

Ricardo made use of empirical examples in which any plausible rise in wages can have only a slight effect on the relative value of commodities, as compared to alterations brought about by changes in the quantity of labor.[2] This enables Ricardo to continue to assume that the relative value of commodities is determined by changes in labor inputs rather than alterations in wages. But this proposition, as Stigler concludes, has empirical and not analytical status. "I can find

[1] The main task of the 1947 article "was a test of the empirical fruitfulness of the theory" (1982, p. 227).

[2] As Ricardo stated with respect to his own example, "The greatest effects which could be produced on the relative prices of these goods from a rise in wages, could not exceed 6 or 7 per cent" (Ricardo 1951, 1:36). Hence the title of Stigler's paper.

no basis for the belief that Ricardo had an *analytical* labor theory of
value, for quantities of labor are *not* the only determinants of relative
values. Such a theory would have to reduce all obstacles to production
to expenditures of labor or assert the irrelevance or non-existence of
non-labor obstacles, and Ricardo does not embrace either view. On
the other hand, there is no doubt that he held what may be called an
empirical labor theory of value, that is, a theory that the relative quantities of labor required in production are the dominant determinants
of relative values" (p. 333).

Stigler's tough-minded empiricism was responsible for fresh insights on almost every subject he approached in the history of economic thought. It enabled him, for example, to deliver the most incisive critical analysis of Thomas Malthus's *Essay on Population* that I
have ever seen. This appeared over the course of several pages of
his 1952 paper "The Ricardian Theory of Value and Distribution."
If I may be indulged just one lengthy quotation—and surely it is an
indulgence that should be granted to someone writing on my present
subject—I call to your attention just two masterly paragraphs. Stigler
is discussing the subsequent history of Malthus's *Essay on Population*
after the great initial success of the first edition, published anony-
mously in 1798.

> The *Essay* became much longer and vastly duller, when
> Malthus added long accounts of population in ancient, prim-
> itive, and modern agricultural and industrial states. These
> descriptive accounts did not demonstrate the principle of
> population, as he claimed; rather, they demonstrated that
> death comes in many forms and that births are influenced
> by social customs. Malthus simply had no canons of evidence.
> He recited—and embroidered—travelers' accounts of prim-
> itive societies, seizing like a gossip columnist upon every ref-
> erence to misery and vice and ignoring those to prosperity
> or virtue. He found the principle of population confirmed
> in the prosperity of England during the twenty years before
> 1811 and also by the depression after the Napoleonic Wars.
>   What evidence could have been used to test the theory?
> If the subsistence level has any stability, and hence any sig-
> nificance, Malthus' theory was wrong if the standard of living
> of the masses rose for any considerable period of time. He
> did not investigate this possibility . . . and ignored the opin-
> ions of such authorities as Sir Frederick Eden that it had
> been rising for a century. His theory was also contradicted
> if population grew at a constant geometrical rate in an "old"
> country, for then the means of subsistence were also growing

at this rate, since population never precedes food. Despite the rapid increase of population in almost all western European nations at the time, which he duly noted, he persisted in considering this as only a confirmation of his fecundity hypothesis. [(1952) 1965, pp. 168–69]

If the reader retains any residual doubts concerning Stigler's evaluation of Malthus, they are removed in his discussion (elsewhere) of Sraffa's wonderful edition of Ricardo's works: Malthus "had one great weakness—he could not reason well. He could not construct a theory that was consistent with either itself or the facts of the world" (1965, p. 311). So much, one is inclined to say, for Malthus!

But Stigler's strong commitment to empirical research led him also to a considerable enlargement of the research agenda of economics scholars with an interest in the history of their subject. In particular, the discovery of significant empirical facts about the structure of economic relationships is itself a subject that has a history. Yet curiously, although the history of economic analysis has attracted many devoted scholars, the history of empirical economics has been largely neglected. Stigler, quite correctly, found this anomalous. The history of such matters as the attempt to estimate the consumption function, or the production function, and the increasing professional sophistication with respect to estimation procedures serve to illuminate some of the most significant aspects of the growth of understanding of economic life.[3]

Stigler was a pioneer in the historical study of empirical research in economics. It was of course, in his view, axiomatic that theoretical and empirical work were complementary. Scarcely any economist would dare disagree with such a statement, but, in fact, theoretical and empirical economists long worked in almost total isolation from one another. Indeed, one would not need to scour the professional journals with enormous care to find continuing evidence of such isolation today.

The benefits of division of labor, while very great, do not presumably extend to the point at which one class of scientists devotes itself exclusively to the collection of data, only to pass them along to an-

---

[3] I have worked hard at resisting the temptation to tell anecdotes, but reference to Stigler's empirical bent compels the telling of just one. Stigler was offered a professorship at the University of Chicago in 1946, but the appointment was contingent on a personal interview with the president of the university. The offer was withdrawn as a result of the interview, on the grounds that Stigler was too empirical! Perhaps it is not totally irrelevant to observe that the president who found Stigler too empirical, Ernest Colwell, was himself a theologian. The professorship was eventually offered to, and accepted by, someone else—a young economist named Milton Friedman (Stigler 1988, p. 40). Thus there is more than one sense in which it is true to say that George Stigler was a founder of the Chicago School.

other class that attempts to divine their meaning. In "The Early History of Empirical Studies of Consumer Behavior" (1954), Stigler explores (1) the early quantitative research on the relationship between income and consumer behavior, in which empirical research preceded, by 70 years, the recognition in formal theory of the role of income in influencing consumer behavior, and (2) the early attempts at the empirical estimation of demand curves in which the development of the purely formal theory preceded the empirical estimation by 40 years. Why, he asks, were the sequences and lags what they were?[4]

The article, an impressive work of historical scholarship, examines the findings of a number of research workers whose names will be mainly unrecognizable to most economists, at least to those who have not read Stigler's article. Indeed, many of the early authors of the budget studies, or the collectors of the data utilized by those studies, could hardly be classified as economists. A number of them were in fact clergymen concerned with the poverty that surrounded them.

Why, Stigler asks, the long delay in incorporating income as an explicit variable in formal theory? Part of the answer, he suggests—perhaps surprisingly, but even the shade of Alfred Marshall can be invoked as supporting evidence—was the belief that real income varied only within a very narrow range in the short run. It was not until the 1920s, according to Stigler, that the full extent of short-term income fluctuations was widely recognized. (I find this explanation not very persuasive, mainly because there is no clear indication of how widely held this belief actually was. And just what constitutes the "very narrow range"? It would not be very difficult to cite a large number of nineteenth-century writers who were concerned over the serious consequences of short-term income fluctuations.)

In any case, this is not Stigler's main point. More important for him is that empirical workers did not know how to convert the particularities of their empirical observations into the wider and more systematic formulations that would be required for conventional economic theory. In the absence of explicit links to theoretical formulations, the empirical research did not become part of a cumulative process. And, as a consequence, the empirical findings could not be readily employed to illuminate issues of larger significance, nor could they become part of generalizations that would have a more direct influence on economic thinking. In Stigler's view, there is no good substitute for empirical research being conducted within the same

---

[4] Two other articles of Stigler's may be treated as useful supplements to this one. They are "Henry L. Moore and Statistical Economics" (1962) and his earlier "Notes on the History of the Giffen Paradox" (1947*b*).

brain that has at least some minimal familiarity with formal theory. While the advantages of an intellectual division of labor are very great, they are not unlimited.

Why the delay of some 40 years between the initiation of formal demand theory, in the 1870s, and the statistical estimation of demand curves? Partly such estimation had to await the birth and subsequent diffusion of the techniques of curve-fitting and correlation analysis. This came with the work of Francis Galton, Francis Edgeworth, Karl Pearson, and George Yule in the last two decades of the nineteenth century. Since important work by both Marcel Lenoir in France and Henry Moore in the United States was underway before the First World War, the lag between the availability of appropriate statistical methods and their utilization by economists cannot be considered to have been unduly long.

A more substantial reason for the lag, in Stigler's view, takes us back once again to his insistence on the inseparability of theory and empirical research. He concludes that "the delay of a generation in empirical work on demand curves was due to the general failure to recognize that economic *functions*, as well as quantities, could be determined empirically" (1965, p. 232). But moving from empirical observations concerning the covariation of prices and quantities to an underlying demand function is no simple matter. And, as Stigler says elsewhere, it was Moore's distinctive accomplishment "to make statistical estimation of economic functions an integral part of modern economics" ([1962] 1965, p. 360).[5]

I would like to turn, finally, to a subject that Stigler immensely enriched by his writings. It is a subject that, while it is an extension of the issues already addressed, raises some of the most profound problems in the realms of scholarship and science. Stigler stood back from the economist's canvas on which he so skillfully painted and asked whether there were laws or regularities shaping the growth of knowledge itself. It is easy to see how his lifelong interest in the emergence of marginal productivity theory might have given rise to much larger questions in the history of science. How does the research agenda of any science get to be determined? By what exogenous or endogenous forces is that research agenda shaped and transformed? Why do discoveries occur where and when they do? How do scientists persuade one another? To put it in its boldest possible form: What are the underlying laws governing the evolution of science?

The attempt to deal with such questions is still in its infancy, although seminal contributions have been made by Thomas Kuhn and,

[5] The classic article on this subject was Working (1927).

especially, Robert K. Merton (i.e., Merton the elder). Stigler's view was that "the evolution of a science is a fascinating area for study: subtle, complex, but surely obeying laws which eventually can be discovered" (1982, p. 86). Stigler has contributed to this emerging field in two distinct roles.

The first is that of a friendly and constructive critic. As one might expect, Stigler has attempted to specify how the hypotheses of Kuhn and Merton would have to be reformulated if they are to become testable (i.e., refutable). Kuhn argued that science progresses, not through the slow, patient accretion of new knowledge, but by occasional drastic revolutionary shifts in which one paradigm is displaced by another (Kuhn 1962). The progress of "normal" science throws up anomalies or contradictory observations that cannot be assimilated by mere modifications or retouching of the established paradigm. In Kuhn's view the old notion that science grows by a steady, cumulative process, adding more and more small bricks to an expanding edifice, is pure fiction.

Stigler's response is that Kuhn has not specified the nature and content of a paradigm in sufficient detail to permit empirical testing.

> If vast changes in the subject and techniques of a science can be accommodated within a paradigm, and hence do not constitute a revolution, Kuhn's assertion that a crisis is necessary to the emergence of a new paradigm is virtually a tautology.[6] If, on the contrary, large change in the science per se constitutes a revolution, Kuhn asserts that there will be an abandonment of the previous paradigm which in actual fact may never have taken place. To be concrete, the marginal utility revolution of the 1870s replaced the individual economic agent as a sociological or historical datum by the utility-maximizing individual. The essential elements of the classical theory were affected in no respect. (A possible, but uncertain, aftereffect in twenty years was the development of the marginal productivity theory.) Until Kuhn gives us criteria of a revolution (or a paradigm) which have direct empirical content, it will not be possible to submit his fascinating hypotheses to test. [1982, p. 114]

Stigler was greatly attracted by Merton's examination of multiples in scientific discovery. Merton has offered the hypothesis that "all scientific discoveries are in principle multiples, including those that

---

[6] Stigler adds at this point, in a note, that "the determination of whether the changes in a science are large or small is itself an extraordinarily subtle and complex task" (p. 114, n. 6). I quite agree. Indeed, I would not have confined the point to a note.

on the surface appear to be singletons" (Merton 1973, p. 356). His basic point is that scientific discoveries are made independently by more than one researcher. But why should the scientific world be one of multiples? The underlying reason is a particular view of science as a social enterprise that evolves in accordance with the changing perceptions and intellectual agenda of the scholars who, at any given time, constitute the scientific community. Multiples are likely because previous scientific advances serve as focusing devices, calling attention to certain problems or, in Kuhn's terminology, anomalies, which the scientific community was unaware of. Scientific research thus exhibits a high degree of path dependence. The research agenda today is powerfully shaped by what happened yesterday, that is, by our particular intellectual inheritance from disciplinary predecessors.

Although Merton's argument for the existence of multiples has received much attention, the justification for such attention is frequently lost from view: whether multiples constitute evidence that would support a particular interpretation of the evolution of science. In Merton's terms, "The sheer fact that multiple discoveries are made by scientists working independently of one another testifies to the further crucial fact that, though remote in space, they are responding to much the same social and intellectual forces that impinge upon them all" (p. 375).

But Stigler sharpens, and indeed substantially modifies, Merton's view in some essential ways. The underlying rationale for multiples "is of course that the discoveries are dictated by the evolving logic of the science—new ideas are not in the air, as it is often said, but near the surface of the work that has just been completed" (Stigler 1982, p. 115). But then he adds that "this is a profoundly correct and illuminating view of science even if there are a substantial number of singletons."

Stigler observes that if the theory of multiples is to be testable in the first place, it is essential to be able to define the "similarity" of the scientific environment on which the theory is supposed to rest. Otherwise it becomes extremely difficult to "*define* multiple discoveries as those which appear at a given stage in the evolution of a science" ([1980] 1982, p. 100). A further difficulty is that Merton places no real restrictions on the time period within which multiples must fall.

> The real problem is that if two discoveries come at very different times (or at the same time in very different intellectual environments) they can no longer be said to be the ripe fruit of that season of the tree of science. The discovery of marginal productivity theory by Longfield in Ireland in 1833 could not be a response to the same scientific environment

as the discovery of the theory by Wicksteed, Clark, Barone, Wood, Marshall, Edgeworth, and others some sixty years later. The proposition that lightning strikes at least twice in every spot where it strikes once is not interesting if a test requires that we wait to the end of time. [1982, pp. 115–16]

In fact, drawing on intellectual progress in economics, Stigler concludes that many of the examples of multiple discovery turn out, on closer inspection, not to be multiples at all. Rather, "most of the multiples were discoveries that had been made earlier but had been ignored" (1982, p. 101). But Stigler, in something of a tour de force, concludes that the fact that they were not really multiples *supports* rather than refutes Merton's basic argument:

> The unsuccessful earlier discoveries are the very evidence for the "inevitability" of scientific progress that the multiple discoveries was supposed to present. If an early, valid statement of a theory falls on deaf ears, and a later restatement is accepted by the science, this is surely proof that the science accepts ideas only when they fit into the then-current state of the science. Gossen, writing in the high tide of German Historical economics, was simply inappropriate to his scientific environment. Longfield in Ireland, and von Thünen in Germany, were presenting a marginal productivity theory for which neither German nor British economic science was ready. And similarly for Slutsky, Cournot and other unsuccessful discoverers. [P. 102]

Stigler also contributed to the emerging discipline of the evolution of science through the application of statistical methods to intellectual history: specifically, to the growth and slow maturing of his own discipline. A key long-term trend that he chooses to approach in quantitative terms is the professionalization of economics.

Stigler shows that, by examining the important English economists from 1766 to 1915 and employing such measures as sources of income and publication practices, it is possible to provide important insights into the professionalization of the discipline. The two basic attributes of professionalization are (1) specialization and (2) persistent application over an extended period of time to one's area of specialization. In the last third of the eighteenth century there were no specialists in economics. Before 1850 only one economist— Malthus—was supported for an extended period of time by his teaching and writing in the field of economics. By the early twentieth century only three of the important English economists (out of eight) were *not* professors. "One may conclude that the specialized writer on economics, with a professional base, was dominant after 1900" (1965, pp. 37–38).

In the first half of the nineteenth century there were no professional journals; that is, there was no clear distinction between specialized scientific journals and those intended for more popular consumption. Or, rather, the former did not exist. Writers on economic issues shared space in the *Edinburgh Review* or *Westminster Review* with authors of political tracts or detailed accounts by travelers recently returned from exotic foreign lands. Serious writers such as Ricardo or Samuel Bailey presented their thoughts to the public in pamphlets or books.[7]

It was not until 1891 that the first fully professional journal (the *Royal Economic Journal*) appeared in England (in the United States the *Quarterly Journal of Economics* had begun publication in 1886). It was not until the early years of the twentieth century that the specialized writer on economics, operating from a professional base, had become dominant.

In the United States, "The periodical has been the main outlet for professional economic writing, especially of a theoretical tendency, since its first appearance in the 1880's" (1965, p. 44). Furthermore, Stigler finds that, in the United States, the journals have been "the almost exclusive possession of the academic economists from the outset" (p. 45).

What have been the consequences of this developing pattern of professionalization on the content of economics? Stigler nowhere attempts to provide a systematic treatment of this big question. But he does offer some tantalizing hints and suggestions in his article "The Adoption of the Marginal Utility Theory" (1972).

Stigler asks why it should have taken at least three-quarters of a century for utility theory to begin to gain acceptance. "Acceptance" is dated by that great "multiple" in the history of economics, the publications of William Jevons, Carl Menger, and León Walras within the 3-year period 1871–74. We may think of utility theory as being in some meaningful sense "accessible" with the publication of Jeremy Bentham's *Introduction to the Principles of Morals and Legislation* in 1789, although the lag would be much longer if we take Daniel Bernoulli's treatment of the St. Petersburg paradox, which first appeared in 1738, as marking the accessibility of the utility approach.

---

[7] Present-day authors will surely envy the remarkable speed with which pamphlets could be produced. Stigler reports that "Ricardo's 'Essay on the Profits of Stock,' published February 24, 1815, contains page references to Malthus' 'Inquiry into Rent,' published February 3, and his 'Grounds of an Opinion,' published February 10" (1965, p. 40). In fact there are, as Stigler points out elsewhere, a relatively small number of famous articles, as contrasted with books, before about 1870 (Stigler and Friedland 1979).

Stigler's explanation is that adoption had to await the transformation of economics into an academic discipline, and this was a development of the closing decades of the nineteenth century. The utility approach was far more intellectually congenial to academics than to earlier generations of economists who were primarily concerned with influencing policy. As the discipline transformed itself into an academic profession, it cultivated academic values. This meant, first of all, a deliberate attempt at disengagement from day-to-day concerns. Second, it meant the attempt to develop a framework of analysis of the widest possible degree of generality.[8]

According to Stigler:

> What utility theory contributed was precisely the values we attribute to the academic world and in particular to the academic sciences. The classical school had advanced one theory of value for producible goods and resorted to other theories (rent) or vague phrases ("passions of the buyer") for non-producible goods. Now the utility theory allowed a unified explanation of the value of shoes, wheat, and Shakespearean folios. The classical school had no central logic of behavior: the entrepreneur was a profit-maximizer while the consumer and laborer were opaque bundles of sociological behavior traits. Now the utility theory allowed a unified explanation of behavior: everyone was a utility-maximizer, and all economic problems became simply problems of tastes and obstacles (so, Pareto). The method of the classical school had been literary and numerical. Now the utility theory obviously permitted and even invited the use of mathematics. [1982, p. 78]

Stigler is left, as he is aware, with the rather thorny problem of explaining why Germany failed to produce a single important utility theorist, in spite of the fact that German economics had achieved an academic status earlier than most other European countries. German economics was "profoundly antitheoretical," basing itself on the models of history and jurisprudence rather than on physics and biology, which served as more rigorous models elsewhere. But the English academic world also housed a historical school that seemed every bit as hostile to utility theory as the German historical school. Why then

---

[8] As Stigler stated elsewhere, "it is a sign of the maturity of a discipline that its main problems are not drawn from immediate, changing events. A genuine and persistent separation of scientific study from the real world leads to sterility, but an immediate and sensitive response to current events stultifies the deepening and widening of analytical principles and techniques" ([1960] 1965, p. 20).

GEORGE J. STIGLER   847

was the English academic world so much more receptive than the German?

Stigler concludes this article by acknowledging that he has offered only "bits of evidence." His main purpose, however, is to insist on the great significance of the problem that he has addressed and to urge that it is "an important and neglected subject of scientific study" (p. 83). His final conclusion can serve as an apt conclusion to the present paper: "The history of economics has become a nearly moribund subject in the United States, and has not failed to decline elsewhere. It is therefore a cause for rejoicing that the extraordinarily complex and subtle forces which dominate a science's evolution present a task of theoretical explanation comparable in intellectual demands to that presented by actual economic life" (p. 83).

I concur. Now if only we can find a few more George Stiglers.

References

Kuhn, Thomas S. *The Structure of Scientific Revolutions.* Chicago: Univ. Chicago Press, 1962.

Merton, Robert K. *The Sociology of Science: Theoretical and Empirical Investigations.* Chicago: Univ. Chicago Press, 1973.

Ricardo, David. *Works and Correspondence of David Ricardo.* Edited by Piero Sraffa. Cambridge: Cambridge Univ. Press (for Royal Econ. Soc.), 1951.

Schumpeter, Joseph A. *History of Economic-Analysis.* New York: Oxford Univ. Press, 1954.

Stigler, George J. "The Economics of Carl Menger." *J.P.E.* 45 (April 1937): 229–50.

———. *Production and Distribution Theories: 1870–1895.* New York: Macmillan, 1941.

———. "The Kinky Oligopoly Demand Curve and Rigid Prices." *J.P.E.* 55 (October 1947): 432–49. (*a*).

———. "Notes on the History of the Giffen Paradox." *J.P.E.* 55 (April 1947): 152–56. (*b*) Reprinted in Stigler (1965).

———. "The Development of Utility Theory" (2 pts.). *J.P.E.* 58 (August 1950): 307–27; (October 1950): 373–96. Reprinted in Stigler (1965).

———. "The Ricardian Theory of Value and Distribution." *J.P.E.* 60 (June 1952): 187–207. Reprinted in Stigler (1965).

———. "The Early History of Empirical Studies of Consumer Behavior." *J.P.E.* 62 (April 1954): 95–113. Reprinted in Stigler (1965).

———. "Ricardo and the 93 Per Cent Labor Theory of Value." *A.E.R.* 48 (June 1958): 357–67. Reprinted in Stigler (1965).

———. "The Influence of Events and Policies on Economic Theory." *A.E.R. Papers and Proc.* 50 (May 1960): 36–45. Reprinted in Stigler (1965).

———. "Henry L. Moore and Statistical Economics." *Econometrica* 30 (January 1962): 1–21. Reprinted in Stigler (1965).

———. *Essays in the History of Economics.* Chicago: Univ. Chicago Press, 1965.

———. "Does Economics Have a Useful Past?" *Hist. Polit. Econ.* 1 (Fall 1969): 217–30. Reprinted in Stigler (1982).

————. "Smith's Travels on the Ship of State." *Hist. Polit. Econ.* 3 (Fall 1971): 265–77. (*a*) Reprinted in Stigler (1982).

————. "The Theory of Economic Regulation." *Bell J. Econ. and Management Sci.* 2 (Spring 1971): 3–21. (*b*)

————."The Adoption of the Marginal Utility Theory." *Hist. Polit. Econ.* 4 (Fall 1972): 571–86. Reprinted in Stigler (1982).

————. "The Scientific Uses of Scientific Biography, with Special Reference to J. S. Mill." In *James and John Stuart Mill: Papers of the Centenary Conference,* edited by John M. Robson and Michael Laine. Toronto: Univ. Toronto Press, 1976. Reprinted in Stigler (1982).

————. "The Literature of Economics: The Case of the Kinked Oligopoly Demand Curve." *Econ. Inquiry* 16 (April 1978): 185–204. Reprinted in Stigler (1982).

————. "Merton on Multiples, Denied and Affirmed." In *Science and Social Structure: A Festschrift for Robert K. Merton.* Transactions of the New York Academy of Sciences, ser. 2, vol. 39. New York: Nat. Acad. Sci., 1980. Reprinted in Stigler (1982).

————. *The Economist as Preacher, and Other Essays.* Chicago: Univ. Chicago Press, 1982.

————. *Memoirs of an Unregulated Economist.* New York: Basic, 1988.

————. "Charles Babbage (1791 + 200 = 1991)." *J. Econ. Literature* 29 (September 1991): 1149–52.

Stigler, George J., and Friedland, Claire. "The Pattern of Citation Practices in Economics." *Hist. Polit. Econ.* 11 (Spring 1979): 1–20. Reprinted in Stigler (1982).

Working, Elmer J. "What Do Statistical 'Demand Curves' Show?" *Q.J.E.* 41 (February 1927): 212–35. Reprinted in *Readings in Price Theory,* edited by Kenneth E. Boulding and George J. Stigler. Homewood, Ill.: Irwin (for American Econ. Assoc.), 1952.

Name index

Abramovitz, Moses 115

Babbage, Charles 94–116, 124, 154, 162, 171, 185
Bailey, Samuel 182
Becker, Gary 100, 164
Bentham, Jeremy 182
Bernal, J.D. 131, 132, 151
Bernoulli, Daniel 182
Blaug, Mark 91, 95, 112
Bober, M.M. 129, 132
Buchanan, James 172

Chalk, A. 1
Clark, John Bates 171, 181
Coats, A.W. 58
Cole, Arthur H. 16
Colwell, Ernest 176

Darwin, Charles 133
Davies, R.W. 22
Davis, Joseph 49, 55

Eden, Sir Frederick 175
Edgeworth, Francis 178, 181
Engels, Frederick 117–54

Ferguson, Adam 29, 37
Friedland, Claire 182, 185
Friedman, Milton 165, 173, 176
Furniss, Edgar S. 58

Galton, Francis 178

Halévy, Elie 9
Hansen, Alvin 151
Hegel, G.W.F. 130
Hirschman, Albert 24
Hume, David 11, 26, 54, 63, 75, 78, 86
Hyman, Anthony 94, 96

Jevons, William 110, 182

Kapp, William K. 17
Knight, Francis 171
Kuhn, Thomas 178, 179, 180, 184
Kuznets, Simon 115, 139, 153

Lenoir, Marcel 178
Lewis, W.A. 28

Machlup, Fritz 28
Malthus, T.R. 54, 55, 67, 175, 176, 181, 182
Mandeville, Bernard 1–14, 34, 38, 39
Marshall, Alfred 177, 181
Marx, Karl 22, 29, 34, 37, 41, 91, 99, 106, 107, 111, 112, 113, 114, 115, 117–54, 166, 167, 168, 169
Maudsley, Henry 96, 103, 146
Meek, Ronald 54, 55, 56
Mendeleev, Dmitri 158
Menger, Carl 171
Merton, Robert K. 179, 180, 184, 185
Mill, John Stuart 95, 111, 112, 113, 167, 171, 185
Mincer, Jacob 100
Mitchell, Wesley 15
Moore, Henry L. 177, 178, 184
Myrdal, Gunnar 17

Needham, Joseph 151
Nelson, Richard R. 158, 160
Newton, Isaac 130

Pearson, Karl 178
Pickering, William 99
Popper, Karl 193
Prony Monsieur 109, 110

Rae, John 54, 55
Ricardo, David 171, 172, 174, 175, 182, 184
Rosenberg, Nathan 8, 13, 34, 51, 55, 56, 62, 67, 68, 69, 75, 76, 101, 105, 153
Rotwein, Eugene 63, 87

Samuels, Warren 78, 91
Schmookler, Jacob 115
Schumpeter, Joseph A. 27, 30, 42, 55, 94, 95, 111, 115, 155–69, 171, 184
Scott, W.R. 31
Senior, Nassau 53, 55
Shaw, Francis 171
Skinner, Andrew 91
Smith, Adam 2, 8, 15–93, 95, 97, 98, 99, 101, 102, 109, 112, 167, 171, 172, 185

Economists of the Twentieth Century

Monetarism and Macroeconomic Policy
Thomas Mayer

Studies in Fiscal Federalism
Wallace E. Oates

The World Economy in Perspective
Essays in International Trade and European Integration
Herbert Giersch

Towards a New Economics
Critical Essays on Ecology, Distribution and Other Themes
Kenneth E. Boulding

Studies in Positive and Normative Economics
Martin J. Bailey

The Collected Essays of Richard E. Quandt (2 volumes)
Richard E. Quandt

International Trade Theory and Policy
Selected Essays of W. Max Corden
W. Max Corden

Organization and Technology in Capitalist Development
William Lazonick

Studies in Human Capital
Collected Essays of Jacob Mincer, Volume 1
Jacob Mincer

Studies in Labor Supply
Collected Essays of Jacob Mincer, Volume 2
Jacob Mincer

Macroeconomics and Economic Policy
The Selected Essays of Assar Lindbeck, Volume I
Assar Lindbeck

The Welfare State
The Selected Essays of Assar Lindbeck, Volume II
Assar Lindbeck

Classical Economics, Public Expenditure and Growth
Walter Eltis

Money, Interest Rates and Inflation
Frederic S. Mishkin

The Public Choice Approach to Politics
Dennis C. Mueller

The Liberal Economic Order
Volume I Essays on International Economics
Volume II Money, Cycles and Related Themes
Gottfried Haberler
Edited by Anthony Y.C. Koo

Economic Growth and Business Cycles
Prices and the Process of Cyclical Development
Paolo Sylos Labini

International Adjustment, Money and Trade
Theory and Measurement for Economic Policy, Volume I
Herbert G. Grubel

International Capital and Service Flows
Theory and Measurement for Economic Policy, Volume II
Herbert G. Grubel

Unintended Effects of Government Policies
Theory and Measurement for Economic Policy, Volume III
Herbert G. Grubel

The Economics of Competitive Enterprise
Selected Essays of P.W.S. Andrews
Edited by Frederic S. Lee and Peter E. Earl

The Repressed Economy
Causes, Consequences, Reform
Deepak Lal

Economic Theory and Market Socialism
Selected Essays of Oskar Lange
Edited by Tadeusz Kowalik

Trade, Development and Political Economy
Selected Essays of Ronald Findlay
Ronald Findlay

General Equilibrium Theory
The Collected Essays of Takashi Negishi, Volume I
Takashi Negishi

The History of Economics
The Collected Essays of Takashi Negishi, Volume II
Takashi Negishi

Studies in Econometric Theory
The Collected Essays of Takeshi Amemiya
Takeshi Amemiya

Exchange Rates and the Monetary System
Selected Essays of Peter B. Kenen
Peter B. Kenen

Econometric Methods and Applications (2 volumes)
G.S. Maddala

National Accounting and Economic Theory
The Collected Papers of Dan Usher, Volume I
Dan Usher

Welfare Economics and Public Finance
The Collected Papers of Dan Usher, Volume II
Dan Usher

Economic Theory and Capitalist Society
The Selected Essays of Shigeto Tsuru, Volume I
Shigeto Tsuru

Methodology, Money and the Firm
The Collected Essays of D.P. O'Brien (2 volumes)
D.P. O'Brien

Economic Theory and Financial Policy
The Selected Essays of Jacques J. Polak (2 volumes)
Jacques J. Polak

Sturdy Econometrics
Edward E. Leamer

The Emergence of Economic Ideas
Essays in the History of Economics
Nathan Rosenberg

Productivity Change, Public Goods and Transaction Costs
Essays at the Boundaries of Microeconomics
Yoram Barzel

Reflections on Economic Development
The Selected Essays of Michael P. Todaro
Michael P. Todaro